DIRE____ ___ON
POPULAR PIETY
AND THE LITURGY

PRINCIPLES AND GUIDELINES

CONGREGATION FOR DIVINE WORSHIP
AND THE DISCIPLINE OF THE SACRAMENTS

*All booklets are published thanks to the generous support
of the members of the Catholic Truth Society*

CATHOLIC TRUTH SOCIETY
PUBLISHERS TO THE HOLY SEE

..S Publications

...uoklets explain the faith, teaching and life of the Catholic Church. They are based on Sacred Scripture, the Second Vatican Council documents, and the *Catechism of the Catholic Church*. Our booklets provide authentic Catholic teaching; they address issues of life and of truth which are relevant to all. They aim to inform and educate readers on the many issues that people have to deal with today.

In addition, CTS nurtures and supports the Christian life through its many spiritual, liturgical, educational and pastoral books. As Publisher to the Holy See, CTS publishes the official documents of the Catholic Church as they are issued.

The CTS is one of the oldest and one of the few sizable publishers of exclusively Catholic publications; its booklets are completely reliable. CTS seeks to communicate and celebrate the riches of the Catholic faith to all.

© 2002 The Incorporated Catholic Truth Society
40-46 Harleyford Road London SE11 5AY

Tel: 020 7640 0042 Fax: 020 7640 0046

website: www.cts-online.org.uk

Front Cover Image: Cimabue's Madonna carried in procession by Frederic Lord Leighton.
The Royal Collection
© 2002, Her Majesty Queen Elizabeth II

ISBN 1 86082 161 8

CONTENTS

INTRODUCTION

PART ONE - EMERGING TRENDS
HISTORY, MAGISTERIUM AND THEOLOGY

CHAPTER ONE
Liturgy and Popular Piety in a Historical Perspective

CHAPTER TWO
Liturgy and Popular Piety in the Church's Magisterium

CHAPTER THREE

For an Evaluation of Renewal of Popular piety

PART TWO - GUIDELINES FOR THE HARMONIZATION OF
POPULAR PIETY WITH THE LITURGY

CHAPTER FOUR

The Liturgical Year and Popular Piety

CHAPTER FIVE

Veneration of the Holy Mother of God

CHAPTER SIX

Veneration of the Saints and Beati

CHAPTER SEVEN

Suffrage for the Dead

CHAPTER EIGHT
Shrines and Pilgrimages

ABBREVIATIONS

AAS   *Acta Apostolicae Sedis*

CCC   *Catechism of the Catholic Church*

CIC   *Codex Iuris Canonici*

CSEL   *Corpus Scriptorum Ecclesiasticorum Latinorum*

DS   H. Denzinger - A. Schoenmetzer, *Enchiridion Symbolorum definitionum et declarationum de rebus fidei et morum.*

EI   *Enchiridon Indulgentiarum. Normae et Concessiones (1999)*

LG   Second Vatican Council, Constitution *Lumen gentium*

PG   *Patrologia greca* (J-P Migne)

PL   *Patrologia latina* (J-P Migne)

SC   Second Vatican Council, Constitution *Sacrosanctum Concilium*

SCh   *Sources chrétiennes*

Extracts from the address of His Holiness Pope John Paul II to the Plenary Meeting of The Congregation for Divine Worship and the Discipline of the Sacraments (21 September 2001)

2. The Sacred Liturgy, described by *Sacrosanctum Concilium* as the summit of the Church's life, can never be reduced to a mere aesthetic reality. Neither can it be considered simply as a means to pedagogical or ecumenical ends. Before all else, the celebration of the sacred mysteries is an act of praise to the Triune God's sovereign majesty, and is willed by God Himself. Through the Sacred Liturgy man, personally and collectively, presents himself before God to render thanksgiving, fully conscious that his existence cannot be complete without praising God and doing His will as he strives for the Kingdom which is already present but whose definitive advent is only to be found in the *Parousia* of the Lord Jesus. Were the Liturgy not to have its effects on life, it would become void and displeasing to God.

3. The celebration of the Liturgy is an act of the virtue of religion which, in keeping with its nature, must be characterised by a profound sense of the sacred. Both the individual and the community must be aware that, in a special way, through the Liturgy they come into the presence of Him who is thrice holy and transcendent. Consequently, the disposition required of them is one that can only flow from that reverence and awe deriving from an awareness of being in the presence of the majesty of Almighty God. Did not God Himself wish to express this when he commanded Moses to remove his sandals in the presence of the burning bush? Was it not because of this same realization that Moses and Elijah did not dare gaze on God *facie in faciem*.

The People of God require a comportment in their priests and deacons that is completely imbued with reverence and dignity since it allows them to penetrate invisible realities without words or explanations. The Roman Missal, promulgated by Saint Pope Pius V, and the various Eastern Liturgies, contain many very beautiful prayers with which the priest expresses a profound sense of reverence and humility before the Sacred Mysteries. These prayers reveal the very substance of every Liturgy.

A liturgical celebration, at which the priest presides, is an assembly of prayer, gathered in faith to hear the Word of God. Its primary object is to offer to God the living, pure and holy Sacrifice made once and for all time by Jesus Christ on Calvary, and which is rendered present at every Holy Mass celebrated by the Church so as to worship God in spirit and in truth.

I am aware of this Congregation's deep commitment, and that of the Bishops, to the promotion and development of the Church's liturgical life. In expressing my appreciation, it is my hope that this valuable work will contribute to make the celebration of the Liturgy ever more dignified and fruitful.

4. With a view to the preparation of a Directory, your Plenary has chosen popular religiosity as its main topic. Popular piety is an expression of faith which avails of certain cultural elements proper to a specific environment which is capable of interpreting and questioning in a lively and effective manner the sensibilities of those who live in that same environment.

Genuine forms of popular piety, expressed in a multitude of different ways, derive from the faith and, therefore, must be valued and promoted. Such authentic expressions of popular piety are not at odds with the centrality of the Sacred Liturgy. Rather, in promoting the faith of the people, who regard popular piety as a natural religious expression, they predispose the people for the celebration of the Sacred Mysteries.

5. The correct relationship between these two expressions of faith must be based on certain firm principles, the first of which recognises that the Liturgy is the centre of the Church's life and cannot be substituted by, or placed on a par with, any other form of

religious expression. Moreover, it is important to reaffirm that popular religiosity, even if not always evident, naturally culminates in the celebration of the Liturgy towards which it should ideally be oriented. This should be made clear through suitable catechesis.

Forms of popular religiosity can sometimes appear to be corrupted by factors that are inconsistent with Catholic doctrine. In such cases, they must be patiently and prudently purified through contacts with those responsible and through careful and respectful catechesis - unless radical inconsistencies call for immediate and decisive measures.

Judgements on these matters is for the diocesan Bishop or for the Bishops of a given territory in which such forms are found. In this case, Bishops should share their experience so as to provide common pastoral guidelines and avoid contradictory positions which can be detrimental for the Christian people. In any event, Bishops should take a positive and encouraging stance with regard to popular religiosity, unless there are patently obvious reasons to the contrary.

Congregation for Divine Worship
and the Discipline of the Sacraments
Prot. N. 1532/00/L

Decree

In affirming the primacy of the Liturgy, "the summit toward which the activity of the Church is directed...and fount from which all her power flows" *(Sacrosanctum Concilium, 10)*, the Second Vatican Council nevertheless reminds us that "the spiritual life, however, is not limited solely to participation in the Liturgy" *(ibidem, 12)*. The spiritual life of the faithful is also nourished by "the pious practices of the Christian people", especially those commended by the Apostolic See and practised in the particular Churches by mandate of the Bishop or by his approval. Mindful of the importance that such cultic expressions should conform to the laws and norms of the Church, the Council Fathers outlined their theological and pastoral understanding of such practices: "pious devotions are to be ordered so as to harmonize with the Sacred Liturgy and lead the Christian people to it, since in fact the Liturgy by its very nature is far superior to any of them" *(ibidem, 13)*.

In the light of this authoritative teaching and of other pronouncements of the Church's Magisterium on the pious practices of the Christian people, and drawing on pastoral cases that have emerged in recent years, the Plenary of the Congregation for Divine Worship and the Discipline of the Sacraments, held September 26-28 2001, approved this present *Directory* which considers, in general terms, the relationship between Liturgy and popular piety, restates the *principles* regulating that nexus, and stipulates *guidelines* for their fruitful implementation in the particular Churches, in accordance with their specific traditions. By cultivation of a positive and encouraging pastoral stance towards popular piety, therefore, it is for the Bishops in a special way to value popular piety, whose fruits have been, and remain, of major importance in conserving the faith of the Christian people.

Having received the approval of the Supreme Pontiff John Paul II to publish this "Directory on Popular Piety. Principles and Guidelines" (Letter of the Secretariat of State, Prot. N. 497.514 of 14 December 2001), the Congregation for Divine Worship and the Discipline of the Sacraments is pleased to publish it in the hope that both Pastors and faithful may draw from this instrument, encouragement to grow in Christ, through him and with him, in the Holy Spirit to the praise of God the Father in heaven.
Anything contrary not withstanding.

From the offices of the Congregation for Divine Worship and the Discipline of the Sacraments, 17 December 2001.

Jorge A. Card. Medina Estévez
Prefect

Francesco Pio Tamburrino
Archbishop Secretary

INTRODUCTION

1. In accordance with the teaching of the Second Vatican Council, this Congregation, in furthering and promoting the Liturgy, "the summit toward which the activity of the Church is directed... and the fount from which all her power flows"[1], wishes to draw attention to the need to ensure that other forms of piety among the Christian people are not overlooked, nor their useful contribution to living in unity with Christ, in the Church, be forgotten[2].

Following on the conciliar renewal, the situation with regard to Christian popular piety varies according to country and local traditions. Contradictory attitudes to popular piety can be noted: manifest and hasty abandonment of inherited forms of popular piety resulting in a void not easily filled; attachments to imperfect or erroneous types of devotion which are estranged from genuine Biblical revelation and compete with the economy of the sacraments; unjustified criticism of the piety of the common people in the name of a presumed "purity" of faith; a need to preserve the riches of popular piety, which is an expression of the profound and mature religious feeling of the people at a given moment in space and time; a need to purify popular piety of equivocation and of the dangers deriving from syncretism; the renewed vitality of popular religiosity in resisting, or in reaction to, a pragmatic technological culture and economic utilitarianism; decline of interest in popular piety ensuing on the rise of secularized ideologies and the aggressive activities of "sects" hostile to it.

The question constantly occupies the attention of Bishops, priests, deacons, pastoral assistants, and scholars, who are concerned both to promote the liturgical life among the faithful and to utilize popular piety.

2. In its constitution on the Liturgy, the Second Vatican Council explicitly touched upon the relationship between the Liturgy and

---

[1] SC 10.
[2] Cf. SC 12 and 13.

pious exercises[3]. The question of popular piety has been more amply considered on various occasions by the Apostolic See[4] and by the Conferences of Bishops[5]. In his Apostolic Letter *Vicesimus Quintus Annus*, John Paul II raised the question again in relation to the liturgical renewal and indicated that it remained among those to be addressed at a future date: "popular piety can neither be ignored nor treated with indifference or disrespect because of its richness and because in itself it represents a religious attitude in relation to God. However, it has to be continually evangelized, so that the faith which it expresses may become more mature and authentic. The pious exercises of the Christian people and other forms of devotion can be accepted and recommended provided that they do not become substitutes for the Liturgy or integrated into the Liturgical celebrations. An authentic pastoral promotion of the liturgy, will know how to build on the riches of popular piety, purify them and direct them towards the Liturgy as an offering of the people"[6].

3. With a view, therefore, to assisting the Bishops in "promoting and honouring the prayers and pious practises of the Christian people, that fully reflect the norms of the Church"[7], in addition to the Liturgy, the preparation of this present *Directory* appears opportune to this Dicastery. In a general way, it considers the various connections between the Liturgy and popular piety. This *Directory* also reaffirms some principles and establishes guidelines for their practical application.

---

[3] Cf. SC 13.
[4] Cf. S. CONGREGATION OF RITES, Instruction *Eucharisticum mysterium* (25.4. 1967), 58-67; PAUL VI, Apostolic Exhortation *Marialis cultus* (2.2.1974), 24-58; Apostolic Exhortation *Evangelii nuntiandi* (8.12.1975), 48; JOHN PAUL II, Apostolic Exhortation *Catechesi tradendae* (16.10.1979), 54; Apostolic Exhortation *Familiaris consorti* (22.11.1981) 59-62; CONGREGATION FOR THE CLERGY, *General Directory on Catechesis* (15.8.1997), Libreria Editrice Vaticana, Città del Vaticano 1997, nn. 195-196.
[5] See, for example, III CONFERENCIA GENERAL DEL EPISCOPADO LATINO-AMERICANO, *Documento de Puebla*, 444-469, 910-915, 935-937, 959-963; CONFERENCIA EPISCOPAL DE ESPANA, Documento pastoral de la Comision episcopal de Liturgia, *Evangelizacion y renovation de la piedad popular*, Madrid 1987; *Liturgia y piedad popular*, Directorio Liturgico-Pastoral, Secretariado Nacional de Liturgia, Madrid 1989; CONFERENCIA GENERAL DEL EPISCOPADO LATINO-AMERICANO, *Documento de Santo Domingo*, 36, 39, 53.
[6] JOHN PAUL II, Apostolic Letter *Vicemus Quintus Annus* (4.12.1988), 18.
[7] JOHN PAUL II, Apostolic Constitution *Pastor Bonus* (28.6.1988), 70.

Nature and Structure

4. This Directory contains two parts. The first, entitled *Emerging trends*, provides the elements necessary for the harmonization of Liturgy and popular piety. It draws on the experience which has matured during the long history and emergence of the contemporary problematic (Chapter 1). The teachings of the Magisterium are systematically restated since they are indispensable for ecclesial communion and fruitful action (Chapter 2). Finally, the theological principles, according to which difficulties concerning the relationship between Liturgy and popular piety are approached and resolved, are stated (Chapter 3). The possibility of realizing a true and fruitful harmonization of Liturgy and popular piety can only be achieved by a wise and committed respect for these presuppositions. Conversely, overlooking them leads to nothing but reciprocal and futile ignorance, damaging confusion and contradictory polemics.

The second part, entitled *Guidelines*, offers a series of practical proposals. It does not claim to be able to include every usage or practice of popular piety to be found in particular locations throughout the world. Mention of particular practices or expressions of popular piety is not to be regarded as an invitation to adopt them where they are not already practised. This section is elaborated in reference to the Liturgical Year (Chapter 4); to the special veneration given by the Church to the Mother of our Saviour (Chapter 5); to devotion to the Holy Angels, the Saints and the Beatified (Chapter 6); to suffrage for the dead (Chapter 7) and to pilgrimage and examples of popular piety connected with shrines (Chapter 8).

The object of this *Directory* is to offer guidelines and, where necessary, to prevent abuses or deviations. Its tone is positive and constructive. In the same context, it provides short historical notes on several popular devotions in its *Guidelines*. It records the various pious exercises attached to these devotions while signalling their theological underpinning, and making practical suggesting in relation to time, place, language and other factors, so as to harmonize them with the Liturgy.

Those to Whom the Directory is Addressed

5. The operative proposals of this Directory, which are intended solely for the Latin Church and primarily for the Roman Rite, are addressed firstly to the Bishops, whose office entails presiding over the worshipping community of the dioceses, promoting the liturgical life and coordinating other forms of worship[8] with it. They are also intended for the Bishops' closest collaborators - their episcopal Vicars, priests, deacons and especially the Rectors of sanctuaries. These proposals are also intended for the major Superiors of the institutes of consecrated life - both male and female, since many forms of popular piety arose within, and were developed by, such institutes, and because the religious and the members of the secular institutes can contribute much to the proper harmonization of the various forms of popular piety with the Liturgy.

6. The history of the Western Church is marked by the flowering among the Christian people of multiple and varied expressions of simple and fervent faith in God, of love for Christ the Redeemer, of invocations of the Holy Spirit, of devotion to the Blessed Virgin Mary, of the veneration of the Saints of commitment to conversion and of fraternal charity. These expressions have grown up alongside the Liturgy. Treatment of this vast and complex material which is sometimes referred to as "popular religiosity" or "popular piety"[9] lacks a uniform terminology. Hence it will be necessary to adopt a certain precision of language. Without pretending to resolve all difficulties in this area, it will be useful to outline the commonly understood meaning of certain terms employed in this document.

---

[8] Cf. LG 21; SC 41; Decree *Christus Dominus*, 15; Sacred Congregation for Bishops, *Directorium de pastorali ministerio* Episcoporum, Typis Polyglotis Vaticanis 1973, 75-76, 82, 90-91; CIC, can. 835, § 1 and can. 839, §2; JOHN PAUL II, Apostolic Letter *Vicesimus quintus annus*, 21.

[9] Treating of the same material, the Apostolic Exhortation, *Evangelii Nuntiandi*, 48, for example, having recalled its richness, states: "because of this we gladly call it *popular piety*, that is, religion of the people, rather than religiosity of the people"; the Apostolic Exhortation *Catechesi tradendae*, 54, uses the expression "popular piety"; *the Code of Canon Law, can. 1234, §1*, adopts the term *"popular piety"*; John Paul II uses the term *"popular piety"* in the Apostolic Letter *Vicesimus quintus annus*; The Catechism of the Catholic Church, 1674-1676, uses the expression "popular religiosity" but is also aware of the term "popular piety" (1679); the fourth Instruction for the correct implementation of the conciliar Constitution on the Sacred Liturgy (37-40) *Varietates legitimae*, published by the Congregation for Divine Worship and the Discipline of the Sacraments (25.1.1994) employs the expression "popular piety" in article 45.

18

Pious Exercise

7. The expression "pious exercise" in this Directory refers to those public or private expressions of Christian piety which, although not part of the Liturgy, are considered to be in harmony with the spirit, norms, and rhythms of the Liturgy. Moreover, such pious exercises are inspired to some degree by the Liturgy and lead the Christian people to the Liturgy[10]. Some pious exercises have been established by mandate of the Apostolic See or by mandate of the Bishops[11]. Many of these exercises are part of the cultic patrimony of particular Churches or religious families. Pious exercises always refer to public divine revelation and to an ecclesial background. They often refer to the grace revealed by God in Jesus Christ and, in conformity with the laws of the Church, they are practised "in accordance with approved customs or books"[12].

Devotions

8. In the present context, this term is used to describe various external practices (e.g. prayers, hymns, observances attached to particular times or places, insignia, medals, habits or customs). Animated by an attitude of faith, such external practices manifest the particular relationship of the faithful with the Divine Persons, or the Blessed Virgin Mary in her privileges of grace and those of her titles which express them, or with the Saints in their configuration with Christ or in their role in the Church's life[13].

Popular Piety

9. The term "popular piety" designates those diverse cultic expressions of a private or community nature which, in the context of the Christian faith, are inspired predominantly not by the Sacred Liturgy but by forms deriving from a particular nation or people or from their culture.

---

[10] Cf. SC 13.
[11] Cf. SC 13.
[12] SC 13.
[13] Cf. COUNCIL OF TRENT, *Decretum de invocatione, veneratione, et reliquiis Sanctorum, et sacris imaginibus* (3. 12. 1563), in DS 1821-1825; Pius XII, Encyclical Letter *Mediator Dei*, in AAS 39 (1947) 581-582; SC 104; LG 50.

Popular piety has rightly been regarded as "a treasure of the people of God"[14] and "manifests a thirst for God known only to the poor and to the humble, rendering them capable of a generosity and of sacrifice to the point of heroism in testifying to the faith while displaying an acute sense of the profound attributes of God: paternity, providence, His constant and loving presence. It also generates interior attitudes otherwise rarely seen to the same degree: patience, an awareness of the Cross in every-day life, detachment, openness to others and devotion"[15].

Popular Religiosity

10. "Popular religiosity" refers to a universal experience: there is always a religious dimension in the hearts of people, nations, and their collective expressions. All peoples tend to give expression to their totalizing view of the transcendent, their concept of nature, society, and history through cultic means. Such characteristic syntheses are of major spiritual and human importance.

Popular religiosity does not always necessarily refer to Christian revelation.

Some Principles

An overview of the present Directory can be obtained from the following principles which are more fully developed and explained in the subsequent text.

The Primacy of the Liturgy

11. History shows that, in certain epochs, the life of faith is sustained by the forms and practices of piety, which the faithful have often felt more deeply and actively than the liturgical celebrations. Indeed, "every liturgical celebration, because it is an action of Christ the Priest and of his Body, which is the Church, it is a sacred action surpassing all others. No other action of the

---

[14] JOHN PAUL II, Homily at the celebration of the Word in La Serena (Chile), 2, in *Insegnamenti di Giovanni Paolo II*, X/1 (1987), Libreria Editrice Vaticana, Città del Vaticano 1988, p. 1078.
[15] PAUL VI, Apostolic Exhortation *Evangelii nuntiandi*, 48.

Church can equal its efficacy by the same title or to the same degree"[16]. Hence, the ambivalence that the Liturgy is not "popular" must be overcome. The liturgical renewal of the Council set out to promote the participation of the people in the celebration of the Liturgy, at certain times and places (through hymns, active participation, and lay ministries), which had previously given rise to forms of prayer alternative to, or substitutive of, the liturgical action itself.

The faithful should be made conscious of the preeminence of the Liturgy over any other possible form of legitimate Christian prayer. While sacramental actions are *necessary* to life in Christ, the various forms of popular piety are properly *optional*. Such is clearly proven by the Church's precept which obliges attendance at Sunday Mass. No such obligation, however, has obtained with regard to pious exercises, notwithstanding their worthiness or their widespread diffusion. Such, however, may be assumed as obligations by a community or by individual members of the faithful.

The foregoing requires that the formation of priests and of the faithful give preeminence to liturgical prayer and to the liturgical year over any other form of devotion. However, this necessary preeminence is not to be interpreted in exclusive terms, nor in terms of opposition or marginalization.

Evaluation and Renewal

12. The optional nature of pious exercises should in no way be taken to imply an under-estimation or even disrespect for such practices. The way forward in this area requires a correct and wise appreciation of the many riches of popular piety, of the potentiality of these same riches and of the commitment to the Christian life which they inspire.

The Gospel is the measure against which all expressions of Christian piety - both old and new - must be measured. The task of evaluating devotional exercises and practices, and of purifying them when necessary, must be conducted against this criterion so as to

---

[16] SC 7.

ensure their proper relationship with the Christian mystery. What is said of the Christian Liturgy is also true of popular piety: "it may never incorporate rites permeated by magic, superstition, animism, vendettas or sexual connotations"[17].

Hence, the liturgical renewal willed by the Second Vatican Council must also inspire a correct evaluation and renewal of pious exercises and devotional practices. Popular piety should be permeated by: a *biblical* spirit, since it is impossible to imagine a Christian prayer without direct or indirect reference to Sacred Scripture; a *liturgical* spirit if it is to dispose properly for or echo the mysteries celebrated in the liturgical actions; an *ecumenical* spirit, in consideration of the sensibilities and traditions of other Christians without, however, being restricted by inappropriate inhibitions; an *anthropological* spirit which both conserves symbols and expressions of importance or significance for a given nation while eschewing senseless archaicisms, and which strives to dialogue in terms redolent with contemporary sensibility. To be successful, such a renewal must be imbued with a pedagogical awareness and realized gradually, always taking into consideration time and particular circumstances.

Distinct from and in harmony with the Liturgy

13. The objective difference between pious exercises and devotional practices should always be clear in expressions of worship. Hence, the formulae proper to pious exercises should not be commingled with the liturgical actions. Acts of devotion and piety are external to the celebration of the Holy Eucharist, and of the other sacraments.

On the one hand, a superimposing of pious and devotional practices on the Liturgy so as to differentiate their language, rhythm, course, and theological emphasis from those of the corresponding liturgical action, must be avoided, while any form of competition with or opposition to the liturgical actions, where such

---

[17] CONGREGATION FOR DIVINE WORSHIP AND THE DISCIPLINE OF THE SACRAMENTS, IV Instruction on the correct application of the Conciliar Constitution on the Sacred Liturgy (nn. 37-40) *Varietates legitimae*, 48.

exists, must also be resolved. Thus, precedence must always be given to Sunday, Solemnities, and to the liturgical seasons and days.

Since, on the other, pious practices must conserve their proper style, simplicity and language, attempts to impose forms of "liturgical celebration" on them are always to be avoided.

The Language of Popular Piety

14. While conserving its simplicity and spontaneity, the verbal and gestural language of popular piety should be careful to ensure the transmission of the truth of the faith together with the greatness of the Christian mysteries.

Gestures

15. Popular piety is characterized by a great variety and richness of bodily, gestural and symbolic expressions: kissing or touching images, places, relics and sacred objects; pilgrimages, processions; going bare-footed or on one's knees; kneeling and prostrating; wearing medals and badges... . These and similar expressions, handed down from father to son, are direct and simple ways of giving external expression to the heart and to one's commitment to live the Christian life. Without this interior aspect, symbolic gesture runs the risk of degenerating into empty customs or mere superstitions, in the worst cases.

Texts and Formulae

16. While drawn up in terms less exacting than those employed for the prayers of the Liturgy, devotional prayers and formulae should be inspired, nonetheless, by Sacred Scripture, the Liturgy, the Fathers of the Church and the Magisterium, and concord with the Church's faith. The established public prayers attached to pious devotions and the various acts associated with pious exercises must always be approved by the local Ordinary[18].

---

[18] Cf. CIC, can 826, § 3.

Song and Music

17. Song, a natural expression of the soul of any nation, plays an important role in popular piety[19]. The conservation of the received corpus of traditional songs must be linked with a biblical and ecclesial spirit which is open to the possibility, where necessary, of their revision or to the composition of new songs.

Among some peoples, song is instinctively linked with hand-clapping, rhythmic corporeal movements and even dance. Such are external forms of interior sentiment and are part of popular traditions, especially on occasions such as patronal feasts. Clearly, such should be genuine expressions of communal prayer and not merely theatrical spectacles. The fact of their prevalence in one area, however, should not be regarded as a reason for their promotion in other areas, especially where they would not be spontaneous.

Sacred Images

18. The use of sacred images is of major importance in the whole area of popular piety, since culturally and artistically they assist the faithful in encountering the mysteries of the Christian faith. Indeed, the veneration of sacred images belongs to the very nature of Catholic piety. Such is clear from its artistic patrimony, which can be seen in many churches and sanctuaries, and to which popular devotion has often contributed.

Here, the principles apply which govern the liturgical use of images of Christ, Our Lady, the Saints. These have been traditionally asserted and defended by the Church in the knowledge that "the honour rendered to the image is directed to the person represented"[20]. The necessary rigour which has to be applied in drawing up the iconographic scheme of churches[21] - in matters relating to the truths of the faith and their hierarchy, beauty and quality- must also be applied to images and objects destined for private and personal devotion.

---

[19] Cf. SC 118.
[20] Cf. COUNCIL OF NICEA II, *Definitio de sacris imaginibus* (23 October 787) in DS 601; COUNCIL OF TRENT *Decretum de invocatione, veneratione, et reliquiis Sanctorum, et sacris imaginibus* (3 December 1563), in DS 1823-1825.
[21] Cf. SC 124-125.

So as to ensure that the iconography used in sacred places is not left to private initiatives, those with responsibility for churches and oratories should safeguard the dignity, beauty and quality of those sacred images exposed for public veneration. Likewise, they should avoid the de facto imposition on the community of pictures or statues inspired by the private devotion of individuals[22].

The Bishops, therefore, and the rectors of sanctuaries are to ensure that the sacred images produced for the use of the faithful, either in their homes or on their persons, or those borne aloft on their shoulders, are not reduced to banalities, nor risk giving rise to error.

Sacred Places

19. Apart from the *church*, sanctuaries -which are sometimes not churches- afford important opportunities for the expression of popular piety, which are often marked by particular devotional forms and practices, among which the most significant is that of pilgrimage. Together with these sacred places, which are clearly reserved for public and private prayer, others exist which are often not less important: e.g. homes, places of life and work. On certain occasions even the streets and squares can become places facilitating the manifestation of the faith.

Sacred Times

20. The rhythm associated with the change from day to night, from one month to another, or of the seasons is often associated with various forms of popular piety. Such can also be true of particular days recalling joyous or tragic personal or community events. Above all, the "the feast days", with their preparations for various religious manifestations, have contributed much in forging the traditions peculiar to a given community.

---

[22] Cf. CIC, can 1188.

Responsibilities and Competencies

21. Manifestations of popular piety are subject to the jurisdiction of the local Ordinary. It is for him to regulate such manifestations, to encourage them as a means of assisting the faithful in living the Christian life, and to purify and evangelize them where necessary. He is also to ensure that they do not substitute for the Liturgy nor become part of the liturgical celebrations[23]. The local ordinary also approves the prayers and formulae associated with acts of public piety and devotional practices[24]. The dispositions given by a particular local Ordinary for the territory of his jurisdiction are for the particular Church entrusted to his pastoral care.

Hence, the faithful - both clerics and laity, either as groups or individuals, may not publically promote prayers, formulae or private initiatives without the permission of the ordinary.

In accordance with the Apostolic Constitution *Pastor Bonus*, n.70, it is the competence of the Congregation for Divine Worship and the Discipline of the Sacraments to assist the Bishops in matters relating to prayers and devotional practices of the Christian people, as well as to issue dispositions in those cases surpassing the bounds of a particular Church, and in imposing subsidiary provisions.

---

[23] Cf. JOHN PAUL II, Apostolic Letter *Vicesimus quintus annus*, 18; CONGREGATION FOR DIVINE WORSHIP AND THE DISCIPLINE OF THE SACRAMENTS, IV Instruction for the correct application of the conciliar Constitution on the Sacred Liturgy (nn. 37-40) *Varietates legitimae*, 45.
[24] Cf. CIC, can 826, § 3.

PART ONE

EMERGING TRENDS
HISTORY, MAGISTERIUM
AND THEOLOGY

CHAPTER ONE

Liturgy and Popular Piety in an Historical Perspective

Liturgy and Popular Piety throughout the Centuries

22. The relationship between Liturgy and popular piety is ancient. It is therefore necessary to begin by surveying, even rapidly, how this relationship has been experienced down through the centuries, since it will often help to resolve contemporary difficulties.

Christian antiquity

23. The Apostolic and post-apostolic periods are marked by a profound fusion of the cultic realities which are now called Liturgy and popular piety. For the earliest Christian communities, Christ alone (cf. *Col* 2:16) was the most important cultic reality, together with his life-giving word (cf. *John* 6:63), his commandment of reciprocal charity (cf. *John* 13:34), and the ritual actions which he commanded in his memory (cf. 1 *Cor* 11:24-26). Everything else - days and months, seasons and years, feasts, new moons, food and drink... (cf. *Gal* 4:10; *Col* 2:16-19) - was of secondary importance.

Nevertheless, the signs of personal piety are already to be found among the first generation of Christians. Inspired by the Jewish tradition, they recommended following the example of incessant prayer of Jesus and St Paul (cf. *Luke* 18:1; *Rm* 12:12; 1 *Thes* 5:17), and of beginning and ending all things with an act of thanksgiving (cf. 1 *Cor* 10:31; 1 *Thes* 2:13; *Col* 3:17). The pious Israelite began the day praising and giving thanks to God. In the same spirit, he gave thanks for all his actions during the day. Hence, every joyful or sorrowful occasion gave rise to an expression of praise, entreaty, or repentance. The Gospels and the writings of the New Testament contain invocations of Jesus, signs of christological devotion, which were repeated spontaneously by the faithful outside of the context of Liturgy. It must be recalled that it was a common usage of the faithful to use biblical phrases such as : "Jesus, Son of David, have mercy on me" (...); "Lord if you wish, you can heal me" (...); "Jesus, remember me when you come into your kingdom" (...); "My Lord and my God" (...); "Lord Jesus, receive my spirit" (...). Innumerable prayers to Christ have been developed by the faithful of every generation on the basis this piety.

Until the second century, expressions of popular piety, whether deriving from Jewish, Greco-Roman or other cultures, spontaneously came together in the Liturgy. It has already been noted, for example, that the *Traditio Apostolica* contains elements deriving from popular sources[25].

The cult of martyrs, which was of great importance for the local Churches, preserves traces of popular usages connected with the memory of the dead[26]. Some of the earliest forms of veneration of the Blessed Virgin Mary[27] also reflect popular piety, among them the *Sub tuum praesidium* and the Marian iconography of the catacombs of St Priscilla in Rome.

While always most vigilant with regard to interior conditions and the prerequisites for a dignified celebration of the sacred mysteries (cf. 1 *Cor* 11:17-32), the Church has never hesitated in incorporating into the liturgical rites forms drawn from individual, domestic and community piety.

In this period Liturgy and popular piety, either conceptually or pastorally, did not oppose each other. Both concurred harmoniously in celebrating the one mystery of Christ, considered as a whole, and in sustaining the supernatural and moral life of the disciples of the Lord.

---

[25] The following examples can be traced to a popular context: the *Benedictio fructuum* (n. 32) in A. BOTTE (ed.) *La Tradition apostolicque de saint Hippolyte. Essai de reconstruction*, Aschendorff, Meunster Westfalen, ed. 1989, pp. 18, 78.

[26] Some customs connected with the cult of the martyrs almost certainly derive from popular practices: lamps placed at their tombs; wreathes of flowers and leaves which lent a festive note to sacred places; fragrant unguents placed on the tombs of the martyrs; various objects, especially cloths called *brandae*, *palliola, nomina* touched to the tombs of the martyrs were regarded as precious, authentic relics; the custom of the *refrigerium* at the tombs of the martyrs.

[27] The famous *De Navitate Mariae* (third century), also known as the *Protoevangelium Iacobi* and numerous accounts of the *De dormitione Mariae* of the second century, all bear witness to early Christian devotion to the Mother of God. According to scholars, these writings refer to many popular traditions which had a significant influence on the development of Marian devotion.

30

24. In the fourth century, given the new politico-social situation of the Church, the question of the relationship between liturgy and popular piety begins to be raised consciously in terms of adaptation and inculturation rather than solely in terms of spontaneous convergence.

The local Churches, guided by clear pastoral and evangelizing principles, did not hesitate to absorb into the Liturgy certain purified solemn and festive cultic elements deriving from the pagan world. These were regarded as capable of moving the minds and imaginations of the people who felt drawn towards them. Such forms, now placed at the service of the mystery of worship, were seen as neither contrary to the Gospel nor to the purity of true Christian worship. Rather, there was a realization that only in the worship of Christ, true God and true Saviour, could many cultic expressions, previously attributed to false gods and false saviours, become true cultic expressions, even though these had derived from man's deepest religious sense.

25. In the fourth and fifth centuries, a greater sense of the sacredness of times and places begins to emerge. Many of the local Churches, in addition to their recollection of the New Testament data concerning the *dies Domini*, the Easter festival and fasting (cf. *Mark* 2:18-22), began to reserve particular days for the celebration of Christ's salvific mysteries (Epiphany, Christmas and Ascension), or to honour the memory of the martyrs on their *dies natalis* or to commemorate the passing of their Pastors on the anniversary of their *dies depositionis*, or to celebrate the sacraments, or to make a solemn undertaking in life. With regard to the socialization of the place in which the community is called to celebrate the divine mysteries and give praise to the Lord, it must be noted that many of these had been transformed from places of pagan worship or profane use and dedicated exclusively to divine worship. They became, often simply by their architectural arrangements, a reflection of the mystery of Christ and an image of the celebrating Church.

26. During this period, the formation of various liturgical families with their consequent differences, matured. The more important metropolitan Churches now celebrate the one worship of the Lord with their own cultural and popular forms which developed from differences of language, theological traditions, spiritual sensibilities, and social contexts. This process gave rise to the progressive development of liturgical systems with their own proper styles of celebration and agglomeration of texts and rites. It is not insignificant to note that even during this golden age for the formation of the liturgical rites, popular elements are also to be found in those rites.

On the other hand, bishops and regional synods began to establish norms for the organization of worship. They became vigilant with regard to the doctrinal correctness of the liturgical texts and to their formal beauty, as well as with regard to the ritual sequences[28]. Such interventions established a liturgical order with fixed forms which inevitably extinguished the original liturgical creativity, which had not been completely arbitrary. Some scholars regard these developments as one of the sources of the future proliferation of texts destined for private and popular piety.

27. Mention must be made of the pontificate of the great pastor and liturgist Pope St Gregory VII (590-604), since it is regarded as an exemplary reference point for any fruitful relationship between the Liturgy and popular piety. Through the organization of processions, stations and rogations, Gregory the Great undertook a major liturgical reform which sought to offer the Roman people structures which resonated with popular sensibilities while, at the same time, remaining securely based on the celebration of the divine mysteries. He gave wise directives to ensure that the conversion of new nations

---

[28] "[Placuit] ut nemo in precibus vel Patrem, vel pro Filio, vel Filium pro Patre nominet. Et cum altari assistitur, semper as patrem dirigatur oratio. Et quicumque sibi preces aliunde describit, non eis utatur, nisi prius cum instructioribus fratribus contulerit": THIRD COUNCIL OF CARTHAGE , can. 23, N. 1, in I. D. Mansi, *Sacrorum Conciliorum nova et amplissima collectio*, III, Florentiae 1759, col. 884; "Placuit etiam hoc, ut preces quae probatae fuerint in concilio celebrentur, sive praefationes sive commendationes, seu manus impositiones, ab omnibus celebrentur, nec aliae omnino contra fidem praeferantur: sed quaecumque a prudentioribus fuerint collectae, dicantur": *Codex canonum Ecclesiae Africae*, can. 103 (*ibid.*, col. 807).

did not happen without regard for their own cultural traditions. Indeed, the Liturgy itself could be enriched by new legitimate cultic expressions and the noble expressions of artistic genius harmonized with more humble popular sensibilities. He established a sense of unity in Christian worship by anchoring it firmly in the celebration of Easter, even if other elements of the one mystery of Salvation (Christmas, Epiphany, and Ascension) were also celebrated and the memorials of the Saints expanded.

The Middle Ages

28. Among the main concerns of the Oriental Christian Churches, especially the Byzantine Church, of the middle ages, mention can be made of both phases of the struggles against the iconaclast heresy (725-787 and 815-843) which was a watershed for the Liturgy. It was also a period of classical commentaries on the Eucharistic Liturgy and on the iconography for buildings set aside for worship.

In the liturgical field, there was a noticeable increase in the Church's iconographical patrimony and in her sacred rites which assumed a definitive form. The Liturgy reflected the symbolic vision of the universe and a sacral hierarchical vision of the world. In this vision, we have the coalescence of all orders of Christian society, the ideals and structures of monasticism, popular aspirations, the intuitions of the mystics and the precepts of the ascetics.

With the decree *De sacris imaginibus* of the Second Council of Nicea (787)[29] and the resolution of the iconaclastic controversy in the "Triumph of Orthodoxy" (843), iconography, having been given doctrinal legitimacy, developed and organized its definitive form. The icon, hieratic and pregnant with symbolic power, itself became part of the celebration of the Liturgy, reflecting, as it did, the mystery celebrated and retaining something of its permanent presence which was exposed for the veneration of the faithful.

In the West, the high middle ages saw the formation of new cultures, and political and civil institution deriving from the

---

[29] In DS 600-603.

encounter of Christianity, already by the fifth century, with peoples such as the Celts, the Visigoths, the Anglosaxons, and the Francogermans.

Between the seventh and the fifteenth century, a decisive differentiation between Liturgy and popular piety began to emerge which gradually became more pronounced, ending eventually in a dualism of celebration. Parallel with the Liturgy, celebrated in Latin, a communitarian popular piety celebrated in the vernacular emerged.

30. The following may be counted among the reasons for the development of this dualism:

• the idea that the Liturgy was the competence of clerics since the laity were no more than spectators at the Liturgy;

• the marked distinction of roles in Christian society - clerics, monks, and laity - gave rise to different styles and forms of prayer;

• in Liturgy and iconography, the distinct and particular consideration given to the various aspects of the one mystery of Christ, while expressing a devotion for the life and work of our Lord, failed to facilitate an explicit realization of the centrality of the Paschal mystery and encouraged a multiplicity of particular times and forms of celebration of a distinctively popular tenor;

• lack of a sufficient knowledge of the Scriptures on the part, not only of the laity, but of many clerics and religious, made access to an understanding of the structure and symbolic language of the Liturgy difficult;

• the diffusion of apocryphal literature containing many stories of miracles and episodic anecdotes, on the other hand, had a significant influence on iconography which, touching the imagination of the faithful, naturally attracted their attention;

• the practical absence of any form of homeletic preaching, the disappearance of mystagogical preaching, and poor catechetical formation, rendered the celebration of the Liturgy closed to the understanding and active participation of the faithful who turned to alternative cultic times and forms;

• a tendencey to allegory, excessively encroaching on the meaning of the liturgical texts and rites, often deviated the faithful from an understanding of the true nature of the Liturgy;

• the discovery of expressive, popular forms and structures unconsciously redrafted the Liturgy which, from many perspectives, had become increasingly incomprehensible and distant from the people.

31. The Middle ages saw the emergence and development of many spiritual movements and associations of different ecclesiastical and juridical form. Their life and activities had notable consequences for the relationship between Liturgy and popular piety.

The new religious orders of evangelical and apostolic life, devoted their efforts to preaching and adopted simpler liturgical forms in comparison to those found in the monasteries. These liturgical forms were often close to the people and to their expressive forms. On the other hand, they also developed and promoted pious exercises that encapsulated their charism, and diffused them among the people.

The emergence of the Confraternities, with their religious and charitable objectives, and of the lay corporations with their professional interests, gave rise to a certain popular liturgical activity. These often erected chapels for their religious needs, chose Patrons and celebrated their feast days. Not infrequently, they compiled the *officia parva* and other prayers for the use of their members. These frequently reflected the influence of the Liturgy as well as containing elements drawn from popular piety.

The various schools of spirituality that had arisen during the middle ages became an important reference point for ecclesial life. They inspired existential attitudes and a multiplicity of ways of interpreting life in Christ and in the Holy Spirit. Such interpretations exercised considerable influence on the choice of celebration (e.g. episodes from the Passion of Christ) and were the basis of many pious exercises.

Civil society, constituted ideally as a *societas Christiana*, modelled many of its structures on ecclesiastical useage and measured itself according to the rhythms of liturgical life. An example of this is to be found in the ringing of bells in the evening which called the peasants from the fields and simultaneously signalled the *Angelus*.

32. Throughout the middle ages many forms of populuar piety gradually emerged or developed. Many of these have been handed down to our times:

• the organization of sacred performances depicting the mysteries celebrated during the liturgical year, especially those surrounding the salvific events of Christ's birth, his passion, death and resurrection;

• the participation of the faithful was encouraged by the emergence of poetry in the vernacular which was widely used in popular piety;

• as a parallel, or even an alternative to many liturgical expressions, several devotional forms appeared; for example, various forms of Eucharistic adoration served to compensate for the rarity with which Holy Communion was received; in the late middle ages, the rosary tended to substitute for the psalter; among the faithful, the pious exercises of Good Friday became a substitute for the Liturgy proper to that day;

36

• the growth in popular forms of devotion to Our Lady and the Saints: pilgrimages to the Holy Land, and to the tombs of the Apostles and martyrs, veneration of relics, litanies, and suffrage for the dead;

• the considerable development of the rites of blessing which, together with Christian elements, also reflected a certain response to a naturalistic sensibility as well to popular pre-Christian beliefs and practices;

• nucleuses of "sacred times" based on popular practices were constituted. These were often marginal to the rhythm of the liturgical year: sacred or profane fair days, tridua, octaves, novenas, months devoted to particular popular devotions.

33. In the middle ages, the relationship between Liturgy and popular piety is constant and complex, but a dual movement can be detected in that same relationship: the Liturgy inspired and nourished various expressions of popular piety; and several forms of popular piety were assumed by, and integrated into the Liturgy. This is especially true with regard to the rites of consecration of persons, the assumption of personal obligations, the dedication of places, the institution of feasts and to the various blessings.

A dualism, however, prevailed between Liturgy and popular piety. Towards the end of the middles ages, both, however, went through a period of crisis. Because of the collapse of cultic unity, secondary elements in the Liturgy acquired an excessive relevance to the detriment of its central elements. In popular piety, because of the lack of adequate catechesis, deviations and exaggerations threatened the correct expressions of Christian worship.

The Modern Period

34. At the dawn of the modern period, a balanced relationship between Liturgy and popular piety did not seem any more likely. The *devotio moderna* of the late fifteenth century was popular with

37

many great spiritual masters and was widespread among clerics and cultivated laymen. It promoted the development of meditative and affective pious exercises based principally on the humanity of Christ - the mysteries of his infancy, his hidden life, his Passion and death. However, the primacy accorded to contemplation, the importance attributed to subjectivity and a certain ascetical pragmatism exalting human endeavour ensured that Liturgy no longer appeared as the primary source of the Christian life in the eyes of men and women advanced in the spiritual life.

35. The *De Imitatione Christi* is regarded as a typical expression of the *devotio moderna*. It has exercised an extraordinary and beneficial influence on many of the Lord's disciples in their quest for Christian perfection. The *De Imitatione Christi* orients the faithful towards a certain type of individual piety which accentuates detachment from the world and the invitation to hear the Master's voice interiorly. Less attention is devoted to the communitarian and ecclesial aspects of prayer and to liturgical spirituality.

Many excellent pious exercises are to be found among those who cultivated the *devotio moderna*, as well as cultic expressions deriving from sincerely devout persons. A full appreciation of the celebration of the Liturgy is not, however, always to be found in such circles.

36. From the end of the fifteenth to the beginning of the sixteenth century, the discovery of Africa, America and the Far East caused the question of the relationship between Liturgy and popular piety to be posed in new terms.

While the work of evangelizing and catechising countries distant from the cultural and cultic centre of the Roman Rite was certainly accomplished through preaching the Word and celebrating the sacraments (cf. *Mt* 28:19), it also came about through the pious exercises popularized by the missionaries.

Pious exercises became a means of transmitting the Gospel message and, following conversion, of preserving the Christian faith. By virtue of the norms designed to preserve the Roman Rite, there were few reciprocal influences between the Liturgy and the autochthonous cultures. In Paraguay, the *Reductiones* are a rare example of this. The encounter with these cultures, however, was easily facilitated in the field of popular piety.

37. Among those most concerned for the reform of the Church at beginning of the sixteenth century, mention must be of two Camoldelesi monks, Paolo Giustiniani and Pietro Querini, authors of the famous *Libellus ad Leonem X*[30] which set out important principles for the revitalization of the Liturgy so as to open its treasures to the entire People of God. They advocated biblical instruction for the clergy and religious, the adoption of the vernacular in the celebration of the divine mysteries and the reform of the liturgical books. They also advocated the elimination of spurious elements deriving from erroneous popular piety, and the promotion of catechesis so as to make the faithful aware of the importance of the Liturgy.

38. Shortly after the close of the fifth Lateran Council (6 March 1517), which had made provisions for the instruction of youth in the Liturgy[31], the crisis leading to the rise of protestantism arose. Its supporters raised many objections to the Catholic doctrine on the sacraments, to the Church's worship, and to popular piety.

The Council of Trent (1545-1563), convoked to resolve the situation facing the People of God as a result of the spread of protestantism, addressed questions relating to the Liturgy and popular piety from the doctrinal and cultic perspective[32], at all three

---

[30] Text in *Annales Camaldulenses*, IX, Venice 1773, coll. 612-719.

[31] Cf. FIFTH LATERAN COUNCIL, [*Bulla reformationis Curiae*] in *Conciliorum Oecumenicorum Decreta*, edited by the Istituto per le scienze religiose di Bologna, Edizioni Dehoniane, Bologna 1991, p. 625.

[32] The *Decretum de sacramentis* DS 1600-1630) and the *Decretum de ss. Eucharistia* (DS 1635-1650), the discussions leading to the *Decretum de sacramento paenitentiae* (DS 1667-1693), the *De doctrina de sacramento extremae unctionis* (DS 1694-1700), the *Doctrina de communione sub utraque specie et parvulorum* (DS 1725-1730), the *Doctrina de ss. Missae sacrificio* (DS 1738-1750) dealing with essential matters of faith on the Catholic doctrine of the Eucharist as a sacrifice, and on points relating to its ritual celebration, the *Decretum super petitione concessionis calicis* (DS 1760), the *Doctrina de sacramento ordinis* (DS 1763-1770), *Doctrina de sacramento matrimonii* (DS 1797-1800), the *Decretum de Purgatorio* (Ds 1820), the *Decretum de invocatione, veneratione, et reliquiis Sanctorum, et sacris imaginibus* (DS 1821-1825), have had wide application in the field of popular piety.

of its phases. Because of the historical context and the doctrinal nature of the matters dealt with by the Council, the liturgical and sacramental questions placed before the Council were answered predominantly from a doctrinal perspective. Errors were denounced and abuses condemned. The Church's faith and liturgical tradition were defended. The decree *De reformatione generali*[33] proposed a pastoral programme, whose activation was entrusted to the Holy See and to the Bishops, which demonstrated concern for the problems arising from the liturgical instruction of the people.

39. In conformity with the dispositions of the Council, synods were held in many of the ecclesiastical provinces. These often demonstrated a concern to bring the faithful to an active participation in the celebration of the divine mysteries. Simultaneously, the Roman Pontiffs began a vast programme of liturgical reform. The Roman Calendar and the liturgical books of the Roman Rite[34] were revised in the relatively short space of time between 1568 and 1614. In 1588 the Sacred Congregation of Rites was established to promote and correctly order the liturgical celebrations of the Roman Church[35]. The *Catechismus ad Parochos* fulfilled the provision of pastoral and liturgical formation.

40. The reform of the Council of Trent brought many advantages for the Liturgy. There was a return to the "ancient norm of the Fathers"[36] in many of the Church's rites, notwithstanding the relatively limited scientific knowledge of the period then available. Elements and impositions extraneous to the Liturgy or excessively connected with popular sensibilities were eliminated. The doctrinal content of the liturgical texts was subjected to examination to

---

[33] In *Conciliorum Oecumenicorum Decreta*, cit., pp. 784-796.
[34] Pius V published the *Breviarium Romanum ex decreto SS. Concilii restitutum* on 9 July 1568 with the Bull *Quod a nobis*, the *Missale Romanum ex decreto sacrosancti Concilii tridentini restitutum* with the Bull *Quo primum tempore* of 14 July 1570; Paul V envisaged a reform of the liturgical books when he promulgted the *Rituale Romanum* on 16 June 1614 with the Apostolic Letters *Apostolicae Sedi*.
[35] The *Sacra Congregatio Rituum* was founded by Sixtus V on 22 January 1588 with the Apostolic Constitution *Immensa aeterni Dei*.
[36] In the Bull promulgting the *Missale Romanum* explicit reference it is explicitly stated that the experts engaged by the Apostolic See *"ad pristinam Missale ipsum sanctorum Patrum normam ac ritum restituerunt"*.

ensure that they reflected the faith in its purity. The Roman Liturgy acquired a notable ritual unity, dignity and beauty.

The reform, however, had a number of indirect negative consequences: the Liturgy seemed to acquire a certain fixed state which derived from the rubrics regulating it rather than from its nature. In its active subject, it seemed to become almost exclusively hierarchical which reinforced the existing dualism between Liturgy and popular piety.

41. The Catholic reform, with its positive concern to promote a doctrinal, moral and institutional reform of the Church and to counteract the spread of protestantism, in a certain sense endorsed the complex cultural phenomenon of the Baroque. This, in turn, exercised a considerable influence on the literary, artistic and musical expressions of Catholic piety.

In the post Tridentine period, the relationship between Liturgy and popular piety acquires some new aspects: the Liturgy entered a static period of substantial uniformity while popular piety entered a period of extraordinary development.

While careful to establish certain limits, determined by the need for vigilance with regard to the exuberant or the fantastic, the Catholic reform promoted the creation and diffusion of pious exercises which were seen as an important means of defending the Catholic faith and of nourishing the piety of the faithful. The rise of Confraternities devoted to the mysteries of the Passion of Our Lord, as well as those of the Blessed Virgin Mary and the Saints are good examples. These usually had the triple purpose of penance, formation of the laity and works of charity. Many beautiful images, full of sentiment, draw their origins from this form of popular piety and still continue to nourish the faith and religious experience of the faithful.

The "popular missions" emerged at this time and contributed greatly to the spread of the pious exercises. Liturgy and popular piety coexist in these exercises, even if somewhat imbalanced at times. The parochial missions set out to encourage the faithful to approach the Sacrament of Penance and to receive Holy Communion. They regarded pious exercises as a means of inducing conversion and of assuring popular participation in an act of worship.

Pious exercises were frequently collected and organized into prayer manuals. Reinforced by due ecclesiastical approval, such became true and proper aids to worship for the various times of the day, month and year, as well as for innumerable circumstances that might arise in life.

The relationship between Liturgy and popular piety during the period of the Catholic Reform cannot be seen simply in contrasting terms of stability and development. Anomalies also existed: pious exercises sometimes took place within the liturgical actions and were superimposed on those same actions. In pastoral practice, they were sometimes more important than the Liturgy. These situations accentuated a detachment from Sacred Scripture and lacked a sufficient emphasis on the centrality of the Paschal mystery of Christ, foundation and summit of all Christian worship, and its privileged expression in Sunday.

42. The age of enlightenment further delineated the separation of "the religion of the learned" which was potentially close to the Liturgy, and the "religion of the simple people" which, of its very nature, was closer to popular piety. Both the "learned" and the "simple people", however, shared the same religious practices. The "learned" promoted a religious practice based on knowledge and the enlightenment of the intelligence and eschewed popular piety which they regarded as superstitious and fanatical.

The aristocratic sense which permeated many aspects of culture had its influence on the Liturgy. The encyclopaedic character of knowledge, coupled with a critical sense and an interest in research, led to the publication of many of the liturgical sources. The ascetical concerns of some movements, often influenced by Jansenism, fuelled a call for a return to the purity of the Liturgy of antiquity. While certainly redolent of the cultural climate, the renewal of interest in the Liturgy was fuelled by a pastoral concern for the clergy and laity, especially from the seventeenth century in France.

In many areas of its pastoral concern, the Church devoted its attention to popular piety. There was an intensification of that form of apostolic activity which tended to integrate, to some degree, the Liturgy and popular piety. Hence, preaching was encouraged at significant liturgical times, such as Advent and on Sundays when adult catechesis was provided. Such preaching aimed at the conversion of the hearts and morals of the faithful, and encouraged them to approach the Sacrament of Penance, attend Sunday Mass regularly, and to demonstrate the importance of the Sacrament of the Anointing of the Sick and Viaticum.

Popular piety, which had been effective in stemming the negative influences of protestantism, now became an effective antidote to the corrosiveness of rationalism and to the baleful consequences of Jansenism within the Church. It emerged strengthened and enriched from this task and from the extensive development of the parish missions. Popular piety emphasized certain aspects of the Christian mystery in a new way, for example, the Sacred Heart of Jesus, and new "days", such as the "first Friday of the month", gained importance in the piety of the faithful.

With regard to the eighteenth century, mention must be made of the work of Ludivico Antonio Muratori who combined erudition with notable pastoral activity. In his famous work, *Della regolata devozione dei cristiani*, he advocated a form of religiosity based on the Liturgy and the Scriptures that eschewed all attachment to superstition and magic. The work of Benedict XIV (Prospero Lambertini) was also significant, especially his authorization of the use of the Bible in the vernacular.

43. The Catholic Reform strengthened the structure and unity of the Roman Rite. Given the notable missionary expansion of the eighteenth century, the Reform spread its proper Liturgy and organizational structure among the peoples to whom the Gospel message was preached.

In the missionary territories of the eighteenth century, the relationship between Liturgy and popular piety was framed in terms similar to, but more accentuated than, those already seen in the sixteenth and seventeenth centuries:

• the Liturgy retained a Roman character and hence remained, at least partially, extraneous to autochthonous culture. The question of inculturation was practically never raised, partly because of the fear of negative consequence for the faith. In this respect, however, mention must be made of the efforts of Matteo Ricci in relation to the question of the Chinese rites, and those of Roberto de' Nobili on the question of the Indian rites;

• popular piety, on the one hand, was subject to the danger of religious syncretism, especially where evangelization was not deeply rooted; while on the other, it became more autonomous and mature: it was not limited to reproducing the pious practices promoted by the missionaries, rather it created other forms of pious exercises that reflected the character of the local culture.

The Contemporary Period

44. Following the French revolution with its objective of eradicating the Christian faith and its overt hostility to Christian worship, the nineteenth century witnessed an important liturgical revival.

This was preceded by the development of a vigorous ecclesiology which saw the Church not only in terms of a hierarchical society but also as the People of God and as a worshipping community. Besides the revival of ecclesiology, mention must also be made of the flowering of biblical and patristic studies, as well as the ecclesial and ecumenical concerns of men such as Antonio Rosmini (d. 1855) and John Henry Newman (d. 1890).

The history of the renaissance of liturgical worship reserves a special place for Dom Prosper Guéranger (d. 1875), who restored the monastic life in France and founded the abbey of Solesmes.

His conception of the Liturgy is permeated by a love for the Church and for tradition. The Roman Rite, he maintained in his writings on Liturgy, was indispensable for unity and, hence, he opposed autochthonous forms of liturgical expression. The liturgical renewal which he promoted has the distinct advantage of not having been an academic movement. Rather, it aimed at making the Liturgy an expression of worship in which the entire people of God participated.

45. The revival of the Liturgy was not the sole activity of the nineteenth century. Independently of that revival, popular piety experienced significant growth. The revival of liturgical song coincided with the development of many popular hymns, the widespread use of liturgical aids such as bilingual missals for the use of the faithful, and a proliferation of devotional booklets.

The culture of Romanticism rediscovered man's religious sense and promoted the quest for, and understanding of, the elements of popular piety, as well as emphasizing their importance in worship.

The nineteenth century experienced a phenomenon of crucial significance: expressions of local cult arising from popular initiatives and often associated with prodigous events such as miracles and apparitions. Gradually, these received official approval as well as the favour and protection of the ecclesial authorities, and were eventually assumed into the Liturgy. Several Marian sanctuaries and centres of pilgrimages, and of Eucharistic and penitential Liturgies as well as Marian centres associated with popular piety are all emblematic of this phenomenon.

While the relationship between popular piety and the Liturgy in the nineteenth century must be seen against the background of a liturgical revival and an ever increasing expansion of popular piety, it has to be noted that that same relationship was affected by the negative influence of an accentuated superimposition of pious exercises on the liturgical actions, a phenomenon already evident during the period of the Catholic Reform.

46. At the outset of the twentieth century, St Pope Pius X (1903-1914) proposed bringing the Liturgy closer to the people, thereby "popularizing" it. He maintained that the faithful assimilated the "true Christian spirit" by drawing from its "primary and indenspensable source, which is active participation in the most holy mysteries and from the solemn public prayer of the Church"[37]. In this way, St Pope Pius X gave authoritative recognition to the objective superiority of the Liturgy over all other forms of piety; dispelled any confusion between Liturgy and popular piety, indirectly clarified the distinction between both and opened the way for a proper understanding of the relationship that must obtain between them.

Thus was born the liturgical movement which was destined to exercise a prominent influence on the Church of the twentieth century, by virtue of the contribution of many eminent men, noted for their learning, piety and commitment, and in which the Supreme Pontiffs recognized the promptings of the Spirit[38]. The ultimate aim of the liturgical movement was pastoral in nature[39], namely, to encourage in the faithful a knowledge of, and love for, the divine mysteries and to restore to them the idea that these same mysteries belong to a priestly people (cf. 1 *Pt* 2:5).

In the context of the liturgical movement, it is easy to understand why some of its exponents assumed a diffident attitude to popular piety and identified it as one of the causes leading to the degeneration of the Liturgy. They faced many of the abuses deriving from the superimposition of pious exercises on the Liturgy as well as instances where the Liturgy was displaced by acts of popular worship. In their efforts to restore the purity of divine worship, they took as their ideal the Liturgy of the early centuries of the Church, and consequently radically rejected any form of popular piety deriving from the middles ages or the post tridentine period.

---

[37] "Motu proprio *Tra le sollecitudini* (22.11.1903), in *Pii X Pontificis Maximi Acta*, I, Akademische Druck-u. Verlagsanstalt, Graz 1971, p. 77.

[38] Cf. Pius XII, Allocution to the participants of the first International congress on pastoral liturgy, Assisi-Rome, (22.9.1956), in AAS 48 (1956) 712; SC 43.

[39] Among those involved with the movement mention must be made of Lambert Beauduin (d. 1960), Odo Casel (d. 1948), Pius Parsch (d. 1954), Bernard Botte (d. 1960), Romano Guardini (d. 1968), Josef A. Jungmann (d. 1975), Cipriano Vagaggini (d. 1999), Aimé-Georges Martimort (d. 2000).

This rejection, however, failed to take sufficient account of the fact that these forms of popular piety, which were often approved and recommended by the Church, had sustained the spiritual life of the faithful and produced unequalled spiritual fruits. It also failed to acknowledge that popular piety had made a significant contribution to safeguarding and preserving the faith, and to the diffusion of the Christian message. Thus, Pope Pius XII, in his encyclical *Mediator Dei* of 21 November 1947[40], with which he assumed leadership of the liturgical movement, issued a defence of pious exercises which, to a certain extent, had become synonymous with Catholic piety in recent centuries.

The Constitution *Sacrosanctum Concilium* of the Second Vatican Council finally defined, in proper terms, the relationship obtaining between the Liturgy and popular piety, by declaring the unquestionable primacy of the Sacred Liturgy and the subordination to it of pious exercises, while emphasizing their validity[41].

Liturgy and Popular Piety: The Current Problematic

47. From the foregoing historical outline, it is clear that the question of the relationship between Liturgy and popular piety is not an exclusively contemporary one. Albeit from different perspectives and in changing terms, the question has constantly arisen. It is now time to draw some conclusions from history so as to address the frequently and urgently asked pastoral questions which arise to-day.

Historical considerations: the causes of imbalances

48. History principally shows that the correct relationship between Liturgy and popular piety begins to be distorted with the attenuation among the faithful of certain values essential to the Liturgy itself. The following may be numbered among the casues giving rise to this:

• a weakened awareness or indeed a diminished sense of the Paschal mystery, and of its centrality for the history of salvation,

---

[40] In AAS 39 (1947) 521-600).
[41] Cf. SC 7, 10, 13.

of which the Liturgy is an actualization. Such inevitably occurs when the piety of the faithful, unconscious of the "hierarchy of truths", imperceptibly turns towards other salvific mysteries in the life of Christ, of the Blessed Virgin Mary or indeed of the Angels and Saints;

• a weakening of a sense of the universal priesthood in virtue of which the faithful offer "spiritual sacrifices pleasing to God, through Jesus Christ" (1 *Pt* 2:5; *Rm* 12:1), and, according to their condition, participate fully in the Church's worship. This is often accompanied by the phenomenon of a Liturgy dominated by clerics who also perform the functions not reserved to them and which, in turn, causes the faithful to have recourse to piuos exercises through which they feel a sense of becoming active participants;

• lack of knowledge of the language proper to the Liturgy - as well as its signs, symbols and symbolic gestures - causing the meaning of the celebration to escape the greater understanding of the faithful. Such can engender a sense of being extraneous to the liturgical action, and hence are easily attracted to pious exercises whose language more easily approaches their own cultural formation, or because certain forms of devotions respond more obviously to daily life.

49. Each of these factors, and both in certain cases, not infrequently produces imbalances in the relationship between the Liturgy and popular piety, to the former's detriment and the latter's impoverishment. These should therefore be corrected through careful and persistent catechetical and pastoral work.

Conversely, the liturgical renewal and the heightened liturgical sense of the faithful have often recontextualized popular piety in its relationship with the Liturgy. Such should be regarded as a positive development and in conformity with the most profound orientation of Christian piety.

The Sacred Constitution on the Liturgy

50. The relationship between the Liturgy and popular piety, in our times, must be approached primarily from the perspective of the directives contained in the constitution *Sacrosanctum Concilium*, which seek to establish an harmonious relationship between both of these expressions of piety, in which popular piety is objectively subordinated to, and directed towards, the Liturgy[42].

Thus, it is important that the question of the relationship between popular piety and the Liturgy not be posed in terms of contradiction, equality or, indeed, of substitution. A realization of the primordial importance of the Liturgy, and the quest for its most authentic expressions, should never lead to neglect of the reality of popular piety, or to a lack of appreciation for it, nor any position that would regard it as superfluous to the Church's worship or even injurious to it.

Lack of consideration for popular piety, or disrespect for it, often betrays an inadequate understanding of certain ecclesial realities and is not infrequently the product not so much of the doctrine of the faith, but of some ideologically inspired prejudice. These give rise to attitudes which:

• refuse to accept that popular piety itself is an ecclesial reality prompted and guided by the Holy Spirit[43];

• do not take sufficient account of the fruits of grace and sanctity which popular piety has produced, and continues to produce, within the ecclesial body;

• not infrequently reflect a quest for an illusory "pure Liturgy", which, while not considering the subjective criteria used to determine purity, belongs more to the realm of ideal aspiration than to historical reality;

---

[42] Cf. SC 13.
[43] Cf. JOHN PAUL II, Homily at the Celebration of the Word in La Serena (Chile), 2, in *Insegnamenti di Giovanni Paolo II*, X/1 (1987), cit., p. 1078.

• and confound, "sense", that noble component of the soul that legitimitatly permeates many expressions of liturgical and popular piety, and its degenerate form which is "sentimentality".

51. In the relationship between the Liturgy and popular piety, the opposite phenomenon is also encountered - the importance of popular piety is overestimated practically to the detriment of the Church's Liturgy.

It has to be said that where such happens, either because of particular circumstances or of a theoretical choice, pastoral deviations emerge. The Liturgy is no longer the "summit towards which the activity of the Church is directed; [and]...the fount from which all her power flows"[44]. Rather it becomes a cultic expression extraneous to the comprehension and sensibility of the people which is destined to be neglected, relegated to a secondary role or even become reserved to particular groups.

52. The laudable idea of making Christian worship more accessible to contemporary man, especially to those insufficiently catechized, should not lead to either a theoretical or practical underestimation of the primary and fundamental expression of liturgical worship, notwithstanding the acknowledged difficulties arising from specific cultures in assimilating certain elements and structures of the Liturgy. In some instances, rather than seeking to resolve such difficulties with patience and farsightedness, recourse is sometimes made to simplistic solutions.

53. In those instances where the liturgical actions have been superseded by popular piety comments, such as the following, are often heard:

• popular piety is sufficient for the free and spontaneous celebration of "Life" and its multiplicity of expressions; Liturgy, on the other hand, centred as it is on the "Mystery of Christ" is essentially anaemic, repetitive, formalistic and inhibits spontaneity;

---

[44] SC 10.

• the Liturgy fails to involve the total being, both corporeal and spiritual, of each member of the faithful; popular piety, because it speaks directly to man, involves his body, heart and mind;

• popular piety is an authentic and real locus for the life of prayer: through pious exercises the faithful truly dialogue with the Lord, in terms which they fully understand and regard as their own; the Liturgy, however, places words on their lips that are not their own or alien to their level of culture, and thereby becomes a hindrance to prayer rather than a means;

• the ritual with which popular piety is expressed is one which is received and accepted by the faithful because of its correspondence between their cultural expectations and ritual language; the ritual proper to the Liturgy is impenetrable because its various expressive forms derive from different cultural sources widely removed from those of the faithful.

54. In an exaggerated and dialectic way, such views reflect the divergence that undeniably exists between the Liturgy and popular piety in some cultural ambits.

Where such views are held, they inevitably indicate that an authentic understanding of the Christian Liturgy has been seriously compromised, or even evacuated of its essential meaning.

Against such views, it is always necessary to quote the grave and well pondered words of the last ecumenical Council: "every Liturgical celebration, because it is an action of Christ the Priest and of his Body, which is the Church, is a sacred action surpassing all others. No other action of the Church can equal its efficacy by the same title and to the same degree"[45].

55. Any unilateral exaltation of popular piety which fails to take account of the Liturgy, is inconsistent with the fact that the essential elements of the Liturgy derive from the will of Christ himself, and

---

[45] SC 7.

is unable to emphasize its indispensable sotereological and doxological importance. Following the Lord's ascension to the glory of the Father, and the descent of the Holy Spirit, the perfect glorification of God and the salvation of man comes about primarily through the celebration of the liturgy[46], which requires an adherence of faith, and brings the believer to participate in the fundamental salvific event: the Passion, Death and Resurrection of Christ (cf. *Rm* 6:2-6, 1 *Cor* 11:23-26).

The Church's understanding of her mystery, and her worshipping and saving actions, constantly affirms that it is through "the Liturgy..., especially in the divine sacrifice of the Eucharist, [that] 'the work of our redemption is accomplished'"[47]. This affirmation, however, does not deny the importance of other forms of piety.

56. Theoretical or practical contempt for the Liturgy inevitably leads to a clouding of the Christian understanding of the mystery of God, Who has mercifully deigned to look down on fallen man and bring him to Himself through the incarnation of His Son and the gift of the Holy Spirit. Such fails to perceive the significance of salvation history and the relationship between Old and New Testaments. It underestimates the saving Word of God which sustains the Liturgy, and to which the Liturgy always refers. Such a disposition attenuates in the faithful any realization of the importance of the work of Christ our only Saviour who is the Son of God and the Son of the Blessed Virgin Mary. Eventually, it leads to a loss of the *sensus Ecclesiae*.

57. Any exclusive promotion of popular piety, which should always be seen in terms of the Christian faith[48], can encourage a process that eventually leads the faithful away from Christian revelation and encourages the undue or distorted use of elements drawn from cosmic or natural religions. It can also give rise to the introduction into Christian worship of elements

---

[46] Cf. SC 5-7.
[47] SC 2.
[48] Cf. supra n. 9.

taken from pre-Christian beliefs, or that are merely cultural, national or ethnic psychological expressions. Likewise, the illusion can be created that the transcendent can be reached through unpurified religious experiences[49], thereby promoting the notion that salvation can be achieved through man's own personal efforts (the constant danger of pelagianism should never be forgotten), thereby compromising any authentic Christian understanding of salvation as a gratuitous gift of God. Indeed, the role of secondary mediators, such as the Blessed Virgin Mary, the Angels and Saints, or even national saints, can surpass that of the Lord Jesus Christ, the one Mediator, in the minds of the faithful.

58. The Liturgy and popular piety, while not conterminous, remain two legitimate expressions of Christian worship. While not opposed to each other, neither are they to be regarded a equiparate to each other. Rather, they are to be seen in harmony with each in accordance with the Council's liturgical constitution: "The popular devotions of the Christian people [...] should accord with the sacred Liturgy...[and] in some way derive from it, and lead people to it, since in fact the Liturgy by its very nature is far superior to any of them"[50].

Hence, the Liturgy and popular piety are two forms of worship which are in mutual and fruitful relationship with each other. In this relationship, however, the Liturgy remains the primary reference point so as "clearly and prudently to channel the yearnings of prayer and the charismatic life"[51] which are found in popular piety. For its part, popular piety, because of its symbolic and expressive qualities, can often provide the Liturgy with important insights for inculturation and stimulate an effective dynamic creativity[52].

---

[49] Cf. CONGREGATION FOR THE DOCTRINE OF THE FAITH, *Lettera "Orationis forma" ai Vescovi della Chiesa cattolica su alcuni aspetti della meditazione cristiana* (15.10.1989): AAS 82 (1990) 362-379.
[50] SC 13.
[51] III CONFERENCIA GENERAL DEL EPISCOPADO LATINO-AMERICANO, *Documento de Puebla*, 465 e.
[52] *Ibid.*

Importance of Formation

59. In the light of the foregoing, it would seem that the formation of both clergy and laity affords a means of resolving many of the reasons underlying the imbalances between the Liturgy and popular piety. Together with the necessary formation in Liturgy, which is a long-term process, provision should also be made to complement it by re-discovering and exploring formation in popular piety[53], especially in view of the latter's importance for the enrichment of the spiritual life[54].

Since "the spiritual life...is not limited solely to participation in the liturgy"[55], restricting the formation of those involved in assisting spiritual growth exclusively to the Liturgy seems inadequate. Moreover, liturgical action, often reduced to participation at the Eucharist, cannot permeate a life lacking in personal prayer or in those qualities communicated by the traditional devotional forms of the Christian people. Current interest in oriental "religious" practices, under various guises, clearly indicates a quest for a spirituality of life, suffering, and sharing. The post-conciliar generation - depending on the country - often has never experienced the devotional practices of previous generations. Clearly, catechesis and educational efforts cannot overlook the patrimony of popular piety when proposing models for the spiritual life, especially those pious exercises commended by the Church's Magisterium.

---

[53] Cf. JOHN PAUL II, Apostolic Letter *Vicesimus Quintus Annus*, 15.
[54] JOHN PAUL II, *Message* to the Plenary meeting of the Congregation for Divine Worship and the Discipline of the Sacraments (21 September 2001), having reiterated the indispensable centrality of the Liturgy in the Church's life, he said "popular piety, although not always concurring with it, has its natural climax in the celebration of the Liturgy, and should ideally be oriented towards it. This should be clearly shown by appropriate catechesis" in *Notitiae* 37 (2001) 403. Cf. also CONGREGATION FOR THE CLERGY, *General Catechetical Directory*, cit., 195-196.
[55] SC 12.

CHAPTER TWO

Liturgy and Popular Piety
in the Church's Magisterium

60. Reference has already been made to the Magisterium of the Second Vatican Council, and to that of the Roman Pontiffs and the bishops, on the subject of popular piety[56]. At this point, it seems opportune to provide an organized synthesis of this material so as to facilitate a common doctrinal orientation for popular piety and to encourage a consistent pastoral approach to it.

Values in Popular Piety

61. Popular piety, according to the Magisterium, is a living reality in and of the Church. Its source is the constant presence of the Spirit of God in the ecclesial community; the mystery of Christ Our Saviour is its reference point, the glory of God and the salvation of man its object, its historical moment "the joyous encounter of the work of evangelisation and culture"[57]. On several occasions, the Magisterium has expressed its esteem for popular piety and its various manifestations, admonishing those who ignore it, or overlook it, or even disdain it, to adopt a more positive attitude towards it, taking due note of its many values[58]. Indeed, the Magisterium sees popular piety as "a true treasure of the People of God"[59].

The Magisterium's esteem for popular piety is principally motivated by the values which it incorporates.

Popular piety has an innate sense of the sacred and the transcendent, manifests a genuine thirst for God and "an acute

---

[56] Cf. supra n. 2.
[57] JOHN PAUL II, Homily given at the shrine of the Virgin Mary of "Zapopang", 2, in AAS, 71 (1979) 228.
[58] Cf. PAUL VI, Apostolic Exhortation *Marialis Cultus*, 31; JOHN PAUL II, Allocution to the Bishops of Basilicata and Apulia, *ad Limina* visit, 4, in *AAS* 74 (1982) 211-213.
[59] JOHN PAUL II, Homily given at the Celebration of the Word in La Serena (Chile), 2, in *Insegnamenti di Giovanni Paolo II*, X/1 (1987), cit., p. 1078.

sense of God's deepest attributes: fatherhood, providence, constant and loving presence",[60] and mercy[61].

The documents of the Magisterium highlight certain interior dispositions and virtues particularly consonant with popular piety and which, in turn, are prompted and nourished by it: patience and "Christian resignation in the face of irremediable situations"[62]; trusting abandonment to God; the capacity to bear sufferings and to perceive "the cross in every-day life"[63]; a genuine desire to please the Lord and to do reparation and penance for the offences offered to Him; detachment from material things; solidarity with, and openness to, others; "a sense of friendliness, charity and family unity"[64].

62. Popular piety can easily direct its attention to the Son of God who, for love of mankind, became a poor, small child, born of a simple humble woman. Likewise, it has a particular sensibility for the mystery of Passion and death of Christ[65].

Contemplation of the mystery of the afterlife is an important feature of popular piety, as is its interest in communion with the Saints in Heaven, the Blessed Virgin Mary, the Angels, and suffrage for the souls of the dead.

63. That harmonious fusion or the Gospel message with a particular culture, which is often found in popular piety, is a further reason for the Magisterium's esteem of popular piety. In genuine forms of popular piety, the Gospel message assimilates expressive forms particular to a given culture while also permeating the consciousness of that culture with the content of the Gospel, and its idea of life and death, and of man's freedom, mission and destiny.

The transmission of this cultural heritage from father to son, from generation to generation, also implies the transmission of Christian principles. In some cases, this fusion goes so deep that

---

[60] Cf. PAUL VI, Apostolic Exhortation *Evangelii nuntiandi*, 48.
[61] Cf. JOHN PAUL II, Apostolic Exhortation *Catechesi tradendae*, 54.
[62] III CONFERENCIA GENERAL DEL EPISCOPADO LATINO-AMERICANO, *Documento de Puebla*, 913.
[63] PAUL VI, Apostolic Exhortation *Evangelii nuntiandi* 48.
[64] III CONFERENCIA GENERAL DEL EPISCOPADO LATINO-AMERICANO, *Documento de Puebla*, 913.
[65] Cf. *Ibid.*, 912.

elements proper to the Christian faith become integral elements of the cultural identity of particular nations[66]. Devotion to the Mother of the God would be an example of this.

64. The Magisterium also highlights the importance of popular piety for the faith-life of the People of God, for the conservation of the faith itself and in inspiring new efforts at evangelization.

It is impossible to overlook "those devotions practised in certain regions by the faithful with fervour and a moving purity of intention"[67]; that authentic popular piety "in virtue of its essentially Catholic roots, is an antidote to the sects and a guarantee of fidelity to the message of salvation"[68]; that popular piety has been a providential means of preserving the faith in situations where Christians have been deprived of pastoral care; that in areas in which evangelization has been deficient, "the people for the most part express their faith primarily through popular piety"[69]; that popular piety is an important and indispensable "starting point in deepening the faith of the people and in bringing it to maturity"[70].

Deviations in Popular Piety

65. While the Magisterium highlights the undeniable qualities of popular piety, it does not hesitate to point out dangers which can affect it: lack of a sufficient number of Christian elements such as the salvific significance of the Resurrection of Christ, an awareness of belonging to the Church, the person and action of the Holy Spirit; a disproportionate interest between the Saints and the absolute sovereignty of Jesus Christ and his mysteries; lack of direct contact with Sacred Scripture; isolation from the Church's sacramental life; a dichotomy between worship and the duties of

---

[66] Cf. JOHN PAUL II, Homily given at the shrine of the Virgin Mary of "Zapopan", 2, in *AAS*, 71 (1979) 228-229; III CONFERENCIA GENERAL DEL EPISCOPADO LATINO-AMERICANO, *Documento de Puebla*, 283.

[67] JOHN PAUL II, Apostolic Exhortation *Catechesi tradendae*, 54.

[68] JOHN PAUL II, Discourse at the inauguration of the IV GENERAL CONFERENCE OF THE LATIN-AMERICAN BISHOPS, Santo Domingo, (12.10.1992), 12: *Insegnamenti di Giovanni Paolo II*, XV/2, Libreria Editrice Vaticana, Città del Vaticano 1994, p. 323.

[69] III CONFERENCIA GENERAL DEL EPISCOPADO LATINO-AMERICANO, *Documento de Puebla*, 913.

[70] *Ibid.*, 960.

Christian life; a utilitarian view of some forms of popular piety; the use of "signs, gestures and formulae, which sometimes become excessively important or even theatrical"[71]; and in certain instances, the risk of "promoting sects, or even superstition, magic, fatalism or oppression"[72].

66. In its attempts to remedy such defects in popular piety, the contemporary Magisterium has insistently stressed the need to "evangelize" popular piety[73], and sees it in relation to the Gospel which "will progressively free it from its defects; purify it, consolidate it and clarify that which is ambiguous by referring it of the contents of faith, hope and charity"[74].

Pastoral sensibility recommends that the work of "evangelizing" popular piety should proceed patiently, tolerantly, and with great prudence, following the methodology adopted by the Church throughout the centuries in matters relating to inculturation of the Christian faith, the Sacred Liturgy[75] and those inherent in popular piety.

The Subject of Popular Piety

67. The Church's Magisterium, mindful that "the spiritual life...is not limited solely to participation in the liturgy" and that "the Christian... must enter into his bedroom to pray to his Father in secret", indeed, "according to the teaching of the apostle, he must pray without ceasing"[76], holds that the subject of the various forms of prayer is every Christian - clerics,

---

[71] JOHN PAUL II, Allocution to the Conference of the Bishops of the Abruzzi and the Molise, *ad Limina* visit, 3, in *AAS*, 78 (1986) 1140.

[72] JOHN PAUL II, Discourse at Popayan (Columbia), in *Insegnamenti di Giovanni Paolo II*, IX/2 (1986), Libreria Editrice Vaticana, Città del Vaticano 1986, p. 115.

[73] Cf. JOHN PAUL II, Apostolic Letter *Vigesimus quintus annus*, 18; Allocution to the Conference of the Bishops of the Abruzzi and the Molise, *ad Limina* visit, 6, in *AAS*, 78 (1986) 1142; III CONFERENCIA GENERAL DEL EPISCOPADO LATINO-AMERICANO, *Documento de Puebla*, 458-459; CONGREGATION FOR DIVINE WORSHIP AND THE DISCIPLINE OF THE SACRAMENTS, Circular letter, *Orientamenti e proposte per la celebrazione dell'anno mariano* (3.4.1987), 68.

[74] JOHN PAUL II, Allocution to the Conference of the Bishops of the Abruzzi and the Molise, *ad Limina* visit, 6, in *AAS* 78 (1986) 1142.

[75] Cf. CONGREGATION FOR DIVINE WORSHIP AND THE DISCIPLINE OF THE SACRAMENTS, IV Instruction for the correct application of the conciliar Constitution on the Liturgy (nn. 37-40) *Varietataes legitimae*, 9-20.

[76] SC 12.

religious and laity - both privately when moved by the Spirit of Christ, and when praying with the community in groups of different origins and types[77].

68. Pope John Paul II has shown how the family can be a subject of popular piety. The exhortation *Familiaris Consortio*, having praised the family as the domestic sanctuary of the Church, emphasizes that "as preparation for worship celebrated in church[78], and as its prolongation in the home, the Christian family makes use of prayer, which presents a variety of forms. While this variety testifies to the extraordinary riches with which the Spirit vivifies Christian prayer, it serves also the various needs and life situations of those who turn to the Lord in prayer". It also observes that "apart from morning and evening prayers, certain prayers are to be expressly encouraged,[...] such as reading and meditating on the word of God, preparation for the reception of the sacraments, devotion and consecration to the Sacred Heart of Jesus, the various forms of the veneration of the Blessed Virgin Mary, grace before and after meals, and observance of popular devotions"[79].

69. Equally important subjects of popular piety are the confraternities and other pious associations of the faithful. In addition to their charitable and social endeavours, they have an institutional commitment to foster Christian cult, in relation to the Trinity, to Christ in his mysteries, to the Blessed Virgin Mary, to the Angels and Saints, in relation to the Beati, and in promoting suffrage for the souls of the faithful departed.

The Confraternities often observe, side by side with the liturgical calendar, their own proper calendars which indicate particular feasts, offices, novenas, setptenaria, tridua, penitential days, processions, pilgrimages, and those days on which specific works

---

[77] Cf. *Institutio generalis de Liturgia Horarum*, 9.
[78] With reference to the Liturgy note should also be made of the recommendation contained in the *Institutio generalis de Liturgia Horarum*, 27: "It is a laudable thing for the family, the domestic sanctuary, where possible, to celebrate in addition to the usual prayers, some parts of the Liturgy of the Hours so as to draw closer to the Church".
[79] JOHN PAUL II, Apostolic Exhortation *Familiaris Consortio*, 61.

of mercy are to be done. They also have their own devotional books and insignia such as medals, habits, cinctures, and even their own places of worship and cemeteries.

The Church recognizes the confraternities and grants juridical personality to them[80], approves their statutes and fosters their cultic ends and activities. They should, however, avoid conflict and isolation by prudent involvement in parochial and diocesan life.

Pious Exercises

70. Pious exercises are typical expressions of popular piety. In origin and content, in language and style, in usage and subject, they greatly differ among each other. The Second Vatican Council gave consideration to pious exercises, reiterating that they were highly to be recommended[81], and indicated those criteria which authenticate their legitimacy and validity.

71. In the light of the nature and of the characteristics proper to Christian worship, pious exercises, clearly must conform to the doctrine, legal discipline and norms of the Church[82]. Moreover, they should be in harmony with the Sacred Liturgy, take into account the seasons of the liturgical calendar, in so far as possible, and encourage "conscious active participation in the prayer of the Church"[83].

72. Pious exercises are part of Christian worship. The Church has always been attentive to ensure that God is glorified worthily through them, and that man derives spiritual benefit from them and is encouraged to live the Christian life.

The actions of Pastors in relation to pious exercises have been many. They have recommended and encouraged them, or guided and corrected them or simply tolerated them. Among the myriad of pious exercises, some must be mentioned, especially those erected by the

---

[80] Cf, CIC, can. 301 and can. 312.
[81] Cf. SC 13; LG 67.
[82] Cf. SC 13.
[83] JOHN PAUL II, Homily at the Celebration of the Word in La Serena (Chile), 2, in *Insegnamenti di Giovanni Paolo II*, X/1 (1987), cit., p. 1079.

Apostolic See, or which have been recommended by the same Apostolic See throughout the ages[84]. Mention must also be made of the pious exercises of the particular Churches "that are undertaken by order of the bishops according to customs or books lawfully approved"[85]; of the pious exercises that are practised in accordance with the particular law or tradition of certain religious families, or confraternities, or other pious associations of the faithful, since such have often received the explicit approbation of the Church; and of the pious exercises practised personally or in the home.

Some pious exercises which grew up among the community of the faithful and have received the approbation of the Magisterium[86], also enjoy the concession of indulgences[87].

Liturgy and Pious Exercises

73. The Church's teaching on the relationship of Liturgy and pious exercises may be summarized as follows: the Sacred Liturgy, in virtue of its very nature, is by far superior to pious exercises[88], and hence pastoral praxis must always accord to the Sacred Liturgy "that preeminent position proper to it in relation to pious exercises"[89]; Liturgy and pious exercises must co-exist in accordance with the hierarchy of values and the nature specific to both of these cultic expressions[90].

74. Careful attention to these principles should lead to a real effort to harmonize, in so far as possible, pious exercises with the rhythm and demands of the Liturgy, thereby avoiding any "mixture or admixture of these two forms of piety"[91]. This in turn ensures that no hybrid, or confused forms emerge from mixing Liturgy and pious

---

[84] Cf. SC 13.
[85] SC 13.
[86] Cf. CIC can. 23.
[87] Cf., EI, *Aliae concessiones*, 54.
[88] Cf. SC 7.
[89] CONGREGATION FOR DIVINE WORSHIP AND THE DISCIPLINE OF THE SACRAMENTS, Circular letter *Orientamenti e proposte per la celebrazione dell'Anno mariano*, 54.
[90] Cf. PAUL VI, Apostolic Exhortation *Marialis Cultus* 31, 48.
[91] THE ITALIAN EPISCOPAL CONFERENCE, EPISCOPAL COMMISSION FOR THE LITURGY, pastoral note *Il rinnovamento liturgico in Italia* (23.9.1983) 18, in *Enchiridion* CEI, 3, Edizioni Dehoniane, Bologna 1986, p. 886.

exercises, not that the latter, contrary to the mind of the Church, are eliminated, often leaving an unfilled void to the great detriment of the faithful[92].

General Principles for the Renewal of Pious Exercises

75. The Apostolic See has not failed to indicate those theological, pastoral, historical, and literary principles by which a renewal of pious exercises is to be effected[93]. It has also signalled the manner in which they should reflect a biblical and liturgical spirit, as well as an ecumenical one. The criteria established by the Holy See emphasize how the essential nucleus of the various pious exercises is to be identified by means of an historical investigation, and also reflect something of contemporary spirituality. Pious exercises are also required to take due account of the implications of a healthy anthropology. They should respect the culture and expressive style of the peoples who use them without, however, losing those traditional elements that are rooted in popular customs.

---

[92] Cf. Apostolic Exhortation *Marialis cultus*, 31; III CONFERENCIA GENERAL DEL EPISCOPADO LATINO-AMERICANO, *Documento de Puebla*, 915.

[93] Cf. SACRED CONGREGATION FOR BISHOPS, *Directorium de pastorali ministerio Episcoporum*, cit., 91; PAUL VI, Apostolic Exhortation *Marialis cultus*, 24-38.

CHAPTER THREE

For an Evaluation of Renewal of Popular piety

The Life of Worship: Communion with the Father, Through Christ, in the Holy Spirit

76. In the history of revelation, man's salvation is constantly presented as a free gift of God, flowing from His mercy, given in sovereign freedom and total gratuity. The entire complex of events and words through which the plan of salvation is revealed and actualized[94], takes the form of a continuous dialogue between God and man. God takes the initiative, and man is asked for an attitude of listening in faith, and a response in "obedience to faith" (*Rm* 1:5; 16:26).

The Covenant stipulated on Sinai between God and His chosen people (cf. *Ex* 19-24) is a singularly important event in this salvific dialogue, and makes the latter a "possession" of the Lord, a "kingdom of priests and a holy people" (*Ex* 19:6). Israel, although not always faithful to the Covenant, finds in it inspiration and the power to model its life on God Himself (cf. *Lk* 11:44-45; 19:2), and the content of that life on His Word.

Israel's worship and prayer are directed towards the commemoration of the *mirabilia Dei*, or God's saving interventions in history, so as to conserve a lively veneration of the events in which God's promises were realized, since these are the constant point of reference both for reflection on the faith and for the life of prayer.

77. In accordance with His eternal plan, "at various times in the past and in various different ways, God spoke to our ancestors through the prophets, but in our own times, these last days, He has spoken to us through His Son, the Son that He has appointed to inherit everything and through whom he made everything there is" (*Heb* 1:1-2).

The mystery of Christ, especially his Passover of death and Resurrection, is the full and definitive revelation and realization of

---

[94] Cf. SECOND VATICAN COUNCIL, Constitution *Dei Verbum*, 2.

God's salvific promises. Since Jesus is the "only Son of God (*John* 3:18), he is the one in whom God has given us all things without reserve" (cf. *Rm* 8:32; *John* 3:16). Hence, the person and works of Christ are the essential reference point for the faith and prayer life of the people of God. In him we find the Teacher of truth (cf. *Mt* 22:16), the faithful Witness (*Aps* 1:5), the High Priest (cf. *Heb* 4:14), the Pastor of our souls (cf. 1 *Pet* 2:25), and the one, perfect Mediator (cf. 1 *Tim* 2:5; *Heb* 8:6; 9:15; 12:24). Through him, man comes to God (cf. *John* 14:6), the Church's praise and supplication rise up to God, and all of the divine gifts are given to man.

In Baptism, we are buried with Christ and rise with him (cf. *Col* 2:12; *Rm* 6:4), we are freed from the dominion of the flesh and introduced to that of the Spirit (cf. *Rom* 8:9), and we are called to a state of perfection whose fulness is in Christ (cf. *Eph* 4:13). We have a model in Christ of a life whose every moment was lived in hearing the word of the Father, and in acceptance of His will. Christ's life is lived as a constant "fiat" to the will of God: "My food is to do the will of the one who sent me (*John* 4:34).

Christ, therefore, is the perfect model of filial piety and of unceasing dialogue with the Father. He is the model of the constant quest for that vital, intimate, and trusting contact with God which enlightens, guides and directs all of man's life.

78. In the life of communion with the Father, the faithful are guided by the Spirit (cf. *Rm* 8:14) who has been given progressively to transform them in Christ. He pours out to them "the spirit of adopted sons", by which they assimilate the filial disposition of Christ (cf. *Rm* 8:15-17), and his sentiments (cf. *Phil* 2:5). He makes present the teaching of Christ to the faithful (cf. *John* 14:26; 16: 13-25) so that they may interpret the events of life in its light. He brings them to a knowledge of the depths of God (cf. 1 *Cor* 2:10) and enables them to transform their lives into a "holy sacrifice" (*Rm* 12:1). He sustains them in rejection and in the trials that must be faced during the process of transforming themselves in Christ. The Spirit is given to sustain, nourish and direct their prayer: "The Spirit

too comes to help us in our weakness. For when we cannot choose words in order to pray properly, the Spirit himself expresses our plea in a way that could never be put into words, and God who knows everything in our hearts knows perfectly well what he means, and that the pleas of the saints expressed by the Spirit are according to the mind of God" (*Rm* 8:26-27).

Christian worship originates in, and draws impetus from the Spirit. That same worship begins, and is brought to completion, in the Spirit. It can therefore be concluded that without the Spirit of Christ there can be neither authentic liturgical worship, nor genuine expressions of popular piety.

79. From the principles already outlined above, popular piety should always be formed as a moment of the dialogue between God and man, through Christ in the Holy Spirit. Despite some deficiencies - such as confusion between God the Father and Jesus Christ - popular piety does bare a Trinitarian mark.

Popular piety, indeed, is especially susceptible to the mystery of God's paternity and arouses a sense of awe for His goodness, power and wisdom. It rejoices in the beauty of creation and gives thanks to God for it. Popular piety can express an awareness of the justice and mercy of God the Father, and of His care for the poor and lowly, and it can proclaim that He commends the good and rewards those who live properly and honestly, while abhorring evil and casting away from Himself those who obstinately follow the path of hatred, violence, injustice and deceit.

Popular piety can easily concentrate on the person of Christ, Son of God and Saviour of mankind. It can movingly recount the birth of Christ and intuit the immense love released by the child Jesus, true God and true man, a true brother in poverty and persecution from the moment of his birth. Innumerable scenes from the public life of Christ, the Good Shepherd who reaches out to sinners and publicans, the Miracle-worker healing the sick and helping the poor, or the Teacher proclaiming the truth, can be represented in popular piety. Above all it has the capacity to contemplate the mysteries of Christ's Passion because in them it can perceive Christ's boundless love and the extent of his solidarity with human suffering: Jesus betrayed and abandoned, scourged and crowned with thorns, crucified between thieves, taken down from the cross and buried in the earth, and mourned by his friends and disciples.

Popular piety is also consciously aware of the person of the Holy Spirit in the mystery of God. It professes that "through the Holy Spirit" the Son of God "became incarnate of Virgin Mary and was made man"[95] and that the Spirit was poured out to the Apostles at the beginning of the Church (cf. *Acts* 2:1-13). Popular piety is especially conscious that the power of the Spirit of God, whose seal is placed on all Christians in the Sacrament of Confirmation, is alive in all of the Church's sacraments; that baptism is conferred, sins forgiven, and the Holy Eucharist begun "in the name of the Father, and of the Son, and of the Holy Spirit"; and that all prayer in the Christian community, and the invocation of divine blessing on mankind and all creatures, is done in the name of the three Divine Persons.

80. Reference to the Most Blessed Trinity, while seminally present in popular piety, is an element requiring further emphasis. The following points offer an outline of how that might be done:

• The faithful require instruction on the character of Christian prayer, which is directed to the Father, through the mediation of the Son, in the power of the Holy Spirit.

• The formulae used in popular piety should give greater emphasis to the person and action of the Holy Spirit. The lack of a "name" for the Spirit of God and the custom of not representing him anthropomorphically have contributed to a certain absence of the Holy Spirit in the texts and formulae of popular piety, while not overlooking the role of music and gestures in expressing our relationship with the Holy Spirit. This lacuna, however, can be overcome by the evangelization of popular piety, as the Magisterium has already recommended on several occasions.

---

[95] DS 150; MISSALE ROMANUM, *Ordo Missae, Symbolum Nicaeno-Constantinopolitanum.*

● It is also necessary for popular piety to emphasize the primary and basic importance of the Resurrection of Christ. The loving devotion for the suffering of Christ, often demonstrated by popular piety, should also be completed by setting it in the context his glorification so as to give integral expression to the salvific plan of God as revealed in Christ, and allow for its inextricable link with his Paschal mystery. Only in this manner can the authentic face of Christianity be seen with its victory over death and its celebration of him who is "God of the living and not of the dead" (*Mt* 22:32), of Christ, the living one, who was dead but now lives forever (cf. *Ap* 1:28) and of the Spirit "who is Lord and giver of life"[96].

● Finally, devotion to the Passion of Christ should lead the faithful to a full and conscious participation in the Eucharist, in which the Body of Christ, sacrificed for our sake (cf. 1 *Cor* 11:24) is given as food; and in which the Blood of Christ, shed on the cross in the new and eternal Covenant and for the remission of sin, is given to drink. Such participation has its highest and most significant moment in the celebration of the Paschal Triduum, apex of the liturgical year, and in the Sunday celebration of the Sacred Mysteries.

The Church: Worshipping Community

81. The Church, "gathered in the name of the Father, and of the Son, and of the Holy Spirit"[97], is a worshipping community. By command of her Lord and Founder, the Church effects many acts of worship whose object is the glory God and the sanctification of man[98]. In different ways and in different measure, these are all celebrations of the Paschal Mystery of Christ, and aimed at realizing the divine will to gather the scattered children [of the Father] into the unity of a single nation.

In her ritual actions, the Church proclaims the Gospel of salvation and announces the Death and Resurrection of Christ, and actualizes the work of his salvation in sacred signs. In the Eucharist she celebrates the memorial of his blessed Passion, his

---

[96] *Ibid.*
[97] St Cyprian, *De oratione dominica*, 23:CSEL 3/1, Vindobonae 1868, p. 285.
[98] Cf. SC 5-7.

glorious Resurrection, and Ascension. In the celebration of the other sacraments she draws from the gifts of the Holy Spirit which flow from the Cross of our Saviour. The Church glorifies the Father in psalms and hymns for the wonders that He has accomplished in the death and exaltation of Christ His Son, and supplicates that the saving mystery of Easter might reach all mankind. With the sacramentals which have been instituted to assist the faithful at various times and in various situations, she prays that their activity might be directed and enlightened by the Spirit of Easter.

82. The celebration of the Liturgy, however, does not exhaust the Church's divine worship. Following the example and the teaching of the Lord, the disciples of Christ pray in the seclusion of their rooms (cf. *Mt* 6:6), they gather to pray according to forms created by men and women of great religious experience, who have encouraged the faithful and oriented their piety towards specific aspects of the mystery of Christ. They also pray according to structures which have emerged practically spontaneously from the collective Christian consciousness, in which the demands of popular culture harmoniously convey the essential data of the Gospel message.

83. Authentic forms of popular piety are also fruits of the Holy Spirit and must always be regarded as expressions of the Church's piety. They are used by the faithful who are in communion with the Church, accept her faith and who are docile to her discipline of worship. Indeed, many forms of popular piety have been approved and recommended by the Church herself[99].

84. Popular piety, as an expression of ecclesial piety, is subject to the general discipline of Christian worship and to the Church's pastoral authority which exercises a role of discernment and authentification in relation to it. The Church renews popular piety

---

[99] Cf. SC 13; LG 67.

by placing it in fertile contact with the revealed Word, tradition and the Sacred Liturgy itself.

On the other hand, expressions of popular piety must always be open to the "ecclesiological principle" of Christian worship. In this way:

• popular piety can have a correct understanding of the relationship between the particular Church and the universal Church. When popular piety concentrates on local or immediate issues, it risks closing itself to universal values and to ecclesiological perspectives;

• the veneration of the Blessed Virgin Mary, of the Angels and Saints, and suffrage for the dead, should be set in the vast context of the relationship between the heavenly Church and the pilgrim Church on earth;

• the relationship between *ministry* and *charism* should be properly understood, while the former is necessary for divine worship, the latter is frequently found in manifestations of popular piety.

Common Priesthood and Popular Piety

85. Through the sacraments of Christian initiation, the faithful become part of the Church, a prophetic, priestly and royal people called to worship God in spirit and in truth (cf. *John* 4:23). The Church exercises this task through Christ in the Holy Spirit, not only in the Sacred Liturgy, especially in the celebration of the Holy Eucharist, but also in other forms of the Christian life, among which are numbered the various forms of popular piety. The Holy Spirit confers the ability to offer sacrifices of praise to God, to offer prayer and entreaty to Him, so as to make of one's life "a living and holy sacrifice, pleasing to God" (Rm 12:1; *Heb* 12:28).

86. On this priestly basis, popular piety assists the faithful in persevering in prayer and in praising God the Father, in witnessing to Christ (cf. *Acts* 2:42-47), and in sustaining their vigilance until He comes again in glory. It also justifies our hope, in the Holy Spirit, of life eternal (cf. 1 *Pet* 3:15) and conserves important aspects of a specific cultic context, and, in different ways and in varying degrees, expresses those ecclesial values which arise and develop within the mystical Body of Christ.

Word of God and Popular Piety

87. The Word of God, as transmitted by Sacred Scripture, as conserved and proposed by the Magisterium of the Church, and as celebrated in the Sacred Liturgy, is the privileged and indispensable instrument of the Holy Spirit in the faithful's worship.

Since the Church is built on, and grows through, listening to the Word of God, the Christian faithful should acquire a familiarity with Sacred Scripture and be imbued with its spirit[100], so as to be able to translate the meaning of popular piety into terms worthy of, and consonant with, the data of the faith, and render a sense of that devotion that comes from God, who saves, regenerates and sanctifies.

The Bible offers an inexhaustible source of inspiration to popular piety, as well as unrivalled forms of prayer and thematic subjects. Constant reference to Sacred Scripture is also a means and a criterion for curbing exuberant forms of piety frequently influenced by popular religion which give rise to ambiguous or even erroneous expressions of piety.

88. Prayer should "accompany the reading of Sacred Scripture, so that a dialogue takes place between God and man"[101]. Thus, it is highly recommended that the various forms of popular piety normally include biblical texts, opportunely chosen and duly provided with a commentary.

---

[100] Cf. SECOND VATICAN COUNCIL, Constitution *Dei Verbum*, 25.
[101] *Ibid.*

70

89. In this respect, the models used in liturgical celebrations can be most useful, since they always contain a text taken from Sacred Scripture, variously chosen for different types of celebration. However, since the different expressions of popular piety already exhibit a legitimate structural and expressional diversity, the disposition of the various biblical pericopes need not necessarily be followed in the same ritual structure with which the Word of God is proclaimed in the Sacred Liturgy.

In any event, the liturgical model can serve as a touchstone for popular piety, against which a correct scale of values can be developed, whose first concern is hearing God when He speaks. It encourages popular piety to discover the harmony between the Old and New Testaments and to interpret one in the light of the other. From its centuries long experience, the liturgical model also provides praiseworthy solutions for the correct application of the biblical message and provides a valid criterion to judge the authenticity of prayer.

In choosing biblical texts, it is always desirable to take short texts, that are easily memorized, incisive, and easily understood, even if difficult to actualize. Certain forms of popular piety, such as the Via Crucis and the Rosary, encourage the use of Sacred Scripture, which can easily be related to particular prayers or gestures that have been learned by heart, especially those biblical passages recounting the life of Christ which are easily remembered.

Popular Piety and Private Revelation

90. Popular piety has always been interested in extraordinary happenings and events that are not infrequently connected with private revelations. While not confined to Marian piety alone, this phenomenon is particularly involved with "apparitions" and "messages". In this regard, it is useful to recall what the Catechism of the Catholic Church says about private revelation: "Throughout the ages, there have been so-called private revelations, some of which have been recognized by the authority of the Church. They do not belong, however, to the deposit of faith. It is not their role to

71

improve or complete Christ's definitive Revelation, but to help live more fully by it in a certain period of history. Guided by the Magisterium of the Church, the *sensus fidelium* knows how to discern and welcome in these revelations whatever constitutes an authentic call of Christ or his saints to the Church" (n. 67)[102].

Inculturation and Popular Piety

91. Popular piety is naturally marked by historical and cultural factors. The sheer variety of its expressions is an indicator of that fact. It reflects forms of popular piety that have arisen and been accepted in many particular Churches throughout the ages, and are a sure sign of the extent to which the faith has taken root in the hearts of particular peoples, and of its influence on the daily lives of the faithful. Indeed, "popular piety is the first and most fundamental form of the faith's "inculturation", and should be continually guided and oriented by the Liturgy, which, in its turn, nourishes the faith through the heart"[103]. The encounter between the innovative dynamism of the Gospel message, and the various elements of a given culture, is affirmed in popular piety[104].

92. The adaptation or inculturation of a particular pious exercise should not present special difficulties at the level of language, musical and artistic forms, or even of adopting certain gestures. While at one level pious exercises do not concentrate on the essential elements of the sacramental life, at another, it has to be remembered, they are in many cases popular in origin and come directly from the people, and have been formulated in the language of the people, within the framework of the Catholic faith.

---

[102] On this question see J. Ratzinger, *Commento teologico*, in CONGREGAZIONE PER LA DOTTRINA DELLA FEDE, *Il messaggio di Fatima*, Libreria Editrice Vaticana, Città del Vaticano 2000, pp. 32-44.
[103] *Ibid.*, p.35.
[104] Cf. PONTIFICAL COUNCIL FOR CULTURE, *Per una Pastorale della Cultura*, Libreria Editrice Vaticana 1999, 28: Popular piety remains one of the principal expressions of a true inculturation of the faith because in it faith and liturgy harmonize, as well as sentiment and the arts, while affirming a consciousness of a proper identity through local traditions. Thus, "America, which historically has been, and still is, a melting-pot of peoples, has recognized in the *mestiza* face of the Virgin of Tepeyac, "in Blessed Mary of Guadalupe, an impressive example of a perfectly inculturated evangelization".... (*Ecclesia in America*, n. 11) Popular piety allows a people to express its faith, its relationship with God and Providence, with Our Lady and the Saints, with neighbours, with the dead, with creation and strengthens membership of the Church."

The fact that pious exercises and devotions express popular sentiment, does not, however, authorize personalistic or subjective approaches to this material. With due respect for the competence proper to local Ordinaries or the Major Superiors of religious orders in cases involving devotions connected with their Orders, the Conference of Bishops should decide in matters relating to pious exercises widely diffused in a particular country or in a vast region.

Great vigilance and a deep sense of discernment are required to ensure that ideas contrary to the Christian faith, or forms of worship vitiated by syncretism, are not insinuated into pious exercises though various forms of language.

It is especially necessary to ensure that those pious exercises undergoing adaptation or inculturation retain their identity and their essential characteristics. In this regard, particular attention must always be given to their historical origin and to the doctrinal and cultic elements by which they are constituted.

With regard to the question of assuming certain elements from popular piety in the process of inculturating the Liturgy, reference should be made to the relative Instruction already published on the subject by this Dicastery[105].

---

[105] Cf. CONGREGATION FOR DIVINE WORSHIP AND THE DISCIPLINE OF THE SACRAMENTS, IV Instruction for the correct application of the conciliar Constitution on the Sacred Liturgy (nn. 37-40) *Varietates legitimate*, 45.

PART TWO

GUIDELINES FOR THE HARMONIZATION OF POPULAR PIETY WITH THE LITURGY

Foreword

93. The following guidelines on the relationship between popular piety and the Sacred Liturgy are offered to facilitate the translation into concrete pastoral action of those principles outlined above, so as to ensure consistency and fruitfulness in pastoral activity. While mentioning the most common pious exercises and devotional practices, the following exposition does not contain an exhaustive account of every possible local form of popular piety or devotional practice. Given the affinity of the material, and the fact that it sometimes falls into categories that are not clearly defined, some mention will be made of the pastoral care of the Liturgy.

The following exposition contains five chapters:

• chapter *four*, on the question of the Liturgical Year, seen from the prospect of the desirability of harmonizing its celebrations with popular piety;

• chapter *five*, on the veneration of the Holy Mother of God, which occupies a singular position both in the Liturgy and popular devotion;

• chapter *six*, on the cult of the Saints and Beati, which also occupies a significant place in the Liturgy and in the devotion of the faithful;

• chapter *seven*, on suffrage for the dead, which occurs in various forms in the Church's worship;

• chapter *eight*, on shrines and pilgrimages; places and expressions characteristic of popular piety, and their liturgical implications.

While referring to very diverse situations, and to the multiplicity of types and forms found in pious exercises, the following text has been developed in constant reference to a number of fundamental

77

presuppositions: the superiority of the Liturgy in respect to other forms of cult[106]; the dignity and legitimacy of popular piety[107]; the pastoral need to avoid any opposition between the Liturgy and popular piety, insurance that their various forms are not confused, so as to eschew the development of hybrid celebrations[108].

---

[106] Cf. SC 7, 13.
[107] Cf. supra nn. 61-64.
[108] Cf. supra n. 74.

CHAPTER FOUR

The Liturgical Year and Popular Piety

94. The liturgical year is the temporal structure within which the Church celebrates the holy mysteries of Christ: "From the Incarnation and the Nativity to the Ascension, to Pentecost and to the wait in joyful hope for the Lord's coming"[109].

In the liturgical year, "the celebration of the Paschal Mystery [...] is the most privileged moment in the daily, weekly and annual celebration of Christian worship"[110]. Consequently, the priority of the Liturgical year over any other devotional form or practice must be regarded as a touchstone for the relationship between Liturgy and popular piety.

Sunday

95. Since the "Lord's day" is the "primordial feast" and "basis and centre of the liturgical year"[111], it cannot be subordinated to popular piety. Hence, pious exercises whose main chronological reference point is Sunday, should not be encouraged.

For the pastoral good of the faithful, it is, however, licit to take up on the Sundays "per annum" those celebrations of the Lord, or in honour of the Blessed Virgin Mary or the Saints which occur during the week and which are particularly significant in popular piety, provided that they have precedence over Sundays in the tables published with the Roman calendar[112].

Given that popular or cultural traditions can sometimes be invasive of the Sunday celebration and deprive it of its Christian character, "There is a need for special pastoral attention to the many situations where there is a risk that the popular and cultural

---

[109] SC 102.
[110] PAUL VI, Apostolic Letter *Mysterii paschalis*, in AAS 61 (1969) 222.
[111] SC 106; CALENDARIUM ROMANUM ex decreto Sacrosancti Oecumenici Concilii Vaticani II instauratum auctoritate Pauli PP. VI promulgatum, Typis Polyglotis Vaticanis 1969, *Normae universales*, 4.
[112] Cf. *ibid.*, 58.

traditions of a region may intrude upon the celebration of Sundays and other liturgical feast-days, mingling the spirit of genuine Christian faith with elements which are foreign to it and may distort it. In such cases, catechesis and well-chosen pastoral initiatives need to clarify these situations, eliminating all that is incompatible with the Gospel of Christ. At the same time, it should not be forgotten that these traditions - and, by analogy, some recent cultural initiatives in civil society - often embody values which are not difficult to integrate with the demands of faith. It rests with the discernment of Pastors to preserve the genuine values found in the culture of a particular social context and especially in popular piety, so that liturgical celebration - above all on Sundays and holy days - does not suffer but rather may actually benefit".[113]

In Advent

96. Advent is a time of waiting, conversion and of hope:

● waiting-memory of the first, humble coming of the Lord in our mortal flesh; waiting-supplication for his final, glorious coming as Lord of History and universal Judge;

● conversion, to which the Liturgy at this time often refers quoting the prophets, especially John the Baptist, "Repent for the kingdom of heaven is at hand" (*Mt* 3:2);

● joyful hope that the salvation already accomplished by Christ (cf. *Rm* 8:24-25) and the reality of grace in the world, will mature and reach their fulness, thereby granting us what is promised by faith, and "we shall become like him for we shall see him as he really is" (*John* 3:2).

97. Popular piety is particularly sensitive to Advent, especially when seen as the memory of the preparation for the coming of the Messiah. The Christian people is deeply conscious of the long

---

[113] JOHN PAUL II, Apostolic Letter, *Dies Domini* (31.5.1998), 80.

period of expectation that preceded the birth of our Saviour. The faithful know that God sustained Israel's hope in the coming of the Messiah by the prophets.

Popular piety is not unaware of this extraordinary event. Indeed, it is awestruck at the prospect of the God of glory taking flesh in the womb of the humble and lowly Virgin Mary. The faithful are particularly sensitive to the difficulties faced by the Virgin Mary during her pregnancy, and are deeply moved by the fact that there was no room at the inn for Joseph and Mary, just as she was about to give birth to the Christ child (cf. *Lk* 2:7).

Various expressions of popular piety connected with Advent have emerged throughout the centuries. These have sustained the faith of the people, and from one generation to the next, they have conserved many valuable aspects of the liturgical season of Advent.

The Advent Wreath

98. Placing four candles on green fronds has become a symbol of Advent in many Christian home, especially in the Germanic countries and in North America.

The Advent wreath, with the progressive lighting of its four candles, Sunday after Sunday, until the Solemnity of Christmas, is a recollection of the various stages of salvation history prior to Christ's coming and a symbol of the prophetic light gradually illuminating the long night prior to the rising of the Sun of justice (cf. *Ml* 3:20; *Lk* 1:78).

Advent processions

99. In many regions, various kinds of processions are held in Advent, publicly to announce the imminent birth of the Saviour (the "day star" in some Italian processions), or to represent the journey to Bethlehem of Joseph and Mary and their search for a place in which Jesus would be born (the *posadas* in the Hispanic and Latin American tradition).

The Winter Interstice

100. Advent is celebrated during the Winter interstice in the northern hemisphere. This indicates a change of seasons and a moment of rest in many spheres of human endeavour. Popular piety is extremely sensitive to the vital cycle of nature. While the Winter interstice is celebrated, the seed lays in the ground waiting for the light and heat of the sun, which begins its ascent with the Winter solstice, and eventually causes it to germinate.

In those areas where popular piety has given rise to the celebration of the changing season, such expressions should be conserved and used as a time to pray the Lord, to reflect on the meaning of human work, which is a collaboration with the creative work of God, a self-realisation of the person, service to the common good, and an actualization of the plan of redemption[114].

The Blessed Virgin Mary and Advent

The Liturgy frequently celebrates the Blessed Virgin Mary in an exemplary way during the season of Advent[115]. It recalls the women of the Old Testament who prefigured and prophesied her mission; it exalts her faith and the humility with which she promptly and totally submitted to God's plan of salvation; it highlights her presence in the events of grace preceding the birth of the Saviour. Popular piety also devotes particular attention to the Blessed Virgin Mary during Advent, as is evident from the many pious exercised practised at this time, especially the novena of the Immaculate Conception and of Christmas.

However, the significance of Advent, "that time which is particularly apt for the cult of the Mother of God"[116], is such that it cannot be represented merely as a "Marian month".

In the calendars of the Oriental Churches, the period of preparation for the celebration of the manifestation (Advent) of divine salvation (Theophany) in the mysteries of Christmas-Epiphany of the Only Son of God, is markedly Marian in character.

---

[114] Cf. SECOND VATICAN COUNCIL, Constitution *Gaudium et Spes*, 34, 35, 67.
[115] Cf. PAUL VI, Apostolic Exhortation *Marialis Cultus*, 4.
[116] *Ibid.*

Attention is concentrated on preparation for the Lord's coming in the *Deipara*. For the Orientals, all Marian mysteries are Christological mysteries since they refer to the mystery of our salvation in Christ. In the Coptic rite, the Lauds of the Virgin Mary are sung in the *Theotokia*. Among the Syrians, Advent is referred to as the *Subbara* or Annunciation, so as to highlight its Marian character. The Byzantine Rite prepares for Christmas with a whole series of Marian feasts and rituals.

102. The Feast of the Immaculate Conception, which is profoundly influential among the faithful, is an occasion for many displays of popular piety and especially for the novena of the Immaculate Conception. There can be no doubt that the feast of the pure and sinless Conception of the Virgin Mary, which is a fundamental preparation for the Lord's coming into the world, harmonizes perfectly with many of the salient themes of Advent. This feast also makes reference to the long messianic waiting for the Saviours's birth and recalls events and prophecies from the Old Testament, which are also used in the Liturgy of Advent.

The novena of the Immaculate Conception, wherever it is celebrated, should highlight the prophetical texts which begin with Genesis 3:15, and end in Gabriel's salutation of the one who is "full of grace" (*Lk* 1:31-33).

The approach of Christmas is celebrated throughout the American continent with many displays of popular piety, centred on the feast of Our Lady of Guadalupe (12 December), which dispose the faithful to receive the Saviour at his birth. Mary, who was "intimately united with the birth of the Church in America, became the radiant Star illuminating the proclamation of Christ the Saviour to the sons of these nations"[117].

The Christmas Novena

103. The Christmas novena began as a means of communicating the riches of the Liturgy to the faithful who were unable easily to grasp it. It has played a very effective role and can continue to play such a

---

[117] JOHN PAUL II, Discourse at the Angelus of 24 January 1999, Mexico City.

role. At the same time, in current conditions where the faithful have easier access to the Liturgy, it would seem desirable that vespers from the 17-23 of December should be more solemn by adopting the use of the "major antiphons", and by inviting the faithful to participate at the celebration. Such a celebration, held either before of after which the popular devotions to which the faithful are particularly attached, would be an ideal "Christmas novena", in full conformity with the Liturgy and mindful of the needs of the faithful. Some elements, such as the homily, the use of incense, and the intercessions, could also be expanded within the celebration of Vespers.

The Crib

104. As is well known, in addition to the representations of the crib found in churches since antiquity, the custom of building cribs in the home was widely promoted from the thirteenth century, influenced undoubtedly by St Francis of Assisi's crib in Greccio. Their preparation, in which children play a significant role, is an occasion for the members of the family to come into contact with the mystery of Christmas, as they gather for a moment of prayer or to read the biblical accounts of the Lord's birth.

Popular piety and the spirit of Advent

105. Popular piety, because of its intuitive understanding of the Christian mystery, can contribute effectively to the conservation of many of the values of Advent, which are not infrequently threatened by the commercialization of Christmas and consumer superficiality.

Popular piety perceives that it is impossible to celebrate the Lord's birth except in an atmosphere of sobriety and joyous simplicity and of concern for the poor and imarginated. The expectation of the Lord's birth makes us sensitive to the value of life and the duties to respect and defend it from conception. Popular piety intuitively understands that it is not possible coherently to celebrate the birth of him "who saves his people from their sins" without some effort to overcome sin in one's own life, while waiting vigilantly for Him who will return at the end of time.

Christmastide

106. During Christmastide, the Church celebrates the mystery of the Lord's manifestation: his humble birth in Bethlehem which was made known to the shepherds, the first of Israel to welcome the Saviour; the Epiphany to the three wise men who had "come from the East" (*Mt* 2:1), the first of the Gentiles who recognised and adored Christ the Messiah in the child of Bethlehem; the theophany at the river Jordan in which the Father declares that Jesus is His "well-beloved Son" (*Mt* 3:17) at the outset of his messianic mission; the miracle of Cana in which Jesus "manifested his glory and his disciples believed in him" (*John* 2:11).

107. In addition to these celebrations recalling the primary meaning of Christmas, there are also other celebrations closely connected with the mystery of the Lord's manifestation: the martyrdom of the Holy Innocents (28 December) whose blood was shed because of hatred for Jesus and because of Herod's rejection of his lordship; the memorial of the Holy Name of Jesus, 13 January; the feast of the Holy Family (Sunday in the octave of Christmas) celebrating the holy family in which Jesus "grew in wisdom and grace before God and men" (*Lk* 2:52); the solemnity of 1 January which recalls the divine, virginal and salvific motherhood of the Blessed Virgin Mary; and, although outside of Christmastide, the feast of the Presentation of the Lord (2 February), celebrating the encounter between the Messiah and his people, represented by Simeon and Anna, and the prophecy of Simeon.

108. Much of the richness and complexity of the mystery of the Lord's manifestation is reflected in displays of popular piety, which is especially sensitive to the childhood of Christ which reveals his love for us. Popular piety intuitively grasps:

• the importance of the "spirituality of gift", which is proper to Christmas: "a child is born for us, a son is given to us" (cf. *Is* 9:5), a gift expressing the infinite love of God, who "so loved the world that he gave his only Son" (*John* 3:16);

• the message of solidarity conveyed by the event of Christmas: solidarity with sinful man, for whom, in Christ, God became man "for us men and for our salvation"[118]; solidarity with the poor, because the Son of God who "was rich but became poor for your sake, to make you rich out of his poverty" (2 *Cor* 8:9);

• the sacredness of human life and the wonderful event that is every birth, since the Word of life came amongst men and was made visible through his birth of the Virgin Mary (cf. 1 *John* 1:2);

• the messianic joy and peace to which man has aspired in every age: the Angels announce the birth of the Saviour of the world to the shepherds, the "Prince of Peace (*Is* 9:5) and proclaim "peace on earth to men of good will" (*Lk* 2:14);

• the spirit of simplicity and poverty, humility and trust in God, suggested by the events surrounding the birth of Christ.

Popular piety, precisely because it can intuit the values inherent in the mystery of Christ's birth, is called upon to cooperate in preserving the memory of the manifestation of the Lord, so as to ensure that the strong religious tradition surrounding Christmas is not secularized by consumerism or the infiltration of various forms of neopaganism.

Christmas Eve

109. In the space of time between the first Vespers of Christmas and Midnight Mass, both the tradition of Christmas carols, which are potent means of conveying the Christmas message of peace and joy, and popular piety propose certain forms of payers, differing from country to country, which should be cherished and, where

---

[118] DS 150; MISSALE ROMANUM, *Ordo Missae Symbolum Nicaeno-Constantinopolitanum.*

necessary, made consonant with the celebration of the Liturgy: These would include:

• "live cribs" and the inauguration of the crib in the homes of the faithful which is an opportunity for family prayer: this prayer should include a reading of St Luke's account of the birth of Christ, the typical Christmas carols, as well as prayers of petition and praise, especially those of children who are the protagonists in such family moments;

• the inauguration of the Christmas tree. This event also offers an opportunity for family prayer. Apart from its historical origins, the Christmas tress has become a potent symbol today and is very diffuse amongst Christians; it evokes both the tree planted in the centre of Eden (*Gen* 2:9), and the tree of the Cross, which lends it a Christological significance: Christ is the true tree of life, born of human stock, of the Virgin Mary, the tree which is always green and productive. In the Nordic countries, the tree is decorated with apples and hosts. "Gifts" can be added; but among the gifts placed under the tree, something should be included for the poor since they belong to every Christian family;

• the Christmas supper. The Christian family, which traditionally blesses the table and gives thanks to the Lord for the gift of food, performs this ceremony with greater intensity at the Christmas supper which gives potent concrete expression to the joy of family ties.

110. Where possible, the Church desires that the faithful should prepare for the celebration of Midnight Mass on the 24 December with the Office of Readings[119]. Where such is not possible, it may be opportune to arrange a vigil of hymns, readings, and elements drawn from popular piety.

---

[119] Cf. *Institutio generalis de Liturgia Horarum*, 215.

111. At Midnight Mass, an event of major liturgical significance and of strong resonance in popular piety, the following could be given prominence:

• at the beginning of Mass, the proclamation of the Saviour's birth according the formula contained in the Roman Martyrology could be made in song;

• the prayer of the faithful should really be universal, and where appropriate, use several languages; and the poor should always be remembered in the presentation of the gifts;

• at the end of Mass, the faithful could be invited to kiss the image of the Child Jesus, which is then placed in a crib erected in the church or somewhere nearby.

The Feast of the Holy Family

112. The feast of the holy family of Jesus, Mary and Joseph (Sunday in the Christmas octave) is a festive occasion particularly suitable for the celebration of rites or moments of prayer proper to the Christian family. The recollection of Joseph, Mary and Jesus' going up to Jerusalem, together with other observant Jewish families, for the celebration of the Passover (cf. *Lk* 2:41-42), should normally encourage a positive acceptance of the pastoral suggestion that all members of the family attend Mass on this day. This feast day also affords an opportunity for the renewal of our entrustment to the patronage of the Holy Family of Nazareth[120]; the blessing of children as provided in the ritual[121]; and where opportune, for the renewal of marriage vows taken by the spouses on their wedding day, and also for the exchange of promises between those engaged to be married in which they formalize their desire to found a new Christian family[122].

---

[120] Cf. *Actus consecrationis familiarum*, in EI, *Aliae concessiones*, 1, p. 50.
[121] Cf RITUALE ROMANUM, *De benedictionibus, Ordo benedictionis filiorum*, Editio Typica, Typis Polyglotis Vaticanis 1985, 174-194.
[122] Cf. *ibid., Ordo benedictionis desponsatorum*, 195-204.

Outside of the feast, the faithful have frequent recourse to the Holy Family of Nazareth in many of life's circumstances: joining the Association of the Holy Family so as to model their own families on the Holy Family of Nazareth[123]; frequent prayers to entrust themselves to the patronage of the Holy Family and to obtain assistance at the hour of death[124].

The Feast of the Holy Innocents

113. Since the sixth century, on 28 December, the Church has celebrated the memory of those children killed because of Herod's rage against Christ (cf. *Mt* 2:16-17). Liturgical tradition refers to them as the "Holy Innocents" and regards them as martyrs. Throughout the centuries Christian art, poetry and popular piety have enfolded the memory of the "tender flock of lambs"[125] with sentiments of tenderness and sympathy. These sentiments are also accompanied by a note of indignation against the violence with which they were taken from their mothers' arms and killed.

In our own times, children suffer innumerable forms of violence which threaten their lives, dignity and right to education. On this day, it is appropriate to recall the vast host of children not yet born who have been killed under the cover of laws permitting abortion, which is an abominable crime. Mindful of these specific problems, popular piety in many places has inspired acts of worship as well as displays of charity which provide assistance to pregnant mothers, encourage adoption and the promotion of the education of children.

31 December

114. Popular piety has given rise to many pious exercises connected with 31 December. In many parts of the Western world the end of the civil year is celebrated on this day. This anniversary affords an opportunity for the faithful to reflect on "the mystery of time",

---

[123] Erected by Leo XIII through the Apostolic Letter *Neminem fugit* (14 June 1892) in *Leonis XIII Pontificis Maximi Acta, XII*, Typographia Vaticana, Romae 1893, pp. 149-158: confirmed by John Paul II with the decree of the *Pontifical Council for the Laity* (25 November 1987).

[124] Cf. EI, *Piae invocationes*, p. 83.

[125] PRUDENTIUS, *Cathemerinon XII*, 130: CCL 126, Turnholti 1966, p. 69; LITURGIA HORARUM: *die 28 Decembris, Ss. Innocentium, martyrum, Ad Laudes, Hymnus* "Audit tyrannus anxius".

which passes quickly and inexorably. Such should give rise to a dual feeling: of penance and sorrow for the sins committed during the year and for the lost occasions of grace; and of thanks to God for the graces and blessings He has given during the past year.

These sentiments have given rise to two pious exercises: prolonged exposition of the Blessed Sacrament, which afford an opportunity for the faithful and many religious communities for silent prayer; and the singing of the *Te Deum* as an act of community praise and thanksgiving to God for the graces received from Him as the year draws to a close[126].

In some places, especially in monasteries and in associations of the faithful with a particular devotion to the Holy Eucharist, 31 December is marked by a vigil of prayer which concludes with the celebration of the Holy Mass. Such vigils are to be encouraged and should be celebrated in harmony with the liturgical content of the Christmas Octave, and not merely as a reaction to the thoughtless dissipation with which society celebrates the passage from one year to another, but as a vigil offering of the new year to the Lord.

The Solemnity of the Holy Mother of God

115. On New Year's Day, the octave day of Christmas, the Church celebrates the Solemnity of the Holy Mother of God. The divine and virginal motherhood of the Blessed Virgin Mary is a singular salvific event: for Our Lady it was the foretaste and cause of her extraordinary glory; for us it is a source of grace and salvation because "through her we have received the Author of life"[127].

The solemnity of the 1 January, an eminently Marian feast, presents an excellent opportunity for liturgical piety to encounter popular piety: the first celebrates this event in a manner proper to it; the second, when duly catechised, lends joy and happiness to the various expressions of praise offered to Our Lady on the birth of her divine Son, to deepen our understanding of many prayers, beginning with that which says: "Holy Mary, Mother of God, pray for us, sinners".

---

[126] Cf. EI, *Aliae concessiones*, 26, p. 71.
[127] MISSALE ROMANUM, *die 1 Ianuarii, In octava Navitatis Domini, Sollemnitas Sanctae Dei Genetricis Mariae, Collecta.*

116. In the West, 1 January is an inaugural day marking the beginning of the civil year. The faithful are also involved in the celebrations for the beginning of the new year and exchange "new year" greetings. However, they should try to lend a Christian understanding to this custom making of these greetings an expression of popular piety. The faithful, naturally, realise that the "new year" is placed under the patronage of the Lord, and in exchanging new year greetings they implicitly and explicitly place the New Year under the Lord's dominion, since to him belongs all time (cf. *Ap* 1:8; 22:13)[128].

A connection between this consciousness and the popular custom of singing the *Veni Creator Spiritus* can easily be made so that on 1 January the faithful can pray that the Spirit may direct their thoughts and actions, and those of the community during the course of the year[129].

117. New year greetings also include an expression of hope for a peaceful New Year. This has profound biblical, Christological and incarnational origins. The "quality of peace" has always been invoked throughout history by all men, and especially during violent and destructive times of war.

The Holy See shares the profound aspirations of man for peace. Since 1967, 1 January has been designated "world day for peace".

Popular piety has not been oblivious to this initiative of the Holy See. In the light of the new born Prince of Peace, it reserves this day for intense prayer for peace, education towards peace and those value inextricably linked with it, such as liberty, fraternal solidarity, the dignity of the human person, respect for nature, the right to work, the sacredness of human life, and the denunciation of injustices which trouble the conscience of man and threaten peace.

Solemnity of the Lord's Epiphany

118. Many traditions and genuine manifestations of popular piety have been developed in relation to the Solemnity of the Lord's

---

[128] Cf. *ibid., In Vigilia paschali, Praeparatio cerei.*
[129] Cf. EI, *Aliae concessiones,* 26, p. 70.

Epiphany, which is of ancient origin and rich in spiritual content. Among such forms of popular piety, mention may be made of:

• the solemn proclamation of Easter and the principal dominical feasts; its revival in many places would be opportune since it served to make the connection between the Epiphany and Easter, and orientate all feasts towards the greatest Christian solemnity;

• the exchange of "Epiphany gifts", which derives from the gifts offered to Jesus by the three kings (cf. *Mt* 2:11) and more radically from the gift made to mankind by God in the birth of Emmanuel amongst us (cf. *Is* 7:14; 9:16; *Mt* 1:23). It is important, however, to ensure that the exchange of gifts on the solemnity of the Epiphany retain a Christian character, indicating that its meaning is evangelical: hence the gifts offered should be a genuine expression of popular piety and free from extravagance, luxury, and waste, all of which are extraneous to the Christian origins of this practice;

• the blessing of homes, on whose lintels are inscribed the Cross of salvation, together with the indication of the year and the initials of the three wise men (C+M+B), which can also be interpreted to mean *Christus mansionem benedicat*, written in blessed chalk; this custom, often accompanied by processions of children accompanied by their parents, expresses the blessing of Christ through the intercession of the three wise men and is an occasion for gathering offerings for charitable and missionary purposes;

• initiatives in solidarity with those who come from afar; whether Christian or not, popular piety has encouraged a sense of solidarity and openness;

• assistance to the work of evangelisation; the strong missionary character of the Epiphany has been well understood by popular piety and many initiatives in support of the missions flourish on 6 January, especially the "Missionary work of the Holy Child", promoted by the Apostolic See;

• the assignation of Patrons; in many religious communities and confraternities, patron saints are assigned to the members for the coming year.

The Feast of the Baptism of the Lord

119. Closely connected with the salvific events of the Epiphany are the mysteries of the Baptism of the Lord and the manifestation of his glory at the marriage feast of Cana.

Christmastide closes with the Baptism of the Lord. Only in recent times has the feast been rehabilitated, and hence has not given rise to any particular displays of popular piety. However, the feast presents an excellent opportunity for the faithful to be reminded of their rebirth as children of God in Baptism. The rite of asperges could be opportunely used at all Masses on this day, and homilies could well concentrate on the symbols associated with Baptism.

The Feast of the Presentation of Our Lord

120. Until 1969, the ancient feast of the presentation of Our Lord[130], which is of Oriental origin, was known in the West as the feast of the Purification of Our Lady, and closed the Christmas season, forty days after the Lord's birth. This feast has for long been associated with many popular devotional exercises. The faithful:

• gladly participate in the processions commemorating the Lord's entry into the Temple in Jerusalem and his encounter with God, whose house he had come to for the first time, and then with Simeon and Anna. Such processions, which in the West had taken the place of licentious pagan events, always had a penitential character, and were later identified with the blessing of candles which were carried in procession in honour of Christ, "the light to enlighten the Gentiles" (*Lk* 2:32);

---

[130] Among the Byzantines, this feast is centred on the *Hypapante*, or the Lord's encounter with those whom he has come to save, who are represented by Simeon and Anna, reflecting the canticle *Nunc dimittis* (Lk 2:29-3), which is frequently repeated in the hymns used on this feast: "The Light to enlighten the gentiles and give glory to your people, Israel".

• are sensitive to the actions of the Blessed Virgin in presenting her Son in the Temple, and to her submission to the Law of Moses (*Lk* 12:1-8) in the rite of purification; popular piety sees in the rite of purification the humility of Our Lady and hence, 2 February has long been regarded as a feast for those in humble service.

121. Popular piety is sensitive to the providential and mysterious event that is the Conception and birth of new life. Christian mothers can easily identify with the maternity of Our Lady, the most pure Mother of the Head of the mystical Body - notwithstanding the notable differences in the Virgin's unique Conception and birth. These too are mothers in God's plan and are about to give birth to future members of the Church. From this intuition and a certain *mimesis* of the purification of Our Lady, the rite of purification after birth was developed, some of whose elements reflect negatively on birth.

The revised *Rituale Romanum* provides for the blessing of women both before[131] and after birth[132], this latter only in cases where the mother could not participate at the baptism of her child.

It is a highly desirable thing for mothers and married couples to ask for these blessings which should be given in accord with the Church's prayer: in a communion of faith and charity in prayer so that pregnancy can be brought to term without difficulty (blessing before birth), and to give thanks to God for the gift of a child (blessing after birth).

122. In some local Churches, certain elements taken from the Gospel account of the Presentation of the Lord (*Lk* 2:22-40), such as the obedience of Joseph and Mary to the Law of the Lord, the poverty of the holy spouses, the virginity of Our Lady, mark out the 2 February as a special feast for those at the service of the brethren in the various forms of consecrated life.

---

[131] RITUALE ROMANUM, *De Benedictionibus, Ordo benedictionis mulieris ante partum*, cit., 219-231.
[132] *Ibid., Ordo benedictionis mulieris post partum*, 236-253.

123. The feast of 2 February still retains a popular character. It is necessary, however, that such should reflect the true Christian significance of the feast. It would not be proper for popular piety in its celebration of this feast to overlook its Christological significance and concentrate exclusively on its Marian aspects. The fact that this feast should be "considered [...] a joint memorial of Son and Mother"[133] would not support such an inversion. The candles kept by the faithful in their homes should be seen as a sign of Christ "the light of the world" and an expression of faith.

Lent

124. Lent precedes and prepares for Easter. It is a time to hear the Word of God, to convert, to prepare for and remember Baptism, to be reconciled with God and one's neighbour, and of more frequent recourse to the "arms of Christian penance"[134]: prayer, fasting and good works (cf. *Mt* 6:1-6, 16-18).

Popular piety does not easily perceive the mystical aspect of Lent and does not emphasize any of its great themes or values, such a relationship between "the sacrament of forty days" and "the sacraments of Christian initiation", nor the mystery of the "exodus" which is always present in the lenten journey. Popular piety concentrates on the mysteries of Christ's humanity, and during Lent the faithful pay close attention to the Passion and Death of Our Lord.

125. In the Roman Rite, the beginning of the forty days of penance is marked with the austere symbol of ashes which are used in the Liturgy of Ash Wednesday. The use of ashes is a survival from an ancient rite according to which converted sinners submitted themselves to canonical penance. The act of putting on ashes symbolizes fragility and mortality, and the need to be redeemed by the mercy of God. Far from being a merely external act, the Church has retained the use of ashes to symbolize that attitude of internal penance to which all the baptized are called during Lent. The faithful who come to receive ashes should be assisted in perceiving

---

[133] PAUL VI, Apostolic Exhortation, *Marialis cultus*, 7.
[134] MISSALE ROMANUM, *Feria IV Cinerum, Collecta*.

the implicit internal significance of this act, which disposes them towards conversion and renewed Easter commitment.

Notwithstanding the secularisation of contemporary society, the Christian faithful, during Lent, are clearly conscious of the need to turn the mind towards those realities which really count, which require Gospel commitment and integrity of life which, through self denial of those things which are superfluous, are translated into good works and solidarity with the poor and needy.

Those of the faithful who infrequently attend the sacraments of Penance and the Holy Eucharist should be aware of the long ecclesial tradition associating the precept of confessing grave sins and receive Holy Communion at least once during the lenten season, or preferably during Eastertide[135.]

126. The existing divergence between the liturgical idea of Lent and the outlook of popular piety need not prevent an effective interaction between Liturgy and popular piety during the forty days of Lent.

An example of such interaction is to be seen in the fact that popular piety often encourages particular observances on certain days, or special devotional exercises, or apostolic or charitable works which are foreseen and recommended by the lenten Liturgy. The practice of fasting, characteristic of the lenten season since antiquity, is an "exercise" which frees the faithful from earthly concerns so as to discover the life that comes from above: "Man does not live on bread alone, but on every word that comes from the mouth of God" (cf. *Dt* 8:3; *Mt* 4:4; *Lk* 4:4; antiphon for the first Sunday of Lent).

Veneration of the Crucified Christ

127. The journey of Lent ends with the Easter Triduum, initiated by the celebration of the *Coena Domini* Mass. During the Triduum, Good Friday which is dedicated to the celebration of the Lord's Passion, is eminently suited for the "Adoration of the Holy Cross".

---

[135] Cf. CIC, canons 989 and 920.

Popular piety tends to anticipate the cultic veneration of the Cross. Throughout Lent, every Friday is observed, since very ancient times, as a commemoration of the Lord's Passion and the faithful easily direct their devotions towards the mystery of the Cross.

They contemplate the crucified Saviour, they sense more easily the great suffering which Jesus, the Holy and Innocent One, suffered for the salvation of mankind. They understand his love and the effectiveness of his redemptive sacrifice.

128. The various and numerous devotions to the crucified Christ acquire a special significance in those churches dedicated to the mystery of the Cross or where authentic relics of the true cross are venerated. The "invention of the Cross" in the early fourth century, and the subsequent diffusion throughout the Church of particles of the true Cross, gave notable impulse to devotion to the Cross.

Devotions to the crucified Christ contain many elements usually found in popular piety: hymns and prayers, acts such as the unveiling and kissing of the Cross, processions and blessing with the Cross. These can lead to the development of pious exercises often containing many valuable formal and material elements.

Devotion to the Cross, however, sometimes requires a certain enlightenment. The faithful should be taught to place the Cross in its essential reference to the Resurrection of Christ: the Cross, the empty tomb, the Death and Resurrection of Christ are indispensable in the Gospel narrative of God's salvific plan. In the Christian faith, the Cross is an expression of the triumph of Christ over the powers of darkness. Hence, it is adorned with precious stones and is a sign of blessing when made upon one's self, or on others or on objects.

129. The Gospel texts of the Passion are especially detailed. Coupled with a tendency in popular piety to isolate specific moments of the narrative, this has induced the faithful to turn their attention to specific aspects of the Passion of Christ, making of them specific devotions: devotion to the "Ecce Homo", Christ despised, "crowned with thorns and clothed in a purple cloak"

(*John* 19:5), and shown to the multitude by Pilate; devotion to the five sacred wounds of Christ, especially to the side of Christ from which flowed blood and water for the salvation of mankind (*John* 19:34); devotion to the instruments of the Passion, the pillar at which Christ was scourged, the steps of the Praetorium, the crown of thorns, the nails, the lance that pierced Him; devotion to the Holy Shroud.

Such expressions of piety, often promoted by persons of great sanctity, are legitimate. However, in order to avoid excessive fragmentation in contemplation of the mystery of the Cross, it is always useful to emphasise the whole event of the Passion, as is the case in biblical and patristic tradition.

Reading of the Lord's Passion

130. The Church exhorts the faithful to frequent personal and community reading of the Word of God. Undoubtedly, the account of the Lord's Passion is among the most important pastoral passages in the New Testament. Hence, for the Christian in his last agony, the *Ordo untionis informorum eorumque pastoralis curae* suggests the reading of the Lord's Passion either in its entirety, or at least some pericopes from it[136].

During Lent, especially on Wednesdays and Fridays, love for our Crucified Saviour should move the Christian community to read the account of the Lord's Passion. Such reading, which is doctrinally significant, attracts the attention of the faithful because of its content and because of its narrative form, and inspires true devotion: repentance for sins, since the faithful see that Christ died for the sins of the entire human race, including their own; compassion and solidarity for the Innocent one who was unjustly condemned; gratitude for the infinite love of Jesus for all the brethren, which was shown by Jesus, the first born Son, in his Passion; commitment to imitating his example of meekness, patience, mercy, forgiveness of offenses, abandonment to the Father, which Jesus did willingly and efficaciously in his Passion.

---

[136] Cf. RITUALE ROMANUM, *Ordo unctionis infirmorum eorumque pastoralis curae*, Editio Typica, Typis Polyglotis Vaticanis 1972, nn. 224-229.

Outside of the liturgical celebration of the Passion, the Gospel narrative can be "dramatized", giving the various parts of the narrative to different persons; or by interspersing it with hymns or moments of silent reflection.

Via Crucis

131. Of all the pious exercises connected with the veneration of the Cross, none is more popular among the faithful than the *Via Crucis*. Through this pious exercise, the faithful movingly follow the final earthly journey of Christ: from the Mount of Olives, where the Lord, "in a small estate called Gethsemane" (*Mk* 14:32), was taken by anguish (cf. *Lk* 22:44), to Calvary where he was crucified between two thieves (cf. *Lk* 23:33), to the garden where he was placed in freshly hewn tomb (*John* 19:40-42).

The love of the Christian faithful for this devotion is amply attested by the numerous *Via Crucis* erected in so many churches, shrines, cloisters, in the countryside, and on mountain pathways where the various stations are very evocative.

132. The *Via Crucis* is a synthesis of various devotions that have arisen since the high middle ages: the pilgrimage to the Holy Land during which the faithful devoutly visit the places associated with the Lord's Passion; devotion to the three falls of Christ under the weight of the Cross; devotion to "the dolorous journey of Christ" which consisted in processing from one church to another in memory of Christ's Passion; devotion to the stations of Christ, those places where Christ stopped on his journey to Calvary because obliged to do so by his executioners or exhausted by fatigue, or because moved by compassion to dialogue with those who were present at his Passion.

In its present form, the *Via Crucis*, widely promoted by St Leonardo da Porto Maurizio (d. 1751), was approved by the Apostolic See and indulgenced[137], consists of fourteen stations since the middle of seventeenth century.

---

[137] Cf. EI, *Aliae concessiones*, 13, pp. 59-60.

133. The *Via Crucis* is a journey made in the Holy Spirit, that divine fire which burned in the heart of Jesus (cf. *Lk* 12:49-50) and brought him to Calvary. This is a journey well esteemed by the Church since it has retained a living memory of the words and gestures of the final earthly days of her Spouse and Lord.

In the *Via Crucis*, various strands of Christian piety coalesce: the idea of life being a journey or pilgrimage; as a passage from earthly exile to our true home in Heaven; the deep desire to be conformed to the Passion of Christ; the demands of following Christ, which imply that his disciples must follow behind the Master, daily carrying their own crosses (cf. *Lk* 9:23).

The Via Crucis is a particularly apt pious exercise for Lent.

134. The following may prove useful suggestions for a fruitful celebration of the *Via Crucis*:

• the traditional form of the Via Crucis, with its fourteen stations, is to be retained as the typical form of this pious exercise; from time to time, however, as the occasion warrants, one or other of the traditional stations might possibly be substituted with a reflection on some other aspects of the Gospel account of the journey to Calvary which are traditionally included in the Stations of the Cross;

• alternative forms of the Via Crucis have been approved by Apostolic See[138] or publicly used by the Roman Pontiff[139]: these can be regarded as genuine forms of the devotion and may be used as occasion might warrant;

• the *Via Crucis* is a pious devotion connected with the Passion of Christ; it should conclude, however, in such fashion as to leave the faithful with a sense of expectation of the resurrection in faith and hope; following the example of the *Via Crucis* in Jerusalem which ends with a station at the *Anastasis*, the celebration could end with a commemoration of the Lord's resurrection.

---

[138] Such is true of the "Via Crucis" in the *Libro del Pellegrino* prepared by the Central Committee for the celebration of the Holy Year of 1975.

[139] Such as the texts used by Pope John Paul II for the "Via Crucis" at the Colosseum in 1991, 1992, and 1994.

135. Innumerable texts exist for the celebration of the *Via Crucis*. Many of them were compiled by pastors who were sincerely interested in this pious exercise and convinced of its spiritual effectiveness. Texts have also been provided by lay authors who were known for their exemplary piety, holiness of life, doctrine and literary qualities.

Bearing in mind whatever instructions might have been established by the bishops in the matter, the choice of texts for the *Via Crucis* should take a count of the condition of those participating in its celebration and the wise pastoral principle of integrating renewal and continuity. It is always preferable to choose texts resonant with the biblical narrative and written in a clear simple style.

The *Via Crucis* in which hymns, silence, procession and reflective pauses are wisely integrated in a balanced manner, contribute significantly to obtaining the spiritual fruits of the pious exercise.

The Via Matris

136. As Christ and Our Lady of Dolours were associated in God's saving plan (*Lk* 2:34-35), so too they are associated in the Liturgy and popular piety.

As Christ was the "man of sorrows" (*Is* 53:3) through whom it pleased God to have "reconciled all things through him and for him, everything in heaven and everything on earth, when he made peace by his death on the cross" (*Col* 1:20), so too, Mary is "the woman of sorrows" whom God associated with his Son as mother and participant in his Passion (socia passionis).

Since the childhood of Christ, the Blessed Virgin Mary's life was entirely lived out under the sign of the sword (cf. *Lk* 2:35). Christian piety has signalled out seven particular incidents of sorrow in her life, known as the "seven sorrows" of the Blessed Virgin Mary.

Modelled on the *Via Crucis*, the pious exercise of the *Via Matris dolorosae*, or simply the *Via Matris*, developed and was subsequently approved by the Apostolic See[140]. This pious exercise already existed

---

[140] Cf. LEO XIII, Apostolic Letter *Deipare Perdolentis*, in *Leonis XIII Pontificis Maximi Acta, III*, Typographia Vaticana 1884, pp. 220-222.

in embryonic form since the sixteenth century, while its present form dates from the nineteenth century. Its fundamental intuition is a reflection on the life of Our Lady from the prophecy of Simeon (cf. *Lk* 2:34-35), to the death and burial of her Son, in terms of a journey in faith and sorrow: this journey is articulated in seven "stations" corresponding to the "seven dolours" of the Mother of Our Saviour.

137. This pious exercise harmonises well with certain themes that are proper to the lenten season. Since the sorrows of Our Lady are caused by the rejection of her Son (cf. *John* 1:11; *Lk* 2:1-7; 2:34-35; 4:28-29; *Mt* 26:47-56; *Acts* 12:1-5), the *Via Matris* constantly and necessarily refers to the mystery of Christ as the suffering servant (cf. *Is* 52:13-53:12). It also refers to the mystery of the Church: the stations of the *Via Matris* are stages on the journey of faith and sorrow on which the Virgin Mary has preceded the Church, and in which the Church journeys until the end of time.

The highest expression of the *Via Matris* is the Pietà which has been an inexhaustible source of inspiration for Christian art since the middles ages.

Holy Week

138. "In Holy Week, the Church celebrates the mysteries of salvation accomplished by Christ in the last days of the earthly life, beginning with his messianic entry into Jerusalem"[141].

The people are notably involved in the rites of Holy Week. Many of them still bear the traces of their origins in popular piety. It has come about, however, that in the course of the centuries, a form of celebrative parallelism has arisen in the Rites of Holy Week, resulting in two cycles each with its own specific character: one is strictly liturgical, the other is marked by particular pious exercise, especially processions.

This divergence should be oriented towards a correct harmonisation of the liturgical celebrations and pious exercises. Indeed, the attention

---

[141] CONGREGATION FOR DIVINE WORSHIP, *Lettera circolare sulla preparazione e celebrazione delle feste pasquali* (16.1.1988), 27.

and interest in manifestations of popular piety, traditionally observed among the people, should lead to a correct appreciation of the liturgical actions, which are supported by popular piety.

Palm Sunday

Palms, olive branches and other fronds

139. Holy Week begins with Palm Sunday, or "Passion Sunday", which unites the royal splendour of Christ with the proclamation of his Passion"[142].

The procession, commemorating Christ's messianic entry into Jerusalem, is joyous and popular in character. The faithful usually keep palm or olive branches, or other greenery which have been blessed on Palm Sunday in their homes or in their work places.

The faithful, however, should be instructed as to the meaning of this celebration so that they might grasp its significance. They should be opportunely reminded that the important thing is participation at the procession and not only the obtaining of palm or olive branches. Palms or olive branches should not be kept as amulets, or for therapeutic or magical reasons to dispel evil spirits or to prevent the damage these cause in the fields or in the homes, all of which can assume a certain superstitious guise.

Palms and olive branches are kept in the home as a witness to faith in Jesus Christ, the messianic king, and in his Paschal Victory.

The Paschal Triduum

140. Every year, the Church celebrates the great mysteries of the redemption of mankind in the "most sacred triduum of the crucifixion, burial and resurrection"[143]. The Sacred Triduum extends from the Mass of the Lord's Supper to Vespers on Easter Sunday and is celebrated "in intimate communion with Christ her Spouse"[144].

[142] *Ibid.*, 28.
[143] St AUGUSTINE, *Epistula*, 55, 24: CSEL 34/2, Vindobonae 1895, p. 195. Cf. SACRED CONGREGATION FOR RITES, general decree *Maxima redemptionis nostrae mysteria*, in AAS 47 (1955) 338.
[144] CONGREGATION FOR DIVINE WORSHIP, *Lettera circolare sulla preparazione e celebrazione delle feste pasquali*, 38.

Holy Thursday

Visiting the Altar of Repose

141. Popular piety is particularly sensitive to the adoration of the Most Blessed Sacrament in the wake of the Mass of the Lord's supper[145]. Because of a long historical process, whose origins are not entirely clear, the place of repose has traditionally been referred to as a "a holy sepulchre". The faithful go there to venerate Jesus who was placed in a tomb following the crucifixion and in which he remained for some forty hours.

It is necessary to instruct the faithful on the meaning of the reposition: it is an austere solemn conservation of the Body of Christ for the community of the faithful which takes part in the liturgy of Good Friday and for the viaticum of the infirmed[146]. It is an invitation to silent and prolonged adoration of the wondrous sacrament instituted by Jesus on this day.

In reference to the altar of repose, therefore, the term "sepulchre" should be avoided, and its decoration should not have any suggestion of a tomb. The tabernacle on this altar should not be in the form of a tomb or funerary urn. The Blessed Sacrament should be conserved in a closed tabernacle and should not be exposed in a monstrance[147].

After mid-night on Holy Thursday, the adoration should conclude without solemnity, since the day of the Lord's Passion has already begun[148].

Good Friday

Good Friday Procession

142. The Church celebrates the redemptive death of Christ on Good Friday. The Church meditates on the Lord's Passion in the

---

[145] The procession and reposition of the Blessed Sacrament are not done in those churches in which the Lord's Passion are not celebrated on Good Friday: cf. CONGREGATION FOR DIVINE WORSHIP, *Lettera circolare sulla preparazione e celebrazione delle feste pasquali*, 54.

[146] Cf. CONGREGATION FOR DIVINE WORSHIP, *Lettera circolare sulla preparazione e celebrazione delle feste pasquali*, 55; SACRED CONGREGATION OF RITES, Instruction on Eucharistic cult *Eucharisticum mysterium*, 49, in AAS 59 (1967) 566-567.

[147] Cf. CONGREGATION FOR DIVINE WORSHIP, *Lettera circolare sulla preparazione e celebrazione delle feste pasquali*, 55.

[148] Cf. ibid., 56.

afternoon liturgical action, in which she prays for the salvation of the word, adores the Cross and commemorates her very origin in the sacred wound in Christ's side (cf. *John* 19:34)[149].

In addition to the various forms of popular piety on Good Friday such as the *Via Crucis*, the passion processions are undoubtedly the most important. These correspond, after the fashion of popular piety, to the small procession of friends and disciples who, having taken the body of Jesus down from the Cross, carried it to the place where there "was a tomb hewn in the rock in which no one had yet been buried" (*Lk* 23:53).

The procession of the "dead Christ" is usually conducted in austere silence, prayer, and the participation of many of the faithful, who intuit much of the significance of the Lord's burial.

143. It is necessary, however, to ensure that such manifestations of popular piety, either by time or the manner in which the faithful are convoked, do not become a surrogate for the liturgical celebrations of Good Friday.

In the pastoral planning of Good Friday primary attention and maximum importance must be given to the solemn liturgical action and the faithful must be brought to realize that no other exercise can objectively substitute for this liturgical celebration.

Finally, the integration of the "dead Christ" procession with the solemn liturgical action of Good Friday should be avoided for such would constitute a distorted celebrative hybrid.

Passion Plays

144. In many countries, passion plays take place during Holy Week, especially on Good Friday. These are often "sacred representations" which can justly be regarded as pious exercises. Indeed, such sacred representations have their origins in the Sacred Liturgy. Some of these plays, which began in the monks' choir, so to speak, have undergone a progressive dramatisation that has taken them outside of the church.

In some places, responsibility for the representations of the

---

[149] Cf. SC 5; St AUGUSTINE, *Ennaratio in Paslmum 138*, 2: CCL 40, Turnholti 1956, p. 1991.

Lord's passion has been given over to the Confraternities, whose members have assumed particular responsibilities to live the Christian life. In such representations, actors and spectators are involved in a movement of faith and genuine piety. It is singularly important to ensure that representations of the Lord's Passion do not deviate from this pure line of sincere and gratuitous piety, or take on the characteristics of folk productions, which are not so much manifestations of piety as tourist attractions.

In relation to sacred "representations" it is important to instruct the faithful on the difference between a "representation" which is commemorative, and the "liturgical actions" which are anamnesis, or mysterious presence of the redemptive event of the Passion.

Penitential practices leading to self-crucifixion with nails are not to be encouraged.

Our Lady of Dolours

145. Because of its doctrinal and pastoral importance, it is recommended that "the memorial of Our Lady of Dolours"[150] should be recalled. Popular piety, following the Gospel account, emphasizes the association of Mary with the saving Passion her Son (cf. *John* 19:25-27; *Lk* 2:34f), and has given rise to many pious exercises, including:

• the *Planctus Mariae*, an intense expression of sorrow, often accompanied by literary or musical pieces of a very high quality, in which Our Lady cries not only for the death of her Son, the Innocent, Holy, and Good One, but also for the errors of his people and the sins of mankind;

• the *Ora della Desolata*, in which the faithful devoutly keep vigil with the Mother of Our Lord, in her abandonment and profound sorrow following the death of her only Son; they contemplate Our Lady as she receives the dead body of Christ (the *Pietà*) realizing

---

[150] CONGREGATION FOR DIVINE WORSHIP, *Lettera circolare sulla preparazione e celebrazione delle feste pasquali*,72.

that the sorrow of the world for the Lord's death finds expression in Mary; in her they behold the personification of all mothers throughout the ages who have mourned the loss of a son. This pious exercise, which in some parts of Latin America is called *El Pésame,* should not be limited merely to the expression of emotion before a sorrowing mother. Rather, with faith in the resurrection, it should assist in understanding the greatness of Christ's redemptive love and his Mother's participation in it.

Holy Saturday

146. "On Holy Saturday, the Church pauses at the Lord's tomb, meditating on his Passion and Death, his descent into Hell, and, with prayer and fasting, awaits his resurrection"[151].

Popular piety should not be impervious to the peculiar character of Holy Saturday. The festive customs and practices connected with this day, on which the celebration of the Lord's resurrection was once anticipated, should be reserved for the vigil and for Easter Sunday.

The "Ora della Madre"

147. According to tradition, the entire body of the Church is represented in Mary: she is the *"credentium collectio universa"*[152]. Thus, the Blessed Virgin Mary, as she waits near the Lord's tomb, as she is represented in Christian tradition, is an icon of the Virgin Church keeping vigil at the tomb of her Spouse while awaiting the celebration of his resurrection.

The pious exercise of the *Ora di Maria* is inspired by this intuition of the relationship between the Virgin Mary and the Church: while the body of her Son lays in the tomb and his soul has descended to the dead to announce liberation from the shadow of darkness to his ancestors, the Blessed Virgin Mary, foreshadowing and representing the Church, awaits, in faith, the victorious triumph of her Son over death.

---

[151] *Ibid.,* 73.
[152] RUPERTUS DI DEUTZ, *De glorificatione Trinitatis,* VIII, 13: PL 169, 155D.

Easter Sunday

148. Easter Sunday, the greatest solemnity in the liturgical year, is often associated with many displays of popular piety: these are all cultic expressions which proclaim the new and glorious condition of the risen Christ, and the divine power released from his triumph over sin and death.

The Risen Christ meets his Mother

149. Popular piety intuits a constancy in the relationship between Christ and his mother: in suffering and death and in the joy of the resurrection.

The liturgical affirmation that God replenished the Blessed Virgin Mary with joy in the resurrection of her Son[153], has been translated and represented, so as to speak, in the pious exercise of the *meeting of the Risen Christ with His Mother*: on Easter morning two processions, one bearing the image of Our Lady of Dolours, the other that of the Risen Christ, meet each other so as to show that Our Lady was the first, and full participant in the mystery of the Lord's resurrection.

What has already been said in relation to the processions of "the dead Christ" also applies to this pious exercise: the observance of the pious exercise should not acquire greater importance than the liturgical celebration of Easter Sunday nor occasion inappropriate mixing of liturgical expressions with those of popular piety[154].

Blessing of the Family Table

150. The Easter liturgy is permeated by a sense of newness: nature has been renewed, since Easter coincides with Spring in the Northern hemisphere; fire and water have been renewed; Christian hearts have been renewed through the Sacrament of Penance, and, where possible, through administration of the Sacraments of Christian initiation; the Eucharist is renewed, so to speak: these are signs and sign-realities of the new life begun by Christ in the resurrection.

---

[153] Cf. LITURGIA HORARUM, *Commune beatae mariae Virginis, II Vesperae, Preces; Collectio missarum de beata maria Virgine, I*, Formula 15. *Beata Maria Virgo in ressurectione Domini, Praefatio.*
[154] Cf. supra n. 143.

Among the pious exercises connected with Easter Sunday, mention must be made of the traditional blessing of eggs, the symbol of life, and the blessing of the family table; this latter, which is a daily habit in many Christian families that should be encouraged[155], is particularly important on Easter Sunday: the head of the household or some other member of the household, blesses the festive meal with Easter water which is brought by the faithful from the Easter Vigil.

Visit to the Mother of the Risen Christ

151. At the conclusion of the Easter Vigil, or following the Second Vespers of Easter, a short pious exercise is kept in many places: flowers are blessed and distributed to the faithful as a sign of Easter joy. Some are brought to the image of Our Lady of Dolours, which is then crowned, as the *Regina Coeli* is sung. The faithful, having associated themselves with the sorrows of the Blessed Virgin in the Lord's Passion and Death, now rejoice with her in His resurrection.

While this pious exercise should not be incorporated into the liturgical action, it is completely in harmony with the content of the Paschal Mystery and is a further example of the manner in which popular piety grasps the Blessed Virgin Mary's association with the saving work of her Son.

Eastertide

The Annual Blessing of Family Homes

152. The annual blessing of families takes places in their homes during Eastertide - or at other times of the year. This pastoral practice is highly recommended to parish priests and to their assistant priests since it is greatly appreciated by the faithful and affords a precious occasion to recollect God's constant presence among Christian families. It is also an opportunity to invite the faithful to live according to the Gospel, and to exhort parents and children to preserve and promote the mystery of being "a domestic church"[156].

---

[155] Cf. RITUALE ROMANUM, *De Benedictionibus, Ordo benedictionis mensae*, cit., 782-784, 806-807.
[156] Cf. *ibid., Ordo benedictionis annuae familiarum in propris domibus*, 68-89.

The Via Lucis

153. A pious exercise called the *Via Lucis* has developed and spread to many regions in recent years. Following the model of the *Via Crucis*, the faithful process while meditating on the various appearances of Jesus - from his Resurrection to his Ascension - in which he showed his glory to the disciples who awaited the coming of the Holy Spirit (cf. *John* 14:26; 16:13-15; *Lk* 24:49), strengthened their faith, brought to completion his teaching on the Kingdom and more closely defined the sacramental and hierarchical structure of the Church.

Through the *Via Lucis*, the faithful recall the central event of the faith - the resurrection of Christ - and their discipleship in virtue of Baptism, the paschal sacrament by which they have passed from the darkness of sin to the bright radiance of the light of grace (cf. *Col* 1:13; *Eph* 5:8).

For centuries the *Via Crucis* involved the faithful in the first moment of the Easter event, namely the Passion, and helped to fixed its most important aspects in their consciousness. Analogously, the *Via Lucis*, when celebrated in fidelity to the Gospel text, can effectively convey a living understanding to the faithful of the second moment of the Pascal event, namely the Lord's Resurrection.

The *Via Lucis* is potentially an excellent pedagogy of the faith, since *"per crucem ad lucem"*. Using the metaphor of a journey, the Via Lucis moves from the experience of suffering, which in God's plan is part of life, to the hope of arriving at man's true end: liberation, joy and peace which are essentially paschal values.

The *Via Lucis* is a potential stimulus for the restoration of a "culture of life" which is open to the hope and certitude offered by faith, in a society often characterized by a "culture of death", despair and nihilism.

Devotion to the Divine Mercy

154. In connection with the octave of Easter, recent years have witnessed the development and diffusion of a special devotion to the Divine Mercy based on the writings of Sr Faustina

Kowalska who was canonized 30 April 2000. It concentrates on the mercy poured forth in Christ's death and resurrection, fount of the Holy Spirit who forgives sins and restores joy at having been redeemed. Since the liturgy of the Second Sunday of Easter or Divine Mercy Sunday - as it is now called[157] - is the natural locus in which to express man's acceptance of the Redeemer's mercy, the faithful should be taught to understand this devotion in the light of the liturgical celebrations of these Easter days. Indeed, "the paschal Christ is the definitive incarnation of mercy, his living sign which is both historico-salvific and eschatological. At the same time, the Easter liturgy places the words of the psalm on our lips: "I shall sing forever of the Lord's mercy" (*Ps* 89[88]:2)"[158].

The Pentecost Novena

155. The New Testament tells us that during the period between the Ascension and Pentecost "all... joined in continuous prayer, together with several women, including Mary the mother of Jesus, and with his brothers" (*Acts* 1:14) while they awaited being "clothed with the power from on high" (*Lk* 24:49). The pious exercise of the Pentecost novena, widely practised among the faithful, emerged from prayerful reflection on this salvific event.

Indeed, this novena is already present in the Missal and in the Liturgy of the Hours, especially in the second vespers of Pentecost: the biblical and eucological texts, in different ways, recall the disciples' expectation of the Paraclete. Where possible, the Pentecost novena should consist of the solemn celebration of vespers. Where such is not possible, the novena should try to reflect the liturgical themes of the days from Ascension to the Vigil of Pentecost.

In some places, the week of prayer for the unity of Christians is celebrated at this time[159].

---

[157] Cf. *Notificazione* of the Congregation for Divine Worship and the Discipline of the Sacraments (5.5.2000).
[158] John Paul II, Encyclical letter *Dives in Misericordia* 8.
[159] Cf. PONTIFICAL COUNCIL FOR THE PROMOTION OF CHRISTIAN UNITY, *Directoire pour l'application des Principes et des Normes sur l'Oecuménisme* (5.3.1993), 110: AAS 85 (1993) 1084.

Pentecost

Pentecost Sunday

156. Eastertide concludes with Pentecost Sunday, the fiftieth day, and its commemoration of the outpouring of the Holy Spirit on the apostles (cf. *Acts* 2:1-4), the Church's foundation, and the beginning of its mission to all nations and peoples. The protracted celebration of the vigil Mass has a particular importance in cathedrals and some parishes, since it reflects the intense persevering prayer of the Christian community in imitation of the Apostles united in prayer with Mother of Jesus[160.]

The mystery of Pentecost exhorts us to prayer and commitment to mission and enlightens popular piety which is a "continued sign of the presence of the Holy Spirit in the Church. He arouses faith, hope and charity, in the hearts [of the faithful] and those ecclesial virtues which make popular piety valuable. The same Spirit ennobles the numerous and varied ways of transmitting the Christian message according to the culture and customs of all times and places"[161].

The faithful are well used to invoking the Holy Spirit especially when initiating new undertakings or works or in times of particular difficulties. Often they use formulas taken from the celebration of Pentecost *(Veni Creator Spiritus, Veni Sancte Spiritus)*[162] or short prayers of supplication *(Emitte Spiritum tuum et creabuntur)*. The third glorious mystery of the Rosary invites the faithful to meditate on the outpouring of the Holy Spirit. In Confirmation they are conscious of receiving the Spirit of wisdom and counsel to guide and assist them; the Spirit of strength and light to help them make important decisions and to sustain the trials of life. The faithful are also aware that through Baptism their bodies become temples of the Holy Spirit to be respected and honoured, even in death, and they know that the body will be raised up on the last day through the power of the Holy Spirit.

---

[160] Cf. CONGREGATION FOR DIVINE WORSHIP *Lettera circolare sulla preparazione e celebrazione delle feste pasquali*, 107; the forms, biblical texts and prayers for the vigil of Pentecost - already published in some editions of the Missale Romanum - are to be found in *Notitiae* 24 (1988) 156-159.

[161] JOHN PAUL II, Homily given at the Celebration of the Word in La Serena (Chile), 2, in *Insegnamenti di Giovanni Paolo II*, X/1 (1987), cit., p. 1078.

[162] Cf. EI, *Aliae concessiones* 26, pp. 70-71.

While the Holy Spirit gives access to communion with God in prayer, he also prompts us towards service of our neighbour by encountering him, by reconciliation, by witness, by a desire for justice and peace, by renewal of outlook, by social progress and missionary commitment[163]. In some Christian communities, Pentecost is celebrated as a "day of intercession for the missions"[164].

Ordinary Time

Solemnity of the Most Holy Trinity

157. The solemnity of the Most Holy Trinity is celebrated on the Sunday after Pentecost. With the growth of devotion to the mystery of God in His Unity and Trinity, John XXII extended the feast of the Holy Trinity to the entire Latin Church in 1334. During the middle ages, especially during the carolingian period, devotion to the Blessed Trinity was a highly important feature of private devotion and inspired several liturgical expressions. These events were influential in the development of certain pious exercises.

In the present context, it would not appear appropriate to mention specific pious exercises connected with popular devotion to the Blessed Trinity, "the central mystery of the faith and of the Christian life"[165]. It suffices to recall that every genuine form of popular piety must necessarily refer to God, "the all-powerful Father, His only begotten Son and the Holy Spirit"[166]. Such is the mystery of God, as revealed in Christ and through him. Such have been his manifestations in salvation history. The history of salvation "is the history of the revelation of the one true God: Father, Son and Holy Spirit, who reconciles and unites to Himself those who have been freed from sin"[167].

Numerous pious exercises have a Trinitarian character or dimension. Most of them begin with the sign of the cross "in the name of the Father, and of the Son, and of the Holy Spirit", the

---

[163] Cf. *Gal* 5, 16.22; SECOND VATICAN COUNCIL, *Ad gentes* 4; *Gaudium et spes*, 26.
[164] JOHN PAUL II, Encyclical letter, *Redemptoris missio* 78: in AAS 83 (1991) 325.
[165] CCC 234.
[166] *Ibid.*, 233.
[167] *ibid.*, 234.

113

same formula with which the disciples of Jesus are baptized (cf. *Mt* 28:19), thereby beginning a life of intimacy with the God, as sons of the Father, brothers of Jesus, and temples of the Holy Spirit. Other pious exercises use formulas similar to those found in the Liturgy of the Hours and begin by giving "Glory to the Father, Son, and Holy Spirit". Some pious exercises end with a blessing given in the name of the three divine Persons. Many of the prayers used in these pious exercises follow the typical liturgical form and are addressed to the "Father, through Christ, in the Holy Spirit", and conserve doxological formulas taken from the Liturgy.

158. Worship, as has been said in the first part of this Directory, is the dialogue of God with man through Christ in the Holy Spirit[168]. A Trinitarian orientation is therefore an essential element in popular piety. It should be clear to the faithful that all pious exercises in honour of the Blessed Virgin May, and of the Angels and Saints have the Father as their final end, from Whom all thing come and to Whom all things return; the incarnate, dead and resurrected Son is the only mediator (1 *Tim* 2:5) apart from whom access to the Father is impossible (cf. *John* 14:6); the Holy Spirit is the only source of grace and sanctification. It is important to avoid any concept of "divinity" which is abstract from the three Divine Persons.

159. Together with the little doxology *(Glory be to the Father, and to the Son, and to the Holy Spirit....)* and the great doxology *(Glory be to God in the highest)*, pious exercises addressed directly to the Most Blessed Trinity often include formulas such as the biblical Trisagion *(Holy, Holy, Holy)* and also its liturgical form *(Holy God, Holy Strong One, Holy Immortal One, have mercy on us)*, especially in the Eastern Churches, in some Western countries as well as among numerous religious orders and congregations.

---

[168] Cf. nn. 76-80.

The liturgical Trisagion is inspired by liturgical hymns and its biblical counterpart. Here mention could be made of the *Sanctus* used in the celebration of the Mass, the *Te Deum*, the *improperia* of Good Friday's veneration of the Cross, all of which are derived from Isaiah 6:3 and Apocalypse 4:8. The Trisagion is a pious exercise in which the faithful, united with the Angels, continually glorify God, the Holy, Powerful and Immortal One, while using expressions of praise drawn from Scripture and the Liturgy.

Solemnity of the Body and Blood of Christ

160. The Solemnity of the Body and Blood of Christ is observed on the Thursday following the solemnity of the Most Blessed Trinity. This feast is both a doctrinal and cultic response to heretical teaching on the mystery of the real presence of Christ in the Eucharist, and the apogee of an ardent devotional movement concentrated on the Sacrament of the Altar. It was extended to the entire Latin Church by Urban IV in 1264.

Popular piety encouraged the process that led to the institution of the feast of *Corpus Christi*, which reciprocally inspired the development of new forms of Eucharistic piety among the people of God.

For centuries, the celebration of *Corpus Christi* remained the principal point of popular piety's concentration on the Eucharist. In the sixteenth and seventeenth centuries, faith, in reaction to various forms of protestantism, and culture (art, folklore and literature) coalesced in developing lively and significant expressions of Eucharistic devotion in popular piety.

161. Eucharistic devotion, which is so deeply rooted in the Christian faithful, must integrate two basic principles:

• the supreme reference point for Eucharistic devotion is the Lord's Passover; the Pasch as understood by the Fathers, is the feast of Easter, while the Eucharist is before all else the celebration of Paschal Mystery or of the Passion, Death and Resurrection of Christ;

• all forms of Eucharistic devotion must have an intrinsic reference to the Eucharistic Sacrifice, or dispose the faithful for its celebration, or prolong the worship which is essential to that Sacrifice.

Hence, the *Rituale Romanum* states "The faithful, when worshipping Christ present in the Sacrament of the Altar, should recall that this presence comes from the Sacrifice of the Eucharist, and tends towards sacramental and spiritual communion"[169].

162. The *Corpus Christi* procession represents the typical form of an Eucharistic procession. It is a prolongation of the celebration of the Eucharist: immediately after Mass, the Sacred Host, consecrated during the Mass, is borne out of the Church for the Christian faithful "to make public profession of faith and worship of the Most Blessed Sacrament"[170].

The faithful understand and appreciate the values inherent in the procession: they are aware of being "the People of God", journeying with the Lord, and proclaiming faith in him who has become truly "God-amongst-us".

It is necessary however to ensure that the norms governing processions be observed[171], especially those ensuring respect for the dignity and reverence of the Blessed Sacrament[172]. It is also necessary to ensure that the typical elements of popular piety accompanying the precession, such as the decoration of the streets and windows with flowers and the hymns and prayers used during the procession, truly "lead all to manifest their faith in Christ, and to give praise to the Lord"[173], and exclude any forms of competition.

163. The Eucharistic procession is normally concluded by a blessing with the Blessed Sacrament. In the specific case of the Corpus Christi procession, the solemn blessing with the Blessed

---

[169] RITUALE ROMANUM, *De sacra communione et de cultu mysterii eucharistici extra Missam*, Editio Typica, Typis Polyglotis Vaticanis 1973, 80.
[170] *Ibid.*, 101; cf. CIC, can. 944.
[171] Cf. RITUALE ROMANUM, *De sacra communione et de cultu mysterii eucharistici extra Missam*, cit., 101-108.
[172] Cf. *ibid.*, 101-102.
[173] *Ibid.*, 104.

Sacrament concludes the entire celebration: the usual blessing by the priest is replaced by the blessing with the Blessed Sacrament.

It is important that the faithful understand that this blessing is not an independent form of Eucharistic piety, but the end of a prolonged act of worship. Hence, liturgical norms prohibit "exposition of the Blessed Sacrament for the purpose of giving the blessing"[174].

Eucharistic Adoration

164. Adoration of the Blessed Sacrament is a form of Eucharistic cult which is particularly widespread in the Church and earnestly recommended to her Pastors and faithful. Its initial form derives from Holy Thursday and the altar of repose, following the celebration of the *Coena Domini* Mass. This adoration is a most apt way of expressing the connection between the celebration of the memorial of the Lord's Sacrifice and his continued presence in the Sacrament of the Altar. The reservation of the Sacred Species, so as to be able to administer Viaticum to the sick at any time, encouraged the practice among the faithful of recollection before the tabernacle and to worship Christ present in the Sacrament[175].

Indeed, this worship of adoration has a sound and firm foundation," [109] especially since faith in the Lord's real presence has as its natural consequence the outward and public manifestation of that belief. Therefore, the devotion prompting the faithful to visit the blessed sacrament draws them into an ever deeper share in the paschal mystery and leads them to respond gratefully to the gift of him who through his humanity constantly pours divine life into the members of his Body. [110] Abiding with Christ the Lord, they enjoy his intimate friendship and pour out their hearts before him for themselves and for those dear to them and they pray for the peace and salvation of the world. Offering their entire lives with Christ to the Father in the Holy

---

[174] *Ibid.*, 81.
[175] Cf. PIUS XII, Encyclical letter *Mediator Dei* in AAS 39 (1947) 568-572; PAUL VI, Encyclical letter *Mysterium fidei* in AAS 57 (1965) 769-772; SACRED CONGREGATION OF RITES, Instruction *Eucharisticum mysterium*, nn. 49-50, in AAS 59 (1967) 566-567; RITUALE ROMANUM, *De sacra communione et de cultu mycteria eucharistici extra Missam*, cit., 5.

Spirit, they derive from this sublime colloquy an increase of faith, hope, and charity. Thus they foster those right dispositions that enable them with due devotion to celebrate the memorial of the Lord and receive frequently the bread given us by the Father.[176]

165. In adoration of the Blessed Sacrament, which can take different forms, several elements deriving from the Liturgy and from popular piety come together and it is not always easy to determine their limits[177]:

• a simple visit to the Blessed Sacrament: a brief encounter with Christ inspired by faith in the real presence and characterized by silent prayer;

• adoration of the Blessed Sacrament exposed for a period of time in a monstrance or pyx in accordance with liturgical norm[178];

• perpetual adoration or the *Quarantore*, involving an entire religious community, or Eucharistic association, or parish, which is usually an occasion for various expressions of Eucharistic piety[179].

The faithful should be encouraged to read the Scriptures during these periods of adoration, since they afford an unrivalled source of prayer. Suitable hymns and canticles based on those of the Liturgy of the Hours and the liturgical seasons could also be encouraged, as well as periods of silent prayer and reflection. Gradually, the faithful should be encouraged not to do other devotional exercises during exposition of the Blessed Sacrament[180]. Given the close relationship between Christ and Our Lady, the rosary can always be

---

[176] SACRED CONGREGATION OF RITES, Instruction *Eucharisticum mysterium*, nn. 49-50.

[177] On the matter of indulgences attached to Eucharistic adoration and processions, cf. EI, *Aliae concessiones*, 7, pp. 54-55.

[178] Cf. RITUALE ROMANUM, *De sacra communione et de cultu mycteria eucharistici extra Missam*, cit., 82-90; CIC, canon 941.

[179] Cf. CIC, canon 942.

[180] Cf. Reply ad dubium on n. 62 of the Instruction *Eucharisticum mysterium*, in *Notitiae* 34 (1998) 133-134; concerning the Rosary, see the following note.

of assistance in giving prayer a Christological orientation, since it contains meditation of the Incarnation and the Redemption[181].

The Sacred Heart of Jesus

166. The Church celebrates the Solemnity of the Sacred Heart of Jesus on the Friday following the second Sunday after Pentecost. In addition to the liturgical celebration, many devotional exercises are connected with the Sacred Heart of Jesus. Of all devotions, devotion to the Sacred Heart was, and remains, one of the most widespread and popular in the Church.

Understood in the light of the Scriptures, the term "Sacred Heart of Jesus" denotes the entire mystery of Christ, the totality of his being, and his person considered in its most intimate essential: Son of God, uncreated wisdom; infinite charity, principal of the salvation and sanctification of mankind. The "Sacred Heart" is Christ, the Word Incarnate, Saviour, intrinsically containing, in the Spirit, an infinite divine-human love for the Father and for his brothers.

167. The Roman Pontiffs have frequently averted to the scriptural basis of devotion to the Sacred Heart of Jesus[182].

Jesus, who is one with the Father (cf. *John* 10:30), invites his disciples to live in close communion with him, to model their lives on him and on his teaching. He, in turn, reveals himself as "meek and humble of heart" (*Mt* 11:29). It can be said that, in a certain sense, devotion to the Sacred Heart of Jesus is a cultic form of the prophetic and evangelic gaze of all Christians on him who was pierced (cf. *John* 19:37; *Zac* 12:10), the gaze of all Christians on the side of Christ, transfixed by a lance, and from which flowed blood

---

[181] Cf. PAUL VI, Apostolic Exhortation *Marialis cultus*, 46; Letter of the Congregation for Divine Worship and the Discipline pf the Sacraments (15.1.1997), in *Notitiae* 34 (1998) 506-510; see also the rescript of the Apostolic Penitentiary of 8 March 1996, in *Notitiae* 34 (1998) 511.

[182] Cf. LEO XIII, Encyclical Letter *Annum sacrum* (25.1889) on the consecration of mankind to the Sacred Heart, in *Leonis XIII Pontificis Maximi Acta* ,XIX, Typographia Vaticana, Romae 1900, pp. 71-80; PIUS XII, Encyclical Letter *Haurietis aquas*, in AAS 48 (1956) 311-329; PAUL VI, Apostolic Letter *Investigabiles divitias Christi* (6.2.1965), in AAS 57 (1965) 298-301; JOHN PAUL II, Message on the centenary of the consecration of mankind to the Sacred Heart of Jesus (11.6.1999), in *L'Osservatore Romano*, 12 June 1999.

and water (cf. *John* 19:34), symbols of the "wondrous sacrament of the Church"[183].

The Gospel of St John recounts the showing of the Lord's hands and his side to the disciples (cf. *John* 20:20), and of his invitation to Thomas to put his hand into his side (cf. *John* 20:27). This event has also had a notable influence on the origin and development of the Church's devotion to the Sacred Heart.

168. These and other texts present Christ as the paschal Lamb, victorious and slain (cf. *Apoc* 5:6). They were objects of much reflection by the Fathers who unveiled their doctrinal richness. They invited the faithful to penetrate the mysteries of Christ by contemplating the wound opened in his side. Augustine writes: "Access is possible: Christ is the door. It was opened for you when his side was opened by the lance. Remember what flowed out from his side: thus, choose where you want to enter Christ. From the side of Christ as he hung dying upon the Cross there flowed out blood and water, when it was pierced by a lance. Your purification is in that water, your redemption is in that blood"[184].

169. Devotion to the Sacred Heart was particularly strong during the middle ages. Many renowned for their learning and holiness developed and encouraged the devotion, among them St Bernard (d. 1153), St Bonaventure (d. 1274), the mystic St Lutgarda (d. 1246), St Mathilda of Marburg (d. 1282), the sainted sisters Mathilda (d. 1299) and Gertrude (d. 1302) of the monastery of Helfta, and Ludolf of Saxony (d. 1380). These perceived in the Sacred Heart a "refuge" in which to recover, the seat of mercy, the encounter with him who is the source of the Lord's infinite love, the fount from which flows the Holy Spirit, the promised land, and true paradise.

170. In the modern period devotion to the Sacred Heart of Jesus underwent new developments. At a time when Jansenism proclaimed the rigours of divine justice, the devotion to the Sacred

---

[183] SC 5; cf. St AUGUSTINE, *Ennaratio in Psalmum 138*, 2: CCL 40, cit.,m p. 1991.
[184] St AUGUSTINE, *Sermo* 311, 3: PL 38, 1415.

Heart of Jesus served as a useful antidote and aroused in the faithful a love for Our Lord and a trust in his infinite mercy symbolized by his Heart. St Francis de Sales (d. 1622) adopted humility, gentleness (cf. *Mt* 11:29) and tender loving mercy, all aspects of the Sacred Heart, as a model for his life and apostolate. The Lord frequently manifested the abundant mercy of his Heart to St Margaret Mary (d. 1690); St John Eudes (d. 1680) promoted the liturgical cult of the Sacred Heart, while St Claude de la Colombière (d. 1682) and St John Bosco (d. 1888) and other saints were avid promoters of devotion to the Sacred Heart.

171. Devotions to the Sacred Heart of Jesus are numerous. Some have been explicitly approved and frequently recommended by the Apostolic See. Among these, mention should be made of the following:

• personal consecration, described by Pius XI as "undoubtedly the principal devotional practice used in relation to the Sacred Heart"[185];

• family consecration to the Sacred Heart, in which the family, by virtue of the Sacrament of Holy Matrimony already participating in the mystery of the unity and love of Christ for the Church, is dedicated to Christ so that he might reign in the hearts of all its members[186];

• the Litany of the Sacred Heart of Jesus, approved for the whole Church in 1891, which is evidently biblical in character and to which many indulgences have been attached;

• the act of reparation, a prayer with which the faithful, mindful of the infinite goodness of Christ, implore mercy for the offences committed in so many ways against his Sacred Heart[187];

---

[185] PIUS XI, Encyclical Letter *Miserentissimus redemptor* AAS 20 (1928) 167.
[186] Cf. EI, *Aliae concessiones* 1, p. 50.
[187] Cf. EI, *Aliae concessiones*, 3, pp. 51-53.

• the pious practice of the first Fridays of the month which derives from the "great promises" made by Jesus to St Margaret Mary. At a time when sacramental communion was very rare among the faithful, the first Friday devotion contributed significantly to a renewed use of the Sacraments of Penance and of the Holy Eucharist. In our own times, the devotion to the first Fridays, even if practised correctly, may not always lead to the desired spiritual fruits. Hence, the faithful require constant instruction so that any reduction of the practice to mere credulity, is avoided and an active faith encouraged so that the faithful may undertake their commitment to the Gospel correctly in their lives. They should also be reminded of the absolute preeminence of Sunday, the "primordial feast"[188], which should be marked by the full participation of the faithful at the celebration of the Holy Mass.

172. Devotion to the Sacred Heart is a wonderful historical expression of the Church's piety for Christ, her Spouse and Lord: it calls for a fundamental attitude of conversion and reparation, of love and gratitude, apostolic commitment and dedication to Christ and his saving work. For these reasons, the devotion is recommended and its renewal encouraged by the Holy See and by the Bishops. Such renewal touches on the devotion's linguistic and iconographic expressions; on consciousness of its biblical origins and its connection with the great mysteries of the faith; on affirming the primacy of the love of God and neighbour as the essential content of the devotion itself.

173. Popular piety tends to associate a devotion with its iconographic expression. This is a normal and positive phenomenon. Inconveniences can sometimes arise: iconographic expressions that no longer respond to the artistic taste of the people can sometimes lead to a diminished appreciation of the devotion's object, independently of its theological basis and its historico-salvific content.

This can sometimes arise with devotion to the Sacred Heart: perhaps certain over sentimental images which are incapable of giving expression

---

[188] SC 106.

to the devotion's robust theological content or which do not encourage the faithful to approach the mystery of the Sacred Heart of our Saviour.

Recent time have seen the development of images representing the Sacred Heart of Jesus at the moment of crucifixion which is the highest expression of the love of Christ. The Sacred Heart is Christ crucified, his side pierced by the lance, with blood and water flowing from it (cf. *John* 19:34).

The Immaculate Heart of Mary

174. The Church celebrates the liturgical memorial of the Immaculate Heart of Mary the day after the Solemnity of the Sacred Heart of Jesus. The contiguity of both celebrations is in itself a liturgical sign of their close connection: the *mysterium* of the Heart of Jesus is projected onto and reverberates in the Heart of His Mother, who is also one of his followers and a disciple. As the Solemnity of the Sacred Heart celebrates the salvific mysteries of Christ in a synthetic manner by reducing them to their fount -the Heart of Jesus, so too the memorial of the Immaculate Heart of Mary is a celebration of the complex visceral relationship of Mary with her Son's work of salvation: from the Incarnation, to his death and resurrection, to the gift of the Holy Spirit.

Following the apparitions at Fatima in 1917, devotion to the Immaculate Heart of Mary became very widespread. On the twenty-fifth anniversary of the apparitions (1942) Pius XII consecrated the Church and the human race to the Immaculate Heart of Mary, and extended the memorial to the entire Church.

In popular piety devotions to the Immaculate Heart of Mary resemble those of the Sacred Heart of Jesus, while bearing in mind the distance between Jesus and his Mother: consecration of individuals and families, of religious communities and nations[189]; reparation for sins through prayer, mortification and alms deeds; the practice of the First Five Saturdays.

---

[189] Among the the various consecrations to the Immaculate Heart of Mary, one of the most important is that of Pius XII's consecration of the world to the Immaculate Heart of Mary on 31 October 1942 (cf. AAS 34 [1942] 318), which was renewed by John Paul II, in communion with the bishops of the Church, on 25 March 1984 (cf. *Insegnamenti di Giovanni Paolo II* VII/1 [1984], Libreria Editrice Vaticana, Città del Vaticano 1984, pp. 774-779).

With regard to receiving Holy Communion on the *Five First Saturdays*, the same as has been said in relation to the Nine First Fridays can be repeated[190]: overestimation of temporal factors should be overcome in favour of re-contextualization of the reception of Holy Communion within the framework of the Eucharist. This pious practice should be seen as an opportunity to live intensely the paschal Mystery celebrated in the Holy Eucharist, as inspired by the life of the Blessed Virgin Mary.

The Most Precious Blood of Christ

175. Biblical revelation, both in its figurative stage in the Old Testament and in its perfect and fulfilled stage in the New Testament, connects blood very closely with life, and authentically with death, exodus and the Pasch, with the priesthood and sacrificial cult, with redemption and the covenant.

The Old Testament figures associated with blood and its redemptive significance are fulfilled perfectly in Christ, especially in his Passion, Death and Resurrection. Thus the mystery of the Blood of Christ is to be found at the very centre of the faith and of our salvation.

The mystery of the Saving Blood of Christ recalls and refers to:

• the Incarnation of the Word (cf. *John* 1:14) and Christ's becoming a member of the people of the Old Testament through circumcision (*Lk* 2:21);

• the Biblical image of the Lamb abounds with implication: "The Lamb of God who takes away the sins of the world" (*John* 1:29), in which Isaiah's Suffering Servant image (*Is* 53) is also to be found, carries upon himself the sins of mankind (cf. *Is* 53:4-5); the "Paschal Lamb", symbol of Israel's redemption (cf. *At* 8:31-35; 1 *Cor* 5:7; 1 *Pet* 1:18-20);

• the "chalice of the passion" of which Jesus spoke in allusion to his imminent redemptive death, when he asked the sons of Zebedee: "Can you drink this chalice that I must drink?" (*Mt* 20:22; cf. *Mk* 10:38) and

---

[190] Cf. supra n. 171.

the chalice of the agony in the garden of olives (cf. *Lk* 22:42-43) which was accompanied by the Lord's sweating blood (cf. *Lk* 22:44);

• the Eucharistic chalice, under the form of wine, contains the Blood of the New Covenant poured out for the remission of sins; is a memorial of the Lord's Pasch (1 *Cor* 11:25); and the drink of salvation according to the Lord's own words: "he who eats my flesh and drinks my blood shall have life eternal and I shall raise him up on the last day" (*John* 6:54);

• the event of the Lord's death, since by pouring out his Blood on the Cross, Christ reconciled heaven and earth (cf. *Col* 1:20);

• the lance which transfixed the immolated Lamb, from whose open side flowed blood and water (cf. *John* 19:34), a sign of the redemption that had been achieved, and of the sacramental life of the Church - blood and water, Baptism and Eucharist -, symbol of the Church born from the side of Christ dying on the Cross[191].

176. The Christological titles associated with the *Redeemer* are particularly associated with the mystery of the Blood of Christ: Christ has redeemed us from an ancient slavery by his most precious and innocent Blood (cf. 1 *Pt* 1:19) and "purifies us of sin" (1 *John* 1:17); *High Priest* "of all blessings to come" since Christ "has entered the sanctuary once and for all, taking with him not the blood of goats and bull calves, but his own blood, having won an eternal redemption for us"; *faithful Witness* vindicating the blood of the martyrs (cf. *Ap* 6:10) "who were slain on account of the word of God, for witnessing to it" (cf. *Aps* 6:9); of King, who as God, "reigns from the wood of the Cross", which is adorned with the purple of his own Blood; *Spouse* and *Lamb of God* in whose Blood the members of the Church -the Bride- have washed their garments (cf. *Ap* 7:14; *Eph* 5:25-27).

---

[191] Cf. SC 5.

177. The extraordinary importance of the saving Blood of Christ has ensured a central place for its memorial in the celebration of this cultic mystery: At the centre of the Eucharistic assembly, in which the Church raises up to God in thanksgiving "the cup of blessing" (1 *Cor* 10:16; cf. 115-116:13) and offers it to the faithful as a "real communion with the Blood of Christ" (1 *Cor* 10:16); and throughout the Liturgical Year. The Church celebrates the saving Blood of Christ not only on the Solemnity of the Body and Blood of Christ, but also on many other occasions, such that the cultic remembrance of the Blood of our redemption (cf. 1 *Pt* 1:18) pervades the entire Liturgical Year. Hence, at Vespers during Christmastide, the Church, addressing Christ, sings: *"Nos quoque, qui sancto tuo redempti sumus sanguine, ob diem natalis tui hymnum novum concinimus"*[192]. In the Paschal Triduum, the redemptive significance and efficacy of the Blood of Christ is continuously recalled in adoration. During the adoration of the Cross on Good Friday the Church sings the hymn: *"Mite corpus perforatur, sanguis unde profluit; terra, pontus, astra, mundus quo lavantur flumine"*[193],and again on Easter Sunday, *"Cuius corpus sanctissimum in ara crucis torridum, sed et cruorem roesum gustando, Deo vivimus"*[194].

In Some places and in certain particular calendars, the feast of the Most Precious Blood of Christ is still observed on 1 July. This feast recalls the various titles of the Redeemer.

178. The veneration of the Blood of Christ has passed from the Liturgy into popular piety where it has been widely diffused in numerous forms of devotional practices. Among these mention can be made of the following:

• the Chaplet of the Most Precious Blood, in which the seven

---

[192] LITURGICAL HORARUM, *Tempus Navitatis I, Ad vesperas, Hymnus "Christe, Redemptor omnium"*.
[193] MISSALE ROMANUM, *Feria VI in Passione Domini, Adoratio sanctae crucis, Hymnus "Crux fidelis"*.
[194] LITURGICAL HORARUM, *Tempus pascale I, Ad Vesperas, Hymnus "Ad cenam Agni providi"*. Analogously, in the alternative hymn"O Rex aeterne, Domine": Tu crucem propter hominem suscipe dignatus es; dedisti tuum sanguinem nostrae salutis pretium.

126

"effusions of the Blood of Christ", implicitly or explicitly mentioned in the Gospels, are recalled in a series of biblical meditations and devotional prayers: the Blood of the Circumcision, the Blood of the Garden of Gethsemane, the Blood of the Flagellation, the Blood of the Crowning of Thorns, the Blood of the Ascent to Calvary, the Blood flowing from Christ's side pierced by the lance;

• the *Litany of the Blood of Christ*, which clearly traces the line of salvation history through a series of biblical references and passages. In its present form it was approved by the Blessed John XXIII on 24 February 1960[195];

• Adoration of the Most Precious Blood of Christ takes a great variety of forms, all of which have a common end: adoration and praise of the Precious Blood of Christ in the Eucharist, thanksgiving for the gift of Redemption, intercession for mercy and pardon; and offering of the Precious Blood of Christ for the good of the Church;

• the *Via Sanguinis*: a recently instituted pious devotion, practised in many Christian communities, whose anthropological and cultural roots are African. In this devotion, the faithful move from place to place, as in the *Via Crucis*, reliving the various moments in which Christ shed his blood for our salvation.

179. Veneration of the Precious Blood of Christ, shed for our salvation, and a realization of its immense significance have produced many iconographical representations which have been approved by the Church. Among these two types can be identified: those representing the Eucharistic cup, containing the Blood of the New Covenant, and those representing the crucified Christ, from whose hands, feet and side flows the Blood of our Salvation. Sometimes, the Blood flows down copiously over the earth, representing a torrent of grace cleansing it of sin; such

---

[195] Text in AAS 52 (1960) 412-413; cf. EI, *Aliae concessiones* 22, p. 68.

representations sometimes feature five Angels, each holding a chalice to collect the Blood flowing from the five wounds of Christ; this task is sometimes given to a female figure representing the Church, the spouse of the Lamb.

Assumption of the Blessed Virgin Mary

180. The Solemnity of the Assumption of the Blessed Virgin Mary clearly stands out in Ordinary Time because of its theological importance. This is an ancient memorial of the Mother of God, which signifies and synthesises many of the truths of the faith. Our Lady assumed into Heaven:

• is "the highest fruit of the redemption"[196], and a supreme testimony to the breath and efficacy of Christ's salvific work (soteriological significance);

• is a pledge of the future participation of the members of the mystical Body of Christ in the paschal glory of the Risen Christ (Christological aspect);

• is for all mankind "the consoling assurance of the coming of our final hope: that full glorification which is Christ's will also be that of his brethren, since He is of the "same flesh and blood" (*Heb* 2:14; cf. *Gal* 4:49)[197] (anthropological aspect);

• is the eschatological icon in which the Church joyfully contemplates "that which she herself desires and hopes wholly to be"[198] (ecclesiological aspect);

• is the guarantee of the Lord's fidelity to his promise: he reserves a munificent reward for his humble Servant because of her faithful cooperation with the divine plan, which is a destiny of fullness, happiness, glorification of her immaculate soul, her

---

[196] SC 103.
[197] PAUL VI, Apostolic Exhortation *Marialis cultus*, 6.
[198] SC 103.

virginal body, perfect configuration to her Risen Son (mariological aspect)[199].

181. The Assumption of the Blessed Virgin Mary (15 August) is deeply imbedded in popular piety. In many places the feast is synonymous with the person of Our Lady, and is simply referred to as "Our Lady's Day" or as the "Immacolada" in Spain and Latin America.

In the Germanic countries, the custom of blessing herbs is associated with 15 August. This custom, received into the *Rituale Romanum*[200], represents a clear example of the genuine evangelization of pre-Christian rites and beliefs: one must turn to God, through whose word "the earth produced vegetation: plants bearing seeds in their several kinds, and trees bearing fruit with their seed inside in their several kinds"(*Gen* 1:12) in order to obtain what was formerly obtained by magic rites; to stem the damages deriving from poisonous herbs, and benefit from the efficacy of curative herbs.

This ancient use came to be associated with the Blessed Virgin Mary, in part because of the biblical images applied to her such as vine, lavender, cypress and lily, partly from seeing her in terms of a sweet smelling flower because of her virtue, and most of all because of Isaiah 11:1, and his reference to the "shoot springing from the side of Jesse", which would bear the blessed fruit of Jesus.

Week of Prayer for Christian Unity

182. At every celebration of the Holy Eucharist, the Church prays for unity and peace[201], mindful of Jesus' prayer. "May they all be one. Father, may they be one in us, as you are in me and I am in you, so that the world may believe it was you who sent me" (*John* 17:21). The Missale Romanum contains three Masses - among

[199] Cf. PAUL VI, Apostolic Exhortation *Marialis cultus*, 6.
[200] Cf. RITUALE ROMANUM Pauli V Pontificis Maximi iussu editum...SS.mi D.N. Pii Papae XII auctoritate auctum et ordinatum, Editio iuxta Typicam, Desclée, Romae 1952, pp. 444-449.
[201] Cf. MISSALE ROMANUM, *Ordo Missae*, the prayer *Domine Jesu Christe*, before the sign of peace.

those for various needs - "for Christian unity". The same intention is remembered in the intercessions of the Liturgy of the Hours"[202].

In deference to the sensibilities of the "separated brethren"[203], expressions of popular piety should take into account the principle of ecumenism[204]. Effectively, "change of heart and holiness of life, along with public and private prayer for the unity of Christians, should be regarded as the soul of the whole ecumenical movement, and merits the name 'spiritual ecumenism'"[205]. The encounter of Catholics with Christians from other Churches or ecclesial communities affords a special occasion for common prayer for the grace of Christian unity, to offer to God their common anxieties, to give thanks to God and to implore his assistance. "Common prayer is particularly recommended during the "Week of Prayer for Christian Unity" or during the period between Ascension and Pentecost"[206]. Prayer for Christian unity also carries several indulgences[207].

[202] See for example: the intercessions at Vespers on Sunday and Monday of the first week, on Wednesday of the third week; and the prayers at Lauds on Wednesday of the fourth week.

[203] Cf. SECOND VATICAN COUNCIL, Decree *Unitatis redintegratio*, 3.

[204] Cf. Paul VI, Apostolic Exhortation *Marialis cultus*, 32-33.

[205] SECOND VATICAN COUNCIL, Decree *Unitatis redintegratio*, 8.

[206] PONTIFICAL COUNCIL FOR THE PROMOTION OF CHRISTIAN UNITY, *Directoire pour l'application des Principes et des Normes sur l'Oecuménisme* (25.3.1993), 110: AAS 85 (1993) 1084.

[207] Cf. EI, *Aliae concessiones*, 11, p. 58.

CHAPTER FIVE

Veneration of the Holy Mother of God

Some Principles

183. Popular devotion to the Blessed Virgin Mary is an important and universal ecclesial phenomenon. Its expressions are multifarious and its motivation very profound, deriving as it does from the People of God's faith in, and love for, Christ, the Redeemer of mankind, and from an awareness of the salvific mission that God entrusted to Mary of Nazareth, because of which she is mother not only of Our Lord and Saviour Jesus Christ, but also of mankind in the order of grace.

Indeed, "the faithful easily understand the vital link uniting Son and Mother. They realise that the Son is God and that she, the Mother, is also their mother. They intuit the immaculate holiness of the Blessed Virgin Mary, and in venerating her as the glorious queen of Heaven, they are absolutely certain that she who is full of mercy intercedes for them. Hence, they confidently have recourse to her patronage. The poorest of the poor feel especially close to her. They know that she, like them, was poor, and greatly suffered in meekness and patience. They can identify with her suffering at the crucifixion and death of her Son, as well as rejoice with her in his resurrection. The faithful joyfully celebrate her feasts, make pilgrimage to her sanctuary, sing hymns in her honour, and make votive offerings to her. They instinctively distrust whoever does not honour her and will not tolerate those who dishonour her"[208].

The Church exhorts all the faithful - sacred minister, religious and laity - to develop a personal and community devotion to the Blessed Virgin Mary through the use of approved and recommended pious exercises[209]. Liturgical worship,

---

[208] CONGREGATION FOR DIVINE WORSHIP, Circular Letter *Guidelines and proposals for the celebration of the Marian Year* (3.4.1987), 67.
[209] Cf. LG 67; Decree *Presbyterorum Ordinis*, 18; Decree *Optatam totius*, 8; Decree *Apostolicam actuositatem*, 4; CIC, canons 76, § 2, 5; 663, §' 2-4; 246 § 3.

notwithstanding its objective and irreplaceable importance, its exemplary efficacy and normative character, does not in fact exhaust all the expressive possibilities of the People of God for devotion to the Holy Mother of God[210].

184. The relationship between the Liturgy and popular Marian piety should be regulated by the principles and norms already mentioned in this document[211]. In relation to Marian devotion, the Liturgy must be the "exemplary form"[212], source of inspiration, constant reference point and ultimate goal of Marian devotion.

185. Here, it will be useful to recall some pronouncements of the Church's Magisterium on Marian devotions. These should always be adhered to when composing new pious exercises or in revising those already in use, or simply in activating them in worship[213]. The care and attention of the Pastors of the Church for Marian devotions are due to their importance, since they are both a fruit and an expression of Marian piety among the people and the ecclesial community, and a significant means of promoting the "Marian formation" of the faithful, as well as in determining the manner in which the piety of the faithful for the Blessed Virgin Mary is moulded.

186. The fundamental principle of the Magisterium with regard to such pious exercises is that they should be derivative from the "one worship which is rightly called Christian, because it efficaciously originates in Christ, finds full expression in Christ, and through Him, in the Holy Spirit leads to the Father"[214]. Hence, Marian devotions, in varying degrees and modes, should:

• give expression to the Trinitarian note which characterises worship of the God revealed in the New Testament, the Father, Son

---

[210] Cf. CCC 971. 2673-2679.
[211] Cf. supra nn. 47-59, 70-75.
[212] Cf. PAUL VI, Apostolic Exhortation *Marialis cultus*, 1; CONGREGATION FOR DIVINE WORSHIP, Circular Letter *Guidelines an proposals for the celebration of the Marian Year 7; Collectio missarum de beata Maria Virgine, Praenotanda*, 9-18.
[213] Cf. PAUL VI, Apostolic Exhortation *Marialis cultus*, 24.
[214] *Ibid, Intro.*

and Holy Spirit; the pneumatological aspect, since every true form of piety comes from the Spirit and is exercised in the Spirit; the ecclesial character, in virtue of which the faithful are constituted as the holy people of God, gathered in prayer in the Lord's name (cf. *Mt* 18:20) in the vital Communion of Saints[215];

• have constant recourse to Sacred Scripture, as understood in Sacred Tradition; not overlook the demands of the ecumenical movement in the Church's profession of faith; consider the anthropological aspects of cultic expressions so as to reflect a true concept of man and a valid response to his needs; highlight the eschatological tension which is essential to the Gospel message; make clear missionary responsibility and the duty of bearing witness, which are incumbent on the Lord's disciples[216].

Times of Pious Marian Exercises

Celebration of feast

187. Practically all Marian devotions and pious exercises are in some way related to the liturgical feasts of the General Calendar of the Roman Rite or of the particular calendars of dioceses and religious families. Sometimes, a particular devotion antedates the institution of the feast (as is the case with the feast of the Holy Rosary), in other instances, the feast is much more ancient than the devotion (as with the *Angelus Domini*). This clearly illustrates the relationship between the Liturgy and pious exercises, and the manner in which pious exercises find their culmination in the celebration of the feast. In so far as liturgical, the feast refers to the history of salvation and celebrates a particular aspect of the relationship of the Virgin Mary to the mystery of Christ. The feast, however, must be celebrated in accordance with liturgical norm, and bear in mind the hierarchal difference between "liturgical acts" and associated "pious exercises"[217].

---

[215] Cf. ibid., 25-39; CONGREGATION FOR DIVINE WORSHIP, Circular letter *Guidelines and proposals for the celebration of the Marian Year*, 8.
[216] Cf. *Ibid.*,8.
[217] Cf. n. 232.

It should not be forgotten that a feast of the Blessed Virgin, in so far as it is popular manifestation, also has important anthropological implications that cannot be overlooked.

Saturdays

188. Saturdays stand out among those days dedicated to the Virgin Mary. These are designated as *memorials of the Blessed Virgin Mary*[218]. This memorial derives from carolingian time (ninth century), but the reasons for having chosen Saturday for its observance are unknown[219.] While many explanation have been advanced to explain this choice, none is completely satisfactory from the point of view of the history of popular piety[220].

Prescinding from its historical origins, today the memorial rightly emphasizes certain values "to which contemporary spirituality is more sensitive: it is a remembrance of the maternal example and discipleship of the Blessed Virgin Mary who, strengthened by faith and hope, on that great Saturday on which Our Lord lay in the tomb, was the only one of the disciples to hold vigil in expectation of the Lord's resurrection; it is a prelude and introduction to the celebration of Sunday, the weekly memorial of the Resurrection of Christ; it is a sign that the "Virgin Mary is continuously present and operative in the life of the Church"[221].

Popular piety is also sensitive to the Saturday memorial of the Blessed Virgin Mary. The statutes of many religious communities and associations of the faithful prescribe that special devotion be paid to the Holy Mother of God on Saturdays, sometimes through specified pious exercises composed precisely for Saturdays[222].

---

[218] The *Missale Romanum* contains diverse formularies for the celebration of Mass in honour of the Blessed Virgin Mary on Saturday mornings during "ordinary time", the use of which is optional. See also the *Collectio missarum de beata Maria Virgine, Praenotanda* 34-36; and the *Liturgia Horarum* for Saturdays of "ordinary time" which permits the Office of the Blessed Virgin Mary on Saturdays.

[219] Cf. ALCUIN, Le sacramentaire grégorien, II, ed. J. DESHUSSES, Editions Universitaires, Fribourg 1988, pp. 25-27 and 45; PL 101, 455-456.

[220] Cf. UMBERTO DE ROMANIS, *De vita regulari*, II, Cap. XXIV, *Quare sabbatum attribuitur Beatae Virgini*, Typis A. BEFANI, Romae 1889, pp. 72-75.

[221] CONGREGATION FOR DIVINE WORSHIP, Circular letter *Guidelines and proposals for the celebration of the Marian Year*, 5.

[222] An example of which is to be found in *Felicitacion sabatina a Maria Inmaculada* compose by Fr Manuel Garcia Navarro, who subsequently entered the Carthusians (d. 1903).

Veneration of the Holy Mother of God

Tridua, Septinaria, Marian Novenas

189. Since it is a significant moment, a feast day is frequently preceded by a preparatory triduum, septinaria or novena. The "times and modes of popular piety", however, should always correspond to the "times and modes of the Liturgy".

Tridua, septinaria, and novenas can be useful not only for honouring the Blessed Virgin Mary through pious exercises, but also to afford the faithful an adequate vision of the positions she occupies in the mystery of Christ and of the Church, as well as the the role she plays in it.

Pious exercises cannot remain indifferent to the results of biblical and theological research on the Mother of Our Saviour. These should become a catechetical means diffusing such information, without however altering their essential nature.

Tridua, septinaria and novenas are truly preparations for the celebration of the various feast days of Our Lady, especially when they encourage the faithful to approach the Sacraments of Penance and Holy Eucharist, and to renew their Christian commitment following the example of Mary, the first and most perfect disciple of Christ.

In some countries, the faithful gather for prayer on the 13th of each month, in honour of the apparitions of Our Lady at Fatima.

Marian Months

190. With regard to the observance of "Marian months", which is widespread in the Latin and Oriental Churches[223], a number of essential points can be mentioned[224].

In the West, the practise of observing months dedicated to the Blessed Virgin emerged from a context in which the Liturgy was

---

[223] In the Byzantine rite, the liturgy for the month of August is centred on the solemnity of the Dormition of Our Lady (15 August). Until the twelfth century, it was observed as a "Marian month"; in the Coptic rite the "Marian month" is that of *kiahk*, corresponding approximately to January-February, and is structured in relation to Christmas. In the West the first indications of a Marian month date from the sixteenth century. By the eighteenth century, the Marian month - in its modern sense - is well attested but during this period the pastors of souls concentrate their apostolic efforts - including Penance and the Eucharist - not so much on the Liturgy but on pious exercises, which were much favoured by the faithful.

[224] Cf. CONGREGATION FOR DIVINE WORSHIP, Circular Letter, *Guidelines and proposals for the celebration of the Marian Year*, 64-65.

not always regarded as the normative form of Christian worship. This caused, and continues to cause, some difficulties at a liturgico-pastoral level that should be carefully examined.

191. In relation to the western custom of observing a "Marian month" during the month of May (or in November in some parts of the Southern hemisphere), it would seem opportune to take into account the demands of the Liturgy, the expectations of the faithful, their maturity in the faith, in an eventual study of the problems deriving from the "Marian months" in the overall pastoral activity of the local Church, as might happen, for example, with any suggestion of abolishing the Marian observances during the month of May.

In many cases, the solution for such problems would seem to lay in harmonizing the content of the "Marian months" with the concomitant season of the Liturgical Year. For example, since the month of May largely corresponds with the fifty days of Easter, the pious exercises practised at this time could emphasize Our Lady's participation in the Paschal mystery (cf. *John* 19:25-27), and the Pentecost event (cf. *Acts* 1:14) with which the Church begins: Our Lady journeys with the Church having shared in the *novum* of the Resurrection, under the guidance of the Holy Spirit. The fifty days are also a time for the celebration of the sacraments of Christian initiation and of the mystagogy. The pious exercises connected with the month of May could easily highlight the earthly role played by the glorified Queen of Heaven, here and now, in the celebration of the Sacraments of Baptism, Confirmation and Holy Eucharist[225].

The directives of *Sacrosanctum Concilium* on the need to orient the "minds of the faithful... firstly to the feasts of the Lord, in which, the mysteries of salvation are celebrated during the year"[226], and with which the Blessed Virgin Mary is certainly associated, should be closely followed.

Opportune catechesis should remind the faithful that the weekly Sunday memorial of the Paschal Mystery is "the primordial feast day". Bearing in mind that the four weeks of Advent are an example

---

[225] For comments on the Blessed Virgin Mary and the Sacraments of Christian initiation cf. *ibid.* 25-31.
[226] SC 108.

of a Marian time that has been incorporated harmoniously into the Liturgical Year, the faithful should be assisted in coming to a full appreciation of the numerous references to the Mother of our Saviour during this particular period.

Pious Exercises Recommended by the Magisterium

192. This is not the place to reproduce the list of Marian exercises approved by the Magisterium. Some, however, should be mentioned, especially the more important ones, so as to make a few suggestions about their practise and emendation.

Prayerfully Hearing the Word of God

193. The Council's call for the "sacred celebration of the word of God" at significant moments throughout the Liturgical Year[227], can easily find useful application in devotional exercises made in honour of the Mother of the Word Incarnate. This corresponds perfectly with the orientation of Christian piety[228] and reflects the conviction that it is already a worthy way to honour the Blessed Virgin Mary, since it involves acting as she did in relation to the Word of God. She lovingly accepted the Word and treasured it in her heart, meditated on it in her mind and spread it with her lips. She faithfully put it into practise and modelled her life on it[229].

194. "Celebrations of the Word, because of their thematic and structural content, offer many elements of worship which are at the same time genuine expressions of devotion and opportunities for a systematic catechesis on the Blessed Virgin Mary. Experience, however, proves that celebrations of the Word should not assume a predominantly intellectual or didactic character. Through hymns, prayers, and participation of the faithful they should allow for simple and familiar expressions of popular piety which speak directly to the hearts of the faithful"[230].

---

[227] Cf. SC 35, 4.
[228] Cf. PAUL VI, Apostolic Exhortation *Marialis Cultus*, 30.
[229] Cf. ibid., 17; *Collectio missarum de beata Virginis Mariae, Praenotanda ad lectionarium*, 10.
[230] CONGREGATION FOR DIVINE WORSHIP, Circular Letter *Guidelines and proposals for the celebration of the Marian Year*, 10.

Angelus Domini

195. The *Angelus Domini* is the traditional form used by the faithful to commemorate the holy annunciation of the angel Gabriel to Mary. It is used three times daily: at dawn, mid-day and at dusk. It is a recollection of the salvific event in which the Word became flesh in the womb of the Virgin Mary, through the power of the Holy Spirit in accordance with the salvific plan of the Father.

The recitation of the *Angelus* is deeply rooted in the piety of the Christian faithful, and strengthened by the example of the Roman Pontiffs. In some places changed social conditions hinder its recitation, but in many other parts every effort should be made to maintain and promote this pious custom and at least the recitation of three *Aves*. The *Angelus* "over the centuries has conserved its value and freshness with its simple structure, biblical character [...] quasi liturgical rhythm by which the various time of the day are sanctified, and by its openness to the Paschal Mystery"[231].

It is therefore "desirable that on some occasions, especially in religious communities, in shrines dedicated to the Blessed Virgin, and at meetings or conventions, the Angelus be solemnly recited by singing the Ave Maria, proclaiming the Gospel of the Annunciation"[232] and by the ringing of bells.

Regina Coeli

196. By disposition of Benedict XIV (2 April 1742), the Angelus is replaced with the antiphon *Regina Coeli* during paschaltide. This antiphon, probably dating from the tenth or eleventh century[233], happily conjoins the mystery of the Incarnation of the Word *(quem meruisti portare)* with the Paschal event *(resurrexit sicut dixit)*. The ecclesial community addresses this antiphon to Mary for the Resurrection of her Son. It adverts to, and depends on, the invitation to joy addressed by Gabriel to the Lord's humble

---

[231] Cf. PAUL VI, Apostolic Exhortation *Marialis cultus*, 41.
[232] CONGREGATION FOR DIVINE WORSHIP, Circular Letter, *Guidelines and proposals for the celebration of the Marian year*, 61.
[233] The antiphon is found in the twelfth century Antiphonary of the Abbey of San Lupo in Benevento. Cf. R. J. HESBERT (ed.) *Corpus Antiphonalium Officii*, vol. II, Herder, Roma 1965, pp. XX-XXIV; vol. III, Herder, Roma 1968, p. 440.

servant who was called to become the Mother of the saving Messiah *(Ave, gratia plena)*.

As with the *Angelus*, the recitation of the *Regina Coeli* could sometimes take a solemn form by singing the antiphon and proclaiming the Gospel of the resurrection.

The Rosary

197. The Rosary, or Psalter of the Blessed Virgin Mary, is one of the most excellent prayers to the Mother of God[234]. Thus, "the Roman Pontiffs have repeatedly exhorted the faithful to the frequent recitation of this biblically inspired prayer which is centred on contemplation of the salvific events of Christ's life, and their close association with the his Virgin Mother. The value and efficacy of this prayer have often been attested by saintly Bishops and those advanced in holiness of life"[235].

The Rosary is essentially a contemplative prayer, which requires "tranquillity of rhythm or even a mental lingering which encourages the faithful to meditate on the mysteries of the Lord's life"[236]. *Its use is expressly recommended in the formation and spiritual life of clerics and religious*[237].

198. The Blessing for Rosary Beads[238] indicates the Church's esteem for the Rosary. This rite emphasises the community nature of the Rosary. In the rite, the blessing of rosary beads is followed by the blessing of those who meditate on the mysteries of the life, death and resurrection of Our Lord so as to "establish a perfect harmony between prayer and life"[239].

As indicated in the *Benedictionale*, Rosary beads can be blessed publicly, on occasions such as a pilgrimage to a Marian shrine, a

---

[234] Regarding indulgences cf. EI, *Aliae concessiones*, 17, p. 62. For a commentary on the *Ave maria* cf. CCC 2676-2677.

[235] CONGREGATION FOR DIVINE WORSHIP, Circular Letter *Guidelines and proposals for the celebration of the Marian Year*, 62.

[236] PAUL VI, Apostolic Exhortation *Marialis Cultus*, 62.

[237] Cf. CIC, canons 246, § 3; 276, § 2,5; 663, § 4; CONGREGATION FOR THE CLERGY, *Directory for the Ministry and Life of Priests*, Libreria Editrice Vaticana, Città del Vaticano 1994, 39.

[238] Cf. RITUALE ROMANUM, *de Benedictionibus, Ordo benedictionis coronarum Roasrii*, cit., 1183-1207.

[239] *Ibid.*

feast of Our Lady, especially that of the Holy Rosary, and at the end of the month of October[240].

199. With due regard for the nature of the rosary, some suggestions can now be made which could make it more proficuous.

On certain occasions, the recitation of the Rosary could be made more solemn in tone "by introducing those Scriptural passages corresponding with the various mysteries, some parts could be sung, roles could be distributed, and by solemnly opening and closing the prayer"[241].

200. Those who recite a third of the Rosary sometimes assign the various mysteries to particular days: joyful (Monday and Thursday), sorrowful (Tuesday and Friday), glorious (Wednesday, Saturday and Sunday).

Where this system is rigidly adhere to, conflict can arise between the content of the mysteries and that of the Liturgy of the day: the recitation of the sorrowful mysteries on Christmas day, should it fall on a Friday. In cases such as this it can be reckoned that "the liturgical character of a given day takes precedence over the usual assignment of a mystery of the Rosary to a given day; the Rosary is such that, on particular days, it can appropriately substitute meditation on a mystery so as to harmonize this pious practice with the liturgical season"[242]. Hence, the faithful act correctly when, for example, they contemplate the arrival of the three Kings on the Solemnity of the Epiphany, rather than the finding of Jesus in the Temple. Clearly, such substitutions can only take place after much careful thought, adherence to Sacred Scripture and liturgical propriety.

201. The custom of making an insertion in the recitation of the Hail Mary, which is an ancient one that has not completely disappeared, has often been recommended by the Pastors of the

---

[240] Cf. *ibid.*,1183-1184.
[241] CONGREGATION FOR DIVINE WORSHIP, Circular Letter *Guidelines and proposals for the celebration of the Marian Year*, 62, a.
[242] *Ibid.*, 62, b.

Church since it encourages meditation and the concurrence of mind and lips[243].

Insertions of this nature would appear particularly suitable for the repetitive and meditative character of the Rosary. It takes the form of a relative clause following the name of Jesus and refers to the mystery being contemplated. The meditation of the Rosary can be helped by the choice of a short clause of a Scriptural and Liturgical nature, fixed for every decade.

202. "In recommending the value and beauty of the Rosary to the faithful, care should be taken to avoid discrediting other forms of prayer, or of overlooking the existence of a diversity of other Marian chaplets which have also been approved by the Church"[244]. It is also important to avoid inculcating a sense of guilt in those who do not habitually recite the Rosary: "The Rosary is an excellent prayer, in regard to which, however, the faithful should feel free to recite it, in virtue of its inherent beauty"[245].

Litanies of the Blessed Virgin Mary

203. Litanies are to be found among the prayers to the Blessed Virgin recommended by the Magisterium. These consist in a long series of invocations of Our Lady, which follow in a uniform rhythm, thereby creating a stream of prayer characterized by insistent praise and supplication. The invocations, generally very short, have two parts: the first of praise *(Virgo clemens)*, the other of supplication *(Ora pro nobis)*.

The liturgical books contain two Marian litanies[246]: *The Litany of Loreto, repeatedly recommended by the Roman Pontiffs; and the Litany for the Coronation of Images of the Blessed Virgin Mary*[247], which can be an appropriate substitute for the other litany on certain occasions[248].

---

[243] Cf. SC 90.

[244] CONGREGATION FOR DIVINE WORSHIP, Circular Letter, *Guidelines and proposals for the celebration of the Marian Year*, 62, c.

[245] PAUL VI, Apostolic Exhortation *Marialis cultus*, 55.

[246] The Litany of Loreto was first included in the *Rituale Romanum* in 1874, as an appendix. Regarding indulgences connected with it cf. EI, *Aliae concessiones*, 22, p. 68.

[247] Cf. *Ordo coronandi imaginem beatae Mariae Virginis*, Editio Typica, Typis Polyglotis Vaticanis 1981, n. 41, pp. 27-29.

[248] Cf. CONGREGATION FOR DIVINE WORSHIP, Circular Letter *Guidelines and proposals for the celebration of the Marian Year*, 63, c.

From a pastoral perspective, a proliferation of litanies would not seem desirable[249], just as an excessive restriction on them would not take sufficient account of the spiritual riches of some local Churches and religious communities. Hence, the Congregation for Divine Worship and the Discipline of the Sacraments recommends "taking account of some older and newer formulas used in the local Churches or in religious communities which are notable for their structural rigour and the beauty of their invocations"[250]. This exhortation, naturally, applies to the specific authorities in the local Churches or religious communities.

Following the prescription of Leo XIII that the recitation of the Rosary should be concluded by the Litany of Loreto during the month of October, the false impression has arisen among some of the faithful that the Litany is in some way an appendix to the Rosary. The Litanies are independent acts of worship. They are important acts of homage to the Blessed Virgin Mary, or as processional elements, or form part of a celebration of the Word of God or of other acts of worship.

Consecration and Entrustment to Mary

204. The history of Marian devotion contains many examples of personal or collective acts of "consecration or entrustment to the Blessed Virgin Mary" *oblatio, servitus, commendatio, dedicatio*). They are reflected in the prayer manuals and statutes of many associations where the formulas and prayers of consecration, or its remembrance, are used.

The Roman Pontiffs have frequently expressed appreciation for the pious practice of "consecration to the Blessed Virgin Mary" and the formulas publicly used by them are well known[251].

---

[249] Litanies multiplied in the sixteenth century. Often, they were in poor taste and the results of an uninformed piety. In 1601, Clement VIII had the Holy Office issue *Quoniam multi* which was intended to curb the excessive and uncontrolled production of litanies. According to the terms of this decree, only the more ancient litanies contained in the Breviary, Missal, Pontifical and Ritual, as well as the Litany of Loreto were approved for the use of the faithful (cf. *Magnum Bullarium Romanum*, III, Lugduni 1656, p. 1609).

[250] CONGREGATION FOR DIVINE WORSHIP, Circular Letter *Guidelines and proposals for the celebration of the Marian Year*, 63, d.

[251] See the *Atto di affidamento alla Beata Vergine Maria* pronounced by John Paul II on Sunday, 8 October 2000, together with the Bishops gathered in Rome for the celebration of the Great Jubilee.

Louis Grignon de Montfort is one of the great masters of the spirituality underlying the act of "consecration to Mary". He " proposed to the faithful consecration to Jesus through Mary, as an effective way of living out their baptismal commitment"[252].

Seen in the light of Christ's words (cf. *John* 19:25-27), the act of consecration is a conscious recognition of the singular role of Mary in the Mystery of Christ and of the Church, of the universal and exemplary importance of her witness to the Gospel, of trust in her intercession, and of the efficacy of her patronage, of the many maternal functions she has, since she is a true mother in the order of grace to each and every one of her children[253].

It should be recalled, however, that the term "consecration" is used here in a broad and non-technical sense: "the expression is use of "consecrating children to Our Lady", by which is intended placing children under her protection and asking her maternal blessing[254] for them". Some suggest the use of the alternative terms "entrustment" or "gift". Liturgical theology and the consequent rigorous use of terminology would suggest reserving the term *consecration* for those self-offerings which have God as their object, and which are characterized by totality and perpetuity, which are guaranteed by the Church's intervention and have as their basis the Sacraments of Baptism and Confirmation.

The faithful should be carefully instructed about the practice of consecration to the Blessed Virgin Mary. While such can give the impression of being a solemn and perpetual act, it is, in reality, only analogously a "consecration to God". It springs from a free, personal, mature, decision taken in relation to the operation of grace and not from a fleeting emotion. It should be expressed in a correct liturgical manner: to the Father, through Christ in the Holy Spirit, imploring the intercession of the Blessed Virgin Mary, to whom we entrust ourselves completely, so as to keep our baptismal commitments and live as her children. The act of consecration should take place outside of the celebration of the Eucharistic Sacrifice, since it is a devotional

---

[252] JOHN PAUL II, Encyclical Letter, *Redemptoris Mater*, 48.

[253] Cf. LG 61; JOHN PAUL II, Encyclical Letter, *Redemptoris Mater*, 40-44.

[254] CONGREGATION FOR DIVINE WORSHIP, Circular letter *Guidelines and proposals for the celebration of the Marian Year*, 86.

act which cannot be assimilated to the Liturgy. It should also be borne in mind that the act of consecration to Mary differs substantially from other forms of liturgical consecration.

The Brown Scapular and other Scapulars

205. The history of Marian piety also includes "devotion" to various scapulars, the most common of which is devotion to the Scapular of Our Lady of Mount Carmel. Its use is truly universal and, undoubtedly, it is one of those pious practices which the Council described as "recommended by the Magisterium throughout the centuries"[255].

The Scapular of Mount Carmel is a reduced form of the religious habit of the Order of the Friars of the Blessed Virgin of Mount Carmel. Its use is very diffuse and often independent of the life and spirituality of the Carmelite family.

The Scapular is an external sign of the filial relationship established between the Blessed Virgin Mary, Mother and Queen of Mount Carmel, and the faithful who entrust themselves totally to her protection, who have recourse to her maternal intercession, who are mindful of the primacy of the spiritual life and the need for prayer.

The Scapular is imposed by a special rite of the Church which describes it as "a reminder that in Baptism we have been clothed in Christ, with the assistance of the Blessed Virgin Mary, solicitous for our conformation to the Word Incarnate, to the praise of the Trinity, we may come to our heavenly home wearing our nuptial garb"[256].

The imposition of the Scapular should be celebrated with "the seriousness of its origins. It should not be improvised. The Scapular should be imposed following a period of preparation during which the faithful are made aware of the nature and ends of the association they are about to join and of the obligations they assume"[257].

---

[255] LG 67; cf. PAUL VI Letter to Cardinal Silva Henriquez, Papal Legate to the Marian Congress in Santo Domingo, in AAS 57 (1965) 376-379.
[256] CONGREGATION FOR DIVINE WORSHIP, Circular Letter *Guidelines and proposals for the celebration of the Marian Year*, 88.
[257] RITUALE ROMANUM, *De Benedictionibus, Ordo benedictionis et impositionis scapularis*, cit., 1213.

Medals

206. The faithful like to wear medals bearing effigies of the Blessed Virgin Mary. These are a witness of faith and a sign of veneration of the Holy Mother of God, as well as of trust in her maternal protection.

The Church blesses such objects of Marian devotion in the belief that "they help to remind the faithful of the love of God, and to increase trust in the Blessed Virgin Mary"[258]. The Church also points out that devotion to the Mother of Christ also requires "a coherent witness of life"[259].

Among the various medals of the Blessed Virgin Mary, the most diffuse must be the "Miraculous Medal". Its origins go back to the apparitions in 1830 of Our Lady to St Catherine Labouré, a humble novice of the Daughters of Charity in Paris. The medal was struck in accordance with the instructions given by Our Lady and has been described as a "Marian microcosm" because of its extraordinary symbolism. It recalls the mystery of Redemption, the love of the Sacred Heart of Jesus and of the Sorrowful Heart of Mary. It signifies the mediatory role of the Blessed Virgin Mary, the mystery of the Church, the relationship between Heaven and earth, this life and eternal life.

St Maximillian Kolbe (d. 1941) and the various movements associated with him, have been especially active in further popularizing the miraculous medal. In 1917 he adopted the miraculous medal as the badge of the "Pious Union of the Militia of the Immaculate Conception" which he founded in Rome while still a young religious of the Conventual Friars Minor.

Like all medals and objects of cult, the Miraculous Medal is never to be regarded as a talisman or lead to any form of blind credulity[260]. The promise of Our Lady that "those who were the medal will receive great graces", requires a humble and tenacious commitment to the Christian message, faithful and persevering prayer, and a good Christian life.

---

[258] RITUALE ROMANUM, *De benedicionibus, Ordo benedictionis rerum quae ad pietatem et devotionem exercendam destinatur*, cit., 1168.

[259] *Ibid.*

[260] Cf. LG 67; PAUL VI, Apostolic Exhortation *Marialis cultus*, 38;CCC 2111.

The "Akathistos" Hymn

207. In the Byzantine tradition, one of the oldest and most revered expressions of Marian devotion is the hymn "Akathistos" - meaning the hymn sung while standing. It is a literary and theological masterpiece, encapsulating in the form of a prayer, the universally held Marian belief of the primitive Church. The hymn is inspired by the Scriptures, the doctrine defined by the Councils of Nicea (325), Ephesus (431), and Chalcedon (451), and reflects the Greek fathers of the fourth and fifth centuries. It is solemnly celebrated in the Eastern Liturgy on the Fifth Saturday of Lent. The hymn is also sung on many other liturgical occasions and is recommended for the use of the clergy and faithful.

In recent times the Akathistos has been introduced to some communities in the Latin Rite[261]. Some solemn liturgical celebrations of particular ecclesial significance, in the presence of the Pope, have also helped to popularize the use of the hymn in Rome[262]. This very ancient hymn[263], the mature fruit of the undivided Church's earliest devotion to the Blessed Virgin Mary, constitutes an appeal and invocation for the unity of Christians under the guidance of the Mother of God: "Such richness of praise, accumulated from the various forms of the great tradition of the Church, could help to ensure that she may once again breath with "both lungs": the East and the West"[264].

---

[261] In addition to the *Akathistos* other prayers deriving from the Oriental traditions have received grants of indulgences: cf. EI *Aliae concessiones*, 23, pp. 68-69.

[262] The singing of the *Akathistos* at Santa Maria Maggiore on 7 June 1981 marked the anniversaries of the Councils of Constantinople (381) and Ephesus (431); the hymn was also sung to commemorate the 450th anniversary of the apparitions of Guadalupe in Mexico, 10-12 December 1981. On 25 March 1988, John Paul II presided at Matins in Santa Maria Supra Minerva during which the hymn was sung in the Slavonic Rite. It is again explicitly mentioned among the indulgenced devotions for the Jubilee Year in the Bull *Incarnationis Mysterium*. It was sung at Santa Maria Maggiore on 8 December 2000 in Greek, Old Slavonic, Hungarian, Romanian and Arabic at a solemn celebration with the representatives of the Byzantine Catholic Churches at which John Paul II presided.

[263] While its author is unknown, modern scholarship tends to place its composition some time after the Council of Chalcedon. A Latin version was written down around 800 by Christopher, Bishop of Venice, which had enormous influence on the piety of the Western middles age. It is associated with Germanus of Constantinople who died in 733.

[264] JOHN PAUL II, Circular Letter *Redemptoris Mater*, 34.

CHAPTER SIX

Veneration of the Saints and Beati

Principles

208. The cult of the Saints, especially of the martyrs, is an ancient ecclesial phenomenon, that is rooted in the Scriptures (cf. *Acts* 7:54-60; *Acts* 6:9-11; 7:9-17) and the practise of the Church of the first half of the second century[265]. Both Eastern and Western Churches have always venerated the Saints. The Church has strenuously defended and explicitated the theological basis of this cult, especially since the rise of protetantism and its objections to certain aspects of the traditional veneration of the Saints. The connection between the cult of the Saints and the doctrine of the Church has also been clearly illustrated. The cultic expressions, both liturgical and devotional, of the veneration have always been carefully disciplined by the Church, which has always stressed the exemplary testimony to genuine Christian life given by these illustrious disciples of the Lord.

209. When treating of the Liturgical Year, *Sacrosanctum Concilium* effectively illustrates this ecclesial reality and the significance of the veneration of the Saints and *Beati*: "The Church has always included in the annual cycle memorial days of the martyrs and other saints. Raised up to perfection by the manifold grace of God and already in possession of eternal salvation, they sing God's perfect praise in heaven and pray for us. By celebrating their anniversaries, the Church proclaims the achievement of the paschal mystery in the saints who have suffered and who have been glorified with Christ. She proposes them to the faithful as examples who draw all men to the Father through Christ, and through their merits she begs God's favours"[266].

---

[265] Cf. St EUSEBIUS OF CAESAREA, *Historia ecclesiastica*, V, XV, 42-47: SCh 31, Paris 1952, pp. 189-190.
[266] SC 104.

210. A correct understanding of the Church's doctrine on the Saints is only possible in the wider context of the articles of faith concerning:

● the "One, Holy Catholic and Apostolic Church"[267], Holy because of the presence in the Church of "Jesus Christ who, with the Father and the Holy Spirit, is proclaimed as the "sole Holy One"[268]; because of the incessant action of the Spirit of holiness[269]; and because the Church has been given the necessary means of sanctification. While the Church does have sinners in her midst, she "is endowed already with a sanctity which is real though imperfect"[270]; she is "the Holy People of God"[271], whose members, according to Scripture, are called "Saints" (cf. *Acts* 9:13; 1 *Cor* 6:1; 16:1).

● the "communion of Saints"[272] through which the Church in heaven, the Church awaiting purification "in the state of Purgatory"[273], and the pilgrim Church on earth share "in the same love of God and neighbour"[274]. Indeed, all who are in Christ and possess his Spirit make up a single Church and are united in him.

● the doctrine of the sole mediation of Christ (cf. 1 *Tim* 2:3), which does not, however, exclude subordinate mediations, which must always be understood in relation to the all embracing mediation of Christ[275].

211. The doctrine of the Church and her Liturgy, propose the Saints and *Beati who already contemplate in the "clarity of His unity and trinity"*[276] to the faithful because they are:

● historical witnesses to the universal vocation to holiness; as eminent fruit of the redemption of Christ, they are a poof and record

---

[267] DS 150; MISSALE ROMANUM, *Ordo Missae, Symbolum Nicaeno-Constantinopolitanum.*
[268] JOHN PAUL II, Apostolic Constitution, *Divinitus pefctionis magister*, in AAS 75 (1983) 349.
[269] Cf. LG 4.
[270] *Ibid.*,48.
[271] *Ibid.*, 48.
[272] *Symbolum Apostolicum*, in DS 19.
[273] CCC 1472.
[274] LG 49.
[275] Cf. *Ibid.*
[276] COUNCIL OF FLORENCE, *Decretum pro Graecis*, in DS 1305.

that God calls his children to the perfection of Christ (cf. *Eph* 4:13; *Col* 1:28), in all times and among all nations, and from the most varied socio-cultural conditions and states of life;

• illustrious disciples of Christ and therefore models of evangelical life[277]; the church recognises the heroicness of their virtues in the canonization process and recommends them as models for the faithful;

• citizens of the heavenly Jerusalem who ceaselessly sing the glory and mercy of God; the Paschal passage from this world to the Father has already been accomplished in them;

• intercessors and friends of the faithful who are still on the earthly pilgrimage, because the Saints, already enraptured by the happiness of God, know the needs of their brothers and sisters and accompany them on their pilgrim journey with their prayers and protection;

• patrons of the Local Churches, of which they were founders (St Eusebius of Vercelli) or illustrious Pastors (St Ambrose of Milan); patrons of nations: apostles of their conversion to the Christian faith (St Thomas and St Bartholomew in India) or expressions of national identity (St Patrick in the case of Ireland); of corporations and professions (St Omobono for tailors); in particular circumstances - in childbirth (St Anne, St Raimondo Nonnato), in death (St Joseph) - or to obtain specific graces (St Lucy for the recovery of eyesight) etc..

In thanksgiving to God the Father, the Church professes all this when she proclaims "You give us an example to follow in the lives of your Saints, assistance by their intercession, and a bond of fraternal love in the communion of grace"[278].

---

[277] Cf. MISSALE ROMANUM, *Die 1 Novembris Omnium Sanctorum Sollemnitas, Paefatio.*
[278] *Ibid., Praefatio I de Sanctis.*

212. The ultimate object of veneration of the Saints is the glory of God and the sanctification of man by conforming one's life fully to the divine will and by imitating the virtue of those who were preeminent disciples of the Lord.

Catechesis and other forms of doctrinal instruction should therefore make known to the faithful that: our relationship with the Saints must be seen in the light of the faith and should not obscure the "cultus latriae due to God the Father through Christ in the Holy Spirit, but intensify it"; "true cult of the Saints consists not so much in the multiplication of external acts but in intensification of active charity", which translates into commitment to the Christian life[279].

Holy Angels

213. With the clear and sober language of catechesis, the Church teaches that "the existence of the spiritual, non-corporeal beings that Sacred Scripture usually calls 'angels' is a truth of faith. The witness of Scripture is as clear as the unanimity of Tradition"[280].

Tradition regards the angels as messengers of God, "potent executives of his commands, and ready at the sound of his words" (*Ps* 103:20. They serve his salvific plan, and are "sent to serve those who will inherit salvation" (*Hb* 1:14).

214. The faithful are well aware of the numerous interventions of angels in the New and Old Covenants. They closed the gates of the earthly paradise (cf. *Gen* 3:24), they saved Hagar and her child Ishmael (cf. *Gen* 21:17), they stayed the hand of Abraham as he was about to sacrifice Isaac (cf. *Gen* 22:7), they announce prodigious births (cf. *Jud* 13:3-7), they protect the footsteps of the just (cf. *Ps* 91:11), they praise God unceasingly (cf. *Is* 6:1-4), and they present the prayer of the Saints to God (cf. *Ap* 8:34). The faithful are also aware of the angel's coming to help Elijah, an exhausted fugitive (cf. 1 *Kings* 19:4-8), of Azariah and his companions in the fiery furnace (cf. *Dan* 3:49-50), and are familiar with the story of Tobias in which Raphael, "one of the seven

---

[279] LG 51.
[280] CCC 328.

Angels who stand ever ready to enter the presence of the glory of God" (cf. *Tb* 12:15), who renders many services to Tobit, his son Tobias and his wife Sarah.

The faithful are also conscious of the roles played by the Angels in the life of Jesus: the Angel Gabriel declared to Mary that she would conceive and give birth to the Son of the Most High (cf. *Lk* 1:26-38), and that an Angel revealed to Joseph the supernatural origin of Mary's conception (cf. *Mt* 1:18-25); the Angels appear to the shepherds in Bethlehem with the news of great joy of the Saviour's birth (cf. *Lk* 2:8-24); "the Angel of the Lord" protected the infant Jesus when he was threatened by Herod (cf. *Mt* 2:13-20); the Angels ministered to Jesus in the desert (cf. *Mt* 4:11) and comforted him in his agony (*Lk* 22:43), and to the women gathered at the tomb, they announced that he had risen (cf. *Mk* 16:1-8), they appear again at the Ascension, revealing its meaning to the disciples and announcing that "Jesus ...will come back in the same way as you have seen him go" (*Acts* 1:11).

The faithful will have well grasped the significance of Jesus' admonition not to despise the least of those who believe in him for "their Angels in heaven are continually in the presence of my Father in heaven" (*Mt* 10:10), and the consolation of his assurance that "there is rejoicing among the Angels of God over one repentant sinner" (*Lk* 15:10). The faithful also realize that "the Son of man will come in his glory with all his Angels" (*Mt* 25:31) to judge the living and the dead, and bring history to a close.

215. The Church, which at its outset was saved and protected by the ministry of Angels, and which constantly experiences their "mysterious and powerful assistance"[281], venerates these heavenly spirits and has recourse to their prompt intercession.

During the liturgical year, the Church celebrates the role played by the Holy Angels, in the events of salvation[282] and commemorates them on specific days: 29 September (feast of the Archangels Michael, Gabriel and Raphael), 2 October (the Guardian Angels). The Church

---

[281] *Ibid.*, 336.
[282] The same is true, for example in the solemnity of Easter and in the solemnities of the Annunciation (25 march), Christmas (25 December), Ascension, the Immaculate Conception (8 December), St Joseph (19 March), Sts. Peter and Paul (29 June), Assumption (15 August) and All Saints (1 November).

has a votive Mass dedicated to the Holy Angels whose preface proclaims that "the glory of God is reflected in his Angels"[283]. In the celebration of the sacred mysteries, the Church associates herself with the angelic hymn and proclaims the thrice holy God (cf. *Isaiah* 6:3)[284] invoking their assistance so that the Eucharistic sacrifice "may be taken [to your] altar in heaven, in the presence of [...] divine majesty"[285]. The office of lauds is celebrated in their presence (cf. *Ps* 137:1)[286]. The Church entrusts to the ministry of the Holy Angels (cf. *Aps* 5:8; 8:3) the prayers of the faithful, the contrition of penitents[287], and the protection of the innocent from the assaults of the Malign One[288]. The Church implores God to send his Angels at the end of the day to protect the faithful as they sleep[289], prays that the celestial spirits come to the assistance of the faithful in their last agony[290], and in the rite of obsequies, invokes God to send his Angels to accompany the souls of just into paradise[291] and to watch over their graves.

216. Down through the centuries, the faithful have translated into various devotional exercises the teaching of the faith in relation to the ministry of Angels: the Holy Angels have been adopted as patrons of cities and corporations; great shrines in their honour have developed such as Mont-Saint-Michel in Normandy, San Michele della Chiusa in Piemonte and San Michele Gargano in Apulia, each appointed with specific feast days; hymns and devotions to the Holy Angels have also been composed.

Popular piety encompasses many forms of devotion to the Guardian Angels. St Basil Great (d. 378) taught that "each and every member of the faithful has a Guardian Angel to protect, guard and guide them through life"[292]. This ancient teaching was

---

[283] MISSALE ROMANUM, *Praefatio de Angelis*.
[284] Cf. *ibid.*, *Prex eucharistica, Sanctus*.
[285] *Ibid.*, *Prex eucharistica I, Supplices te rogamus*.
[286] Cf. St BENEDICT, *Regula*, 19, 5: CSEL 75, Vindobonae 1960, p. 75.
[287] Cf. RITUALE ROMANUM, *Ordo Paenitentiae*, Editio Typica, Typis Polyglotis Vatacanis 1974, 54.
[288] Cf. LITURGIA HORARUM, *Die 2 Octobris, Ss Angelorum Custodum memoria, Ad Vesperas, Hymnus*, "Custodes hominum psallimus angelos".
[289] Cf. ibid., *Ad Completorium post II Vesperas Dominicae et Sollemnitatum, Oratio "Visita quaesumus"*.
[290] Cf. RITUALE ROMANUM, *Ordo unctionis informorum eorumque patoralis curae*, cit., 147.
[291] Cf. RITUALE ROMANUM, *Ordo exsequiarum*, Editio Typica, Typis Polyglottis Vaticanis 1969, 50.
[292] St BASIL OF CAESAREA, *Adversus Eunomium III, 1: PG 29, 656*.

consolidated by biblical and patristic sources and lies behind many forms of piety. St Bernard of Clairvaux (d. 1153) was a great master and a notable promoter of devotion to the Guardian Angels. For him, they were a proof "that heaven denies us nothing that assists us", and hence, "these celestial spirits have been placed at our sides to protect us, instruct us and to guide us"[293].

Devotion to the Holy Angels gives rise to a certain form of the Christian life which is characterized by:

● devout gratitude to God for having placed these heavenly spirits of great sanctity and dignity at the service of man;

● an attitude of devotion deriving from the knowledge of living constantly in the presence of the Holy Angels of God;- serenity and confidence in facing difficult situations, since the Lord guides and protects the faithful in the way of justice through the ministry of His Holy Angels.Among the prayers to the Guardian Angels the *Angele Dei*[294] is especially popular, and is often recited by families at morning and evening prayers, or at the recitation of the *Angelus*.

217. Popular devotion to the Holy Angels, which is legitimate and good, can, however, also give rise to possible deviations:

● when, as sometimes can happen, the faithful are taken by the idea that the world is subject to demiurgical struggles, or an incessant battle between good and evil spirits, or Angels and daemons, in which man is left at the mercy of superior forces and over which he is helpless; such cosmologies bear little relation to the true Gospel vision of the struggle to overcome the Devil, which requires moral commitment, a fundamental option for the Gospel, humility and prayer;

● when the daily events of life, which have nothing or little to do with our progressive maturing on the journey towards Christ are

---

[293] St BERNARD OF CLAIRVAUX, *Sermo XII in Psalmum "Qui habitat", 3: Sancti Bernardi Opera, IV,* Editiones Cistercienses, Romae 1966, p. 459.
[294] Cf. EI, *Normae et concessiones,* 18, p. 65.

read schematically or simplistically, indeed childishly, so as to ascribe all setbacks to the Devil and all success to the Guardian Angels. The practice of assigning names to the Holy Angels should be discouraged, except in the cases of Gabriel, Raphael and Michael whose names are contained in Holy Scripture.

St Joseph

218. In activating His plan of salvation, God, in His sapient providence, assigned to Joseph of Nazareth, "the just man" (cf. *Mt* 1:19), and spouse of the Virgin Mary (cf. *ibid*; *Lk* 1:27), a particularly important mission: legally to insert Jesus Christ into the line of David from whom, according to the prophets, the Messiah would be born, and to act as his father and guardian.

In virtue of this mission, St Joseph features in the mysteries of the infancy of Jesus: God revealed to him that Jesus had been conceived by the Holy Spirit; (cf. *Mt* 1:20-21); he witnessed the birth of Christ in Bethlehem (cf. *Lk* 2:6-7), the adoration of the shepherds (cf. *Lk* 2:15-16), the adoration of the Magi (cf. *Mt* 2:11); he fulfilled his mission religiously with regard to the rearing of Christ, having had him circumcised according to the discipline of the Covenant of Abraham (*Lk* 2:21) and in giving him the name of Jesus (*Mt* 1:21); in accordance with the Law of the Lord, he presented Christ in the Temple and made the offering prescribed for the poor (cf. *Lk* 2:22-24; *Ex* 13:2, 12-13), and listened in wonder to the prophecy of Simeon (cf. *Lk* 2:25-33); he protected the Mother of Christ and her Son from the persecution of Herod by taking them to Egypt (cf. *Mt* 2:13-23); together with Mary and Jesus, he went every year to Jerusalem for the Passover, and was distraught at having lost the twelve year old Jesus in the Temple (*Lk* 2:43-50); he lived in Nazareth and exercised paternal authority over Jesus who was submissive to him (*Lk* 2:51); he instructed Jesus in the law and in the craft of carpentry.

219. The virtues of St Joseph have been the object of ecclesial reflection down through the centuries, especially the more recent centuries. Among those virtues the following stand out: faith, with which he fully accepted God's salvific plan; prompt and silent

obedience to the will of God; love for and fulfilment of the law, true piety, fortitude in time of trial; chaste love for the Blessed Virgin Mary, a dutiful exercise of his paternal authority, and fruitful reticence.

220. Popular piety has grasped the significance, importance and universality of the patronage of St Joseph "to whose care God entrusted the beginning of our redemption",[295] "and his most valuable treasures"[296]. The following have been entrusted to the patronage of St Joseph: the entire Church was placed under the patronage and protection of this Holy patriarch[297] by the Blessed Pius IX; those who are consecrated to God by celibacy for the sake of the Kingdom of Heaven (cf. *Mt* 19:12): "in St Joseph they have [...] a type and a protector of chaste integrity"[298]; workers and craftsmen, for whom the carpenter of Nazareth is a singular model[299]; the dying, since pious tradition holds that he was assisted by Mary and Jesus in his last agony[300].

221. The person and role of St Joseph is frequently celebrated in the Liturgy, especially in connection with nativity and infancy of Christ: during Advent[301]; Christmastide, especially the feast of the Holy Family, on the Solemnity of St Joseph (19 March), and on his memorial (1 May).

---

[295] MISSALE ROMANUM, *Die 19 Martii, Sollemnitas S. Iosephi sposi beatae Mariae Virginis, Collecta.*
[296] SACRED CONGREGATION FOR RITES, Decree *Quemadmodum Deus*, in *Pii IX Pontificis Maximi Acta*, Pars Prima, vol. 5, Akademische Druck - u. Verlagsanstalt, Graz 1971, p. 282; cf. JOHN PAUL II, Apostolic Exhortation Redemptoris custos, 1, in AAS 82 (1990) 6.
[297] The declaration of St Joseph as patron of the universal Church took place on 8 December 1870 with the Decree *Quemadmodum Deus* to which reference was already been made.
[298] LEO XIII, Encyclical Letter *Quamquam pluries* (15 August 1889) in *Leonis XIII Pontificis Maximi Acta*, IX, Typographia Vaticana, Romae 1890, p. 180.
[299] Cf. Pius XII, *Allocutio ad adscriptos Societatibus Christianis Operariorum Italicorum* (A:C:L:I:) (1 May 1955), in AAS 47 (1955) 402-407, *declaring the institution of the feast of St Joseph the Worker for the 1 May* (cf. SACRED CONGREGATION FOR RITES, *Decree* [24 April 1956] in AAS 48 [1956] 237); JOHN PAUL II Apostolic Exhortation *Redemptoris Custos*, 22-24, in AAS 82 (1990) 26-28.
[300] Cf. St BERNARDINE OF SIENA, *De Sancto Joseph sponso beatae Virginis*, art. II, cap. III, in *S. Bernardini Opera omnia*, t. VII, Typis Collegii Sancti Bonaventurae, Ad Claras Aquas 1959, p. 28.
[301] Especially on days when the central theme of the liturgy is the genealogy of Our Lord (Mt 1:1-17): 17 December) or the angel's message to St Joseph (Mt 1:18-4: 18 December); IV Sunday in Advent A): both pericopes underline that Jesus is the Messiah, "the Son of David" (Mt 1:1) through Joseph who was of the house of David (cf. Mt 1:20; Lk 1:27.32).

St Joseph is also mentioned in the *Communicantes* of the Roman Canon and in the *Litany of the Saints*[302]. The invocation of the Holy Patriarch[303] is suggested in the *Commendation of the Dying*, as well as the community's prayer that the souls of the dead, having left this world, may "be taken to the peace of the new and eternal Jerusalem, and be with Mary, the Mother of God, St Joseph, and all of the Angels and Saints"[304].

222. St Joseph plays a prominent part in popular devotion: in numerous popular traditions; the custom of reserving Wednesdays for devotion to St Joseph, popular at least since the end of the seventeenth century, has generated several pious exercises including that of the *Seven Wednesdays*; in the pious aspirations made by the faithful[305]; in prayers such as that of Pope Leo XIII, *A te, Beate Ioseph*, which is daily recited by the faithful[306]; in the Litany of St Joseph, approved by St Pope Pius X[307]; and in the recitation of the chaplet of St Joseph, recollecting the *Seven agonies and seven joys of St Joseph*.

223. That the solemnity of St Joseph (19 March) falls in Lent, when the Church concentrates her attention on preparation for Baptism and the memorial of the Lord's Passion, inevitably gives rise to an attempt to harmonize the Liturgy and popular piety. Hence, the traditional practices of a "month of St Joseph" should be synchronized with the liturgical Year. Indeed, the liturgical renewal movement attempted to instill among the faithful a realization of the importance of the meaning of Lent. Where the necessary adaptations can be made to the various expressions of popular piety, devotion to St Joseph should naturally be encouraged among the faithful who should be constantly remained of this "singular example [...] which, surpassing all states of life, should be

---

[302] cf. CALENDARIUM ROMANUM, *Litanae Sanctorum*, cit., 1969, pp 33-39.
[303] Cf. RITUALE ROMANUM, *Ordo unctionis infirmorum eorumque pastoralis curae*, cit., 143.
[304] *Ibid.*, 146.
[305] Cf. EI, *Piae invocationes*, p. 83.
[306] Cf. EI, *Aliae concessiones*, 19, p. 66.
[307] cf. EI, *Aliae concessiones*, 22, p. 68.

recommended to the entire Christian community, whatever their condition or rank"[308].

St John the Baptist

224. St John the Baptist, the son of Zachary and Elizabeth, straddles both the Old and New Testaments. His parents were reckoned as "just before God" (*Lk* 1:6). John the Baptist is a major figure in the history of salvation. While in his mother's womb, he recognised the Saviour, as he was borne in his mother's womb (cf. *Lk* 1:39-45); his birth was accompanied by great signs (cf. *Lk* 1:57-66); he retired to the desert where he led a life of austerity and penance (cf. *Lk* 1:80; *Mt* 3:4); "Prophet of the Most High" (*Lk* 1:76), the word of God descended on him (*Lk* 3:2); "he went through the whole of the Jordan district proclaiming a baptism of repentance for the forgiveness of sins" (*Lk* 3:3); like the new Elijah, humble and strong, he prepared his people to receive the Lord (cf. *Lk* 1:17); in accordance with God's saving plan, he baptized the Saviour of the World in the waters of the Jordan (cf. *Mt* 3:13-16); to his disciples, he showed that Jesus was "the Lamb of God" (John 1:29), "the Son of God" (*John* 1:34), the Bridegroom of the new messianic community (cf. *John* 3:28-30); he was imprisoned and decapitated by Herod for his heroic witness to the truth (cf. *Mk* 6:14-29), thereby becoming the Precursor of the Lord's own violent death, as he had been in his prodigious birth and prophetic preaching. Jesus praised him by attributing to him the glorious phrase "of all children born to women, there is no one greater than John" (*Lk* 7:28).

225. The cult of St John the Baptist has been present in the Christian Church since ancient time. From a very early date, it acquired popular forms and connotations. In addition to the celebration of his death (29 August), of all the Saints he is the only one whose birth is also celebrated (24 June) - as with Christ and the Blessed Virgin Mary.

---

[308] JOHN PAUL II, Apostolic Exhortation *Redemptoris Custos*, 1, in AAS 82 (1990) 31.

In virtue of having baptised Jesus in the Jordan, many baptisteries are dedicated to him and his image as "baptizer" is to be found close to many baptismal founts. He is the patron Saint of those condemned to death or who have been imprisoned for the witness to the faith, in virtue of the harsh prison which he endured and of the death which he encountered.

In all probability, the date of John the Baptists' birth (24 June) was fixed in relation to that of Christ (25 December): according to what was said by the Angel Gabriel, when Mary conceived Our Saviour, Elizabeth had already been with child for six months (cf. *Lk* 1:26.36). The date of 24 June is also linked to the solar cycle of the Northern hemisphere. The feast is celebrated as the Sun, turning towards the South of the zodiac, begins to decline: a phenomenon that was taken to symbolize John the Baptist who said in relation to Jesus: *"illum oportet crescere, me autem minui"* (*John* 3:30).

John's mission of witnessing to the light (cf. *John* 1:7) lies at the origin of the custom of blessing bonfires on St John's Eve - or at least gave a Christian significance to the practice. The Church blesses such fires, praying God that the faithful may overcome the darkness of the world and reach the "indefectible light" of God[309].

Cult due to the Saints and to the *Beati*

226. The reciprocal influence of Liturgy and popular piety is particularly noticeable in the various forms of cult given to the saints and to the Beati. Here, it would seem opportune to recall, however briefly, the principle forms of the Church's veneration of the Saints in the Liturgy: these should enlighten and guide expressions of popular piety.

Celebration of Saints

227. The celebration of a feast in honour of a Saint - and what is said in this regard also applies to the *Beati, servatis servandis* - is undoubtedly the most eminent expression of cult that the ecclesial

---

[309] Cf. RITUALE ROMANUM *Pauli V Pontificis Maximi iussu editum... Pii XII auctoritate ordinatum et auctum.* Tit. IX, cap. III, 13: *Benedictio rogi in Vigilia Navitatis S. Ioannis Baptistae.*

community can give: in many cases it implicitly involves the celebration of the Holy Eucharist. Determining a day for such an observance is a relevant, and sometimes complicated, cultic event, in which various historical, liturgical, and cultic factors cannot always be easily accommodated.

In the Roman Church and in other local Churches, the celebration of the memorial of the martyrs on the anniversary of their passion (their assimilation with Christ and heavenly birth)[310], the recollection of the *Ecclesiae conditor* or of other saintly Bishops who ruled these sees, the memorial of Confessors for the faith or of anniversaries such as the dedication of the Cathedral, progressively gave rise to the development of local calendars, which kept the date and place of the deaths of particular Saints, or groups of Saints.

The martyrologies quickly evolved from the local calendars: the Syriac Martyrology (fifth century), the *Martyrologium Hieronymianum* (sixth century), the Martyrology of Bede (eighth century), the Martyrology of Lyons (ninth century), the Martyrology of Usardo (ninth century) and that of Adon (ninth century).

On 14 January 1584, Gregory XIII promulgated the *editio typica* of the *Martyrologium Romanum* for liturgical use. On 29 June 2001, John Paul II promulgated the first post-Conciliar revision of the *Martyrologium Romanum*[311]. The revision was based on the Roman tradition and incorporated the dates of many historical martyrdoms, and collects the names of many Saints and *Beati*. The *Martyrologium Romanum* bears witness to the extraordinary wealth of sanctity which the Spirit of the Lord has raised up in the Church in different places, and at different times in her history.

228. The development of the *Calendarium Romanum*, which indicates the date and grade of the celebrations in honour of the Saints, is closely related to the history of the *Martyrologium Romanum*.

---

[310] The tradition of the *"dies natalis"* or date of death of the martyrs. This usage dates at least from the fifth century. Cf. St AUGUSTINE, *Sermo* 310, 1: PL 38, 1412-1413.
[311] MARTYROLOGIUM ROMANUM *ex decreto Sacrosancti Oecumenici Concilii Vaticani Secundi instauratum auctoritate Ioannis Pauli PP. II promulgatum*, Editio Typica, Typiis Vaticanis 2001.

In accordance with the desire of the Second Vatican Council, the present *Calendarium Romanum*[312] contains only those memorials of the "Saints of a truly universal importance"[313], and leaves mention of other Saints to the particular calenders of a given nation, region, diocese or religious family.

It would seem convenient to recall, at this point, the reasons leading to the reduction in the number of commemorations in the *Calendarium Romanum* so as to translate it into pastoral praxis: the reduction was made because "the feasts of the Saints may not take precedence over commemorations of the mysteries of salvation"[314]. Throughout the centuries, "the multiplication of feasts, vigils, and octaves, and the growing complexity of the various parts of the liturgical year" often "led the faithful to observe particular devotions so that the impression was given of their detaching themselves from the fundamental mysteries of divine redemption"[315].

229. From the foregoing reflection on the origin and development of the *Calendarium Romanum Generale* a number of useful pastoral inferences can be made:

● it is necessary to instruct the faithful on the links between the feasts of the Saints and the commemoration of the mystery of salvation of Christ. The *raison d'etre* for the feasts of the Saints is to highlight concrete realizations of the saving plan of God and "to proclaim the marvels of Christ in his servants"[316]; the feasts accorded to the Saints, the members of the Body of Christ, are ultimately feasts of the Head who is Christ;

● it is always useful to teach the faithful to realize the importance and significance of the feasts of those Saints who have had a

---

[312] The *Calendarium Romanum* was published by Paul VI on 14 February 1969, with the Apostolic Letter *Mysterii paschalis*, in AAS 61 (1969) 222-226.
[313] SC 111.
[314] *Ibid.*
[315] PAUL VI, Apostolic Letter *Mysterii paschalis*, 1, in AAS 61 (1969) 222.
[316] SC 111.

particular mission in the history of Salvation, or a singular relationship with Christ such as St John the Baptist (24 June), St Joseph (19 March), Sts. Peter and Paul (29 June), the Apostles and Evangelists, St Mary Magdalen (22 July), St Martha (29 July) and St Stephen (26 December);

• it is also important to exhort the faithful to have a particular devotion to the Saints who have had an important role in the particular Churches, for example, the Patrons of a particular Church or those who first proclaimed the Gospel to the original community;

• finally, it is useful to explain the notion of the "universality" of the Saints inscribed in the *Calendarium Romanum Generale* to the faithful, as well as the significance of the grades with which their feasts are observed: solemnity, feast and memorial (obligatory or optional).

Feast Days

230. Both the Liturgy and popular piety attach great importance to the feast days assigned to the Saints. The "Saint's day" is marked with numerous cultic displays, some liturgical, others deriving from popular piety. Such cultic expressions can sometimes conflict.

Conflicts of this nature must be resolved by application of the norms contained in the *Missale Romanum* and in the *Calendarium Romanum Generale* on the grades assigned to the celebration of Saints and Beati. In this, account must be taken of the their relationship with a particular Christian community (principal Patron of a place, Title of a Church, Founder of a religious family, or their Principal Patron); the conditions governing the transfer of certain feasts to the subsequent Sunday, and of norms on the celebration of the feasts of Saints at certain particular times during the liturgical year[317].

The aforementioned norms should be respected not only from a sense of respect for the liturgical authority of the Apostolic See, but

---

[317] Cf. CALENDARIUM ROMANUM, cit., *Normae universales*, 58-59; S.CONGREGATION FOR DIVINE WORSHIP, Instruction *De Calendariis particularibus*, 8-12, in AAS 62 (1970) 653-654).

above all from a sense of reverence for the mystery of Christ and a desire to promote the spirit of the Liturgy.

It is especially necessary to ensure that the reasons which have led to the transfer of some feasts, for example from Lent to ordinary time, are not nullified in pastoral practice: follow the liturgical celebration of the Saint on the new date while continuing to observe the old date in popular piety. Such practices not only severely affect the harmony that should obtain between the Liturgy and popular piety, but also create duplication, confusion and disorder.

231. It is always necessary to ensure that the feast days of the Saints are carefully prepared both liturgically and pastorally.

Such requires a correct presentation of the objectives of the cult of the Saints, i.e. the glorification of God "in His Saints"[318], a commitment to live the Christian life following the example of Christ, of whose mystical Body the Saints are preeminent members.

It is also necessary to represent the figure of the Saint in a correct manner. Bearing in mind the prospect of contemporary society, this presentation should not only contain an account of the legendary events associated with the Saint, or of his thaumaturgic powers, but should also include an evaluation of his significance for the Christian life, the greatness of his sanctity, the effectiveness of his Christian witness, and of the manner in which his particular charism has enriched the Church.

232. A "Saint's day" also has an anthropological significance: it is a feast day. The feast also echoes man's vital needs, and is deeply rooted in his longing for the transcendent. The feast, with its manifestations of joy and rejoicing, is an affirmation of the value of life and creation. The feast is also an expression of integral freedom and of man's tendency towards true happiness, with its interruption of daily routine, formal conventions, and of the need to earn a living. As a cultural expression, the feast highlights the particular genius of a certain people and their cultural characteristics, and

---

[318] LITURGIA HORARUM, *Commune Sanctorum virorum, Ad Invitatorium.*

their true folk customs. As a social moment, the feast is an occasion to strengthen family relations and to make new contacts.

233. From a religious and anthropological perspective, several elements serve to undermine the genuine nature of the "Saint's day".

In a religious perspective, the "Saint's feast" of the "patronal feast" of the parish, when emptied of the Christian content that lies at its origin - the honour given to Christ in one of his members - becomes a mere popular observance or a social occasion, serving, in the best instances, as little other than a social occasion for the members of a particular community.

In an anthropological perspective, "to celebrate", not infrequently, is defined by the behaviour assumed by particular individuals or groups which can be widely at variance with the true significance of the feast. To celebrate a feast is to allow man to participate in God's lordship over creation, and in His active "rest", rather than in any form of laziness. It is an expression of simple joy, rather than unlimited selfishness. It is an expression of true liberty rather than an occasion for ambiguous amusement which creates new and more subtle forms of enslavement. It can safely be said that: transgressions of the norms for ethical behaviour not only contradict the law of the Lord, but also injure the anthropological fibre of celebration.

Celebration of the Eucharist

234. The celebration of the feast of a Saint or *Beatus* is not the only manner in which the Saints are present in the liturgy. The celebration of the Eucharist is the singular moment of communion with the Saints in heaven.

In the Liturgy of the Word, the Old Testament readings frequently refer to the great Patriarchs and prophets, and to other persons distinguished by their virtue and by their love for the law of the Lord. The New Testament recounts the deeds of the Apostles and other Saints who enjoyed the Lord's friendship. The lives of the Saints sometimes reflect the Gospel so closely that their very personality becomes apparent from merely reading the pages.

163

The relationship between Sacred Scripture and Christian hagiography, in the context of the celebration of the Eucharist, has given rise to the composition of a number of Commons which provide a synopsis of a particular biblical text which illustrates the lives of the Saints. With regard to this relationship, it has been said that Sacred Scripture orients and indicates the journey of the Saints to perfect charity. The Saints, in turn, become a living exegesis of the Word.

Reference is made to the Saints at various points during the celebration of the Eucharist. The Canon mentions "the gifts of your servant Abel, the sacrifice of Abraham our father in faith and the bread and wine offered by your priest Melchizedek"[319]. The same Eucharistic prayer becomes an occasion to express our communion with the Saints, by venerating their memory and pleading for their intercession, since "in union with the whole Church, we honour Mary, the Virgin Mother of God, we honour Joseph her husband, the Apostles and martyrs: Peter and Paul, Andrew [...] and all the Saints, may their prayers and intercession gain us your constant help and protection"[320].

The Litany of the Saints

235. The Litany of the Saints has been used in the Roman Church since the seventh century[321]. Its liturgical structure is subtle, simple and popular. Through the litany, the Church invokes the Saints on certain great sacramental occasions and on other occasions when her imploration is intensified: at the Easter vigil, before blessing the Baptismal font; in the celebration of the Sacrament of Baptism; in conferring Sacred Orders of the episcopate, priesthood and diaconate; in the rite for the consecration of virgins and of religious profession; in the rite of dedication of a church and consecration of an altar; at rogation; at the station Masses and penitential

---

[319] MISSALE ROMANUM, *Prex eucharistica I, Supra quae propitio.*
[320] *Ibid., Communicantes.* Provision is made for a memorial of the Saint or patron of the day in *Prex eucharistica III.*
[321] Cf. *Ordo Romanus* in A. ANDRIEU (ed.), *Les "Ordines Romani" du Haut Moyen-Age, III*, Spicilegium Sacrum Lovaniense, Lovain 1951, p. 249. For indulgences cf. EI, *Aliae concessiones*, 22, p. 68.

processions; when casting out the Devil during the rite of exorcism; and in entrusting the dying to the mercy of God.

The Litanies of the Saints contain elements deriving from both the liturgical tradition and from popular piety. They are expressions of the Church's confidence in the intercession of the Saints and an experience of the communion between the Church of the heavenly Jerusalem and the Church on her earthly pilgrim journey. The names of the *Beati* that have been inscribed in the calendars of particular Churches or religious institutes may be invoked in the litanies of the Saints[322]. Clearly, the names of those whose cult has not received ecclesial recognition should not be used in the litanies.

The Relics of the Saints

236. The Second Vatican Council recalls that "the Saints have been traditionally honoured in the Church, and their authentic relics and images held in veneration"[323]. The term "relics of the Saints" principally signifies the bodies - or notable parts of the bodies - of the Saints who, as distinguished members of Christ's mystical Body and as Temples of the Holy Spirit (cf. 1 *Cor* 3:16; 6:19; 2 *Cor* 6:16)[324] in virtue of their heroic sanctity, now dwell in Heaven, but who once lived on earth. Objects which belonged to the Saints, such as personal objects, clothes and manuscripts are also considered relics, as are objects which have touched their bodies or tombs such as oils, cloths, and images.

237. The *Missale Romanum* reaffirms the validity "of placing the relics of the Saints under an altar that is to be dedicated, even when not those of the martyrs"[325]. This usage signifies that the sacrifice of the members has its origin in the Sacrifice of the altar[326], as well as

---

[322] Cf. CONGREGATION FOR DIVINE WORSHIP AND THE DISCIPLINE OF THE SACRAMENTS, *Notificatio de cultu Beatorum*,13, in *Notitiae* 35 (1999) 446.
[323] SC 111; cf THE COUNCIL OF TRENT, *Decretum de invocatione, veneratione et reliquiis Sanctorum, et sacris imaginibus* (3 December 1563), in DS 1822.
[324] Cf. *ibid*.
[325] *Institutio generalis Missalis Romani*, 302.
[326] Cf. PONTIFICALE ROMANUM, *Ordo dedicationis ecclesiae et* altaris, Editio Typica, Typis Polyglotis Vaticanis 1977, cap. IV, *Praenotanda*, 5.

symbolising the communion with the Sacrifice of Christ of the entire Church, which is called to witness, event to the point of death, fidelity to her Lord and Spouse.

Many popular usages have been associated with this eminently liturgical cultic expression. The faithful deeply revere the relics of the Saints. An adequate pastoral instruction of the faithful about the use of relics will not overlook:

• ensuring the authenticity of the relics exposed for the veneration of the faithful; where doubtful relics have been exposed for the veneration of the faithful, they should be discreetly withdrawn with due pastoral prudence[327];

• preventing undue dispersal of relics into small pieces, since such practice is not consonant with due respect for the human body; the liturgical norms stipulate that relics must be "of a sufficient size as make clear that they are parts of the human body"[328];

• admonishing the faithful to resist the temptation to form collections of relics; in the past this practise has had some deplorable consequences;

• preventing any possibility of fraud, trafficking[329], or superstition.

The various forms of popular veneration of the relics of the Saints, such as kissing, decorations with lights and flowers, bearing them in processions, in no way exclude the possibility of taking the relics of the Saints to the sick and dying, to comfort them or use the intercession of the Saint to ask for healing. Such should be conducted with great dignity and be motivated by faith.

The relics of the Saints should not be exposed on the mensa of the altar, since this is reserved for the Body and Blood of the King of Martyrs[330].

---

[327] Cf. *ibid.*,cap. II, *Praenotanda*, 5.
[328] *Ibid.*
[329] Cf. CIC, can. 1190.
[330] Cf. St AMBROSE, *Epistula LXXVII* (MAUR. 22), 13: CSEL 82/3, Vindobonae 1982, pp. 134-135; PONTIFICALE ROMANUM, *Ordo dedicationis ecclesiae et* altaris, cit., cap. IV, *Praenotanda*, 10.

Sacred Images

238. The Second Council of Nicea, "following the divinely inspired teaching of our Holy Fathers and the tradition of the Catholic Church", vigorously defended the veneration of the images of the Saints: "we order with every rigour and exactitude that, similar to the depictions of the precious and vivifying Cross of our redemption, the sacred images to be used for veneration, are to be depicted in mosaic or any other suitable material, and exposed in the holy churches of God, on their furnishings, vestments, on their walls, as well as in the homes of the faithful and in the streets, be they images of Our Lord God and Saviour Jesus Christ, or of Our Immaculate Lady, the holy Mother of God, or of the Angels, the Saints and the just"[331].

The Fathers of Nicea see the basis for the use of sacred images in the mystery of the Incarnation of Christ, "the image of the invisible God" (*Col* 1:15): "the Incarnation of the Son of God initiated a new "economy" of images"[332].

239. The veneration of sacred images, whether paintings, statues, bas reliefs or other representations, apart from being a liturgical phenomenon, is an important aspect of popular piety: the faithful pray before sacred images, both in churches and in their homes. They decorate them with flowers, lights, and jewels; they pay respect to them in various ways, carrying them in procession, hanging *ex votos* near them in thanksgiving; they place them in shrines in the fields and along the roads.

Veneration of sacred images requires theological guidance if it is to avoid certain abuses. It is therefore necessary that the faithful be constantly remained of the doctrine of the Church on the veneration of sacred images, as exemplified in the ecumenical Councils[333], and in the *Catechism of the Catholic Church*[334].

---

[331] SECOND COUNCIL OF NICEA, *Definitio de sacris imaginibus* (23 October 787), in DS 600.

[332] CCC 1161.

[333] Cf. COUNCIL OF NICEA II, *Definitio de sacris imaginibus* (23 October 787) in DS 600-603; COUNCIL OF TRENT *Decretum de invocatione, veneratione, et reliquiis Sanctorum et sacris imaginibus* (3 December 1562), in DS 1821-1825; SC 111.

[334] Cf. CCC nn. 1159-1162.

240. According to the teaching of the Church, sacred images are:

• iconographical transcriptions of the Gospel message, in which image and revealed word are mutually clarified; ecclesiastical tradition requires that images conform "to the letter of the Gospel message"[335];

• sacred signs which, in common with all liturgical signs, ultimately refer to Christ; images of the Saints "signify Christ who is glorified in them"[336];

• memorials of our brethren who are Saints, and who "continue to participate in the salvation of the world, and to whom we are united, above all in sacramental celebrations"[337];

• an assistance in prayer: contemplation of the sacred images facilitates supplication and prompts us to give glory to God for the marvels done by his grace working in the Saints; - a stimulus to their imitation because "the more the eye rests on these sacred images, the more the recollection of those whom they depict grows vivid in the contemplative beholder"[338]; the faithful tend to imprint on their hearts what they contemplate with the eye: "a true image of the new man", transformed in Christ, through the power of the Holy Spirit, and in fidelity to his proper vocation;

• and a form of catechesis, because "through the history of the mysteries of our redemption, expressed in pictures and other media, the faithful are instructed and confirmed in the faith, since they are afforded the means of meditating constantly on the articles of faith"[339].

---

[335] COUNCIL OF NICEA II, *Definitio de sacris* imaginibus, in *Conciliorum Oecumeniorum Decreta*, cit., p. 135 (not contained in DS).
[336] CCC 1161.
[337] *Ibid.*
[338] COUNCIL OF NICEA II, *Definitio de sacris imaginibus*, in DS 601.
[339] COUNCIL OF TRENT, *Decretum de sacris invocatione, veneratione et reliquiis Sanctorum, et sacris imaginibus*, in DS 1824.

241. It is necessary for the faithful to understand the relative nature of the cult of images. The image is not venerated in itself. Rather, that which it represents is venerated. Thus, sacred images "are given due honour and veneration, not because there are believed to contain some divinity or power justifying such cult, nor because something has to be requested of an image, nor because trust is reposed in them, as the pagans used to do with idols, but because the honour given to sacred images is given to the prototypes whom they represent"[340].

242. In the light of the foregoing, the faithful should be careful not to fall into the error of raising sacred images to the level of paragons. The fact that some sacred images are the object of such devotion that they have become embodiments of the religious culture of nations or cities or particular groups, should be explained in the light of the grace which is at the basis of the veneration accorded them, and of the historical and social circumstances of the history surrounding them. It is good that a people should recall such events, to strengthen its faith, glorify God, conserve its cultural identity, and pray incessantly with confidence to the Lord who, according to his own words (cf. *Mt* 7:7; *Lk* 11:9; *Mk* 11:24), is always prepared to hear them; thereby causing an increase of charity and hope, and the growth of the spiritual life of the Christian faithful.

243. By their very nature, sacred images belong to the realm of sacred signs and to the realm of art. These "are often works of art infused with innate religious feeling, and seem almost to reflect that beauty that comes from God and that leads to God"[341]. The primary function of sacred images is not, however, to evince aesthetic pleasure but to dispose towards Mystery. Sometimes, the artistic aspects of an image can assume a disproportionate importance, seeing the image as an "artistic" theme, rather conveying a spiritual message.

---

[340] *Ibid.*, 1823.
[341] RITUALE ROMANUM, *De Benedictionibus, Ordo as benedicendas imagines quae fidelium venerationi publicae exhibentur*, cit., 985.

The production of sacred images in the West is not governed by strict canons that have been in place for centuries, as is the case in the Eastern Church. This does not imply that the Latin Church has overlooked or neglected its oversight of sacred images: the exposition of images contrary to the faith, or indecorous images, or images likely to lead the faithful into error, or images deriving from a disincarnate abstraction or dehumanizing images, have been prohibited on numerous occasions. Some images are examples of anthropocentric humanism rather than reflections of a genuine spirituality. The tendency to remove sacred images from sacred places is to be strongly condemned, since this is detrimental for the piety of the Christian faithful.

Popular piety encourages sacred images which reflect the characteristics of particular cultures; realistic representations in which the saints are clearly identifiable, or which evidently depict specific junctures in human life: birth, suffering, marriage, work, death. Efforts should be made, however, to ensure that popular religious art does not degenerate into mere oleography: in the Liturgy, there is a correlation between iconography and art, and the Christian art of specific cultural epochs.

244. The Church blesses sacred images because of their cultic significance. This is especially true of the images of the Saints which are destined for public veneration[342], when she prays that, guided by a particular Saint, "we may progress in following the footsteps of Christ, so that the perfect man may be formed in us to the full measure of Christ"[343]. The Church has published norms for the exposition of sacred images in churches and other sacred places which are to be diligently observed[344]. No statue or image is to be exposed on the table of an altar. Neither are the relics of the Saints to be exposed on the table of an altar[345]. It is for the local ordinary

[342] Cf. RITUALE ROMANUM, *De Benedictionibus, Ordo benedictionis imaginis Sanctorum*, cit., 1018-1031.
[343] *Ibid.*, 1027.
[344] Cf. CIC, can. 1188; *Institutio generalis Missalis Romani*, 318.
[345] Cf. PONTIFICALE ROMANUM, *Ordo dedicationis ecclesiae et altaris*, cit., cap. IV, *Praenotanda*, 10.

to ensure that inappropriate images or those leading to error or superstition, are not exposed for the veneration of the faithful.

Processions

245. Processions are cultic expressions of a universal character and have multiple social and religious significance. In them, the relationship between Liturgy and popular piety is especially important. Inspired by biblical examples (cf. *Ex* 14:8-31; 2 *Sam* 6:12-19; 1 *Cor* 15:25-16:3), the Church has instituted a number of liturgical processions which have differing emphases:

● some recall salvific events in the life of Christ, among them: the procession on 2 February commemorating the Lord's presentation in the Temple (cf. *Lk* 2:22-38); Palm Sunday, in evocation of the Lord's messianic entry into Jerusalem (cf. *Mt* 21:1-10; *Mk* 11:1-11; *Lk* 19:28-38; *John* 12:12-16); the procession at the Easter Vigil commemorating the Lord's passage from the darkness of the tomb to the glory of the Resurrection, synthesising and surpassing everything that had happened in the Old Testament, and standing as a necessary prelude to the sacramental "passages" accomplished in the disciples of Christ, especially in the celebration of Baptism and in the rite of exequies;

● others are votive processions, such as the Eucharistic procession on the feast of Corpus Christi: the Blessed Sacrament passing through the streets arouses sentiments of gratitude and thanksgiving in the minds and hearts of the faithful, it arouses in them faith-adoration and is a source of grace and blessing (*Acts* 10:38)[346]; the rogation processions, whose dates are to be established by the respective Conferences of Bishops, are both public implorations of God's blessing on the fields and on man's work, and penitential in character; the procession to the cemeteries on 2 November are commemorations of the faithful departed;

---

[346] Cf. RITUALE ROMANUM, *De sacra communione et de cultu Mysterii eucharistici extra Missam*, cit., 101; CIC, can. 944; supra note 162.

• others again are required by certain liturgical actions, such as: the stational processions during Lent, at which the worshipping community leaves from the established gathering point *(collectio)* for the church of the *statio*; the procession for the reception at the parish churches of the Holy Oils blessed on Holy Thursday; the procession for the veneration of the Cross on Good Friday; the procession of the baptized at the Vespers of Easter Sunday, during which psalms and canticles are sung on the way to the baptistery[347]; the processions associated with the celebration of the Holy Eucharist, such as the entrance of the Sacred Ministers, the proclamation of the Gospel, the presentation of the gifts, the communion with the Body of Christ; the procession carrying the Viaticum to the sick, where still practised; funeral corteges accompanying the bodies of the faithful departed from their homes to the church, and from the church to the cemetery; the procession for the translation of relics.

246. From the middle ages, votive processions acquired a particular importance in popular piety, and reached their apogee during the age of the Baroque. The Patron Saints of a city, or streets, or guild were honoured by carrying their relics, or image, or effigy in procession.

In their true form, processions are a manifestation of the faith of the people. They often have cultural connotations and are capable of re-awakening the religious sense of the people. From the perspective of the Christian's faith, votive processions, like other pious exercises, are exposed to certain risks: the precedence of devotions over the sacraments, which are relegated to second place, of external displays over interior disposition; regarding the procession as the apogee of a feast; the impression given to some of the less competently instructed of the faithful that Christianity is merely a "religion of Saints"; the degeneration of the procession itself from a manifestation of faith to a mere spectacle or a purely secular parade.

---

[347] *Institutio generalis de Liturgia Horarum*, 213.

247. To preserve the character of processions as manifestations of faith, it is necessary for the faithful to be carefully instructed on their theological, liturgical and anthropological aspects.

From a theological perspective, it is important to emphasise that a procession is a sign of the Church's condition, the pilgrimage of the People of God, with Christ and after Christ, aware that in this world it has no lasting dwelling. Through the streets of this earth it moves towards the heavenly Jerusalem. It is also a sign of the witness to the faith that every Christian community is obliged to give to the Lord in the structures of civil society. It is also a sign of the Church's missionary task which reaches back to her origins and the Lord's command (cf. *Mt* 28:19-20), which sent her to proclaim the Gospel message of salvation.

From a liturgical point of view, processions, even those of a popular tenor, should be oriented towards the Liturgy. The journey from church to church should be presented as the journey of the community living in this world towards the community living in Heaven. Such processions should be conducted under ecclesiastical supervision so as to avoid anything unsuitable or degenerative. They should begin with a moment of prayer during which the Word of God should be proclaimed. Hymns and canticles should be sung and instrumental music can also be used. Lighted candles or lamps should be carried by the faithful during the procession. Pauses should be arranged along the way so as to provide for alternative paces, bearing in mind that such also reflects the journey of life. The procession should conclude with a doxology to God, source of all sanctity, and with a blessing given by a Bishop, Priest or Deacon.

From an anthropological perspective, the procession should make it evident that it is "a commonly undertaken journey". The participants join in the same atmosphere of prayer and are united in singing, and concentrated on arriving at the same goal. Thus the faithful feel united with each other, and intent in giving concrete expression to their Christian commitment throughout the journey of life.

CHAPTER SEVEN

Suffrage for the Dead

Faith in the Resurrection of the Dead

248. "It is in regard to death that man's condition is most shrouded in doubt"[348]. However, faith in Christ changes that doubt into the certainty of life without end. Christ has told us that he came from the Father "so that whosoever believes in him might not die but have eternal life" (*John* 3:16). Again he says, "it is my Father's will that whoever sees the Son and believes in him shall have eternal life; and I shall raise him up on the last day"[349].

Based on the Word of God, the Christian firmly believes and hopes that "just as Christ is truly risen from the dead and lives for ever, so after death the righteous will live for ever with the risen Christ and he will raise them up on the last day"[350].

249. Belief in the resurrection of the dead is an essential part of Christian revelation. It implies a particular understanding of the ineluctable mystery of death.

Death is the end of earthy life, but "not of our existence"[351] since the soul is immortal. "Our lives are measured by time, in the course of which we change, grow old and, as with all living beings on earth, death seems like the normal end of life"[352]. Seen from the perspective of the faith, "death is the end of man's earthly pilgrimage, of the time of grace and mercy which God offers him so as to work out his earthly life in keeping with the divine plan, and to decide his ultimate destiny"[353].

In one light death can seem natural, in another it can be seen as "the wages of sin" (*Rm* 6:23). Authentically interpreting the

---

[348] SECOND VATICAN COUNCIL, *Constitution Gaudium et spes* 18.
[349] DS 150: MISSALE ROMANUM, *Ordo Missae, Symbolum Nicaeno-Constantinopolitanum.*
[350] CCC 989.
[351] St AMBROSE, *De excessu fratris*, I, 70: CSEL 73, Vindobonae 1955, p. 245.
[352] CCC 1007.
[353] *Ibid.*,1013.

175

meaning of Scripture (cf. *John* 2:17; 3:3; 3:19; *Wis* 1:13; *Rm* 5:12; 6:23), the Church teaches that "death entered the world on account of man's sin"[354].

Jesus, the Son of God, "born of a woman and subject to the law" (*Gal* 4:4) underwent death which is part of the human condition; despite his anguish in the face of death (*Mk* 14:33-34; *Heb* 5:7-8), "he accepted it in an act of complete and free submission to his Father's will. The obedience of Jesus has transformed the curse of death into a blessing"[355].

Death is the passage to the fullness of true life. The Church, subverting the logic of this world, calls the Christian's day of death his *dies natalis*, the day of his heavenly birth, where "there will be no more death, and no more mourning or sadness [for] the world of the past has gone" (*Aps* 21:4). Death is the prolongation, in a new way, of life as the Liturgy says: "For your faithful, O Lord, life has changed not ended; while our earthly dwelling is destroyed, a new and eternal dwelling is prepared for us in Heaven"[356].

The death of a Christian is an event of grace, having, as it does, a positive value and significance in Christ and through Christ. Scripture teaches that: "Life to me, of course, life is Christ, but then death would bring me something more" (*Phil* 1:21); "here is a saying you can rely on: if we have died with him, then we shall live with him" (2 *Tim* 2:11).

250. According to the faith of the Church, "to die in Christ" begins at Baptism. In Baptism, the Lord's disciples sacramentally die in Christ so as to live a new life. If the disciples die in the grace of Christ, physical death seals that "dying with Christ", and consummates it by incorporating them fully and definitively into Christ the Redeemer.

The Church's prayer of suffrage for the souls of the faithful departed implores eternal life not only for the disciples of Christ who have died in his peace, but for the dead whose faith is known to God[357].

---

[354] *Ibid.*, 1008; cf. COUNCIL OF TRENT, *Decretum de peccato originali* (17 Iunii 1546), in DS 1511.
[355] CCC 1009.
[356] MISSALE ROMANUM, *Praefatio defunctorum*, I.
[357] Cf. *ibid.*, *Prex eucharistica IV, Commemoratio pro defunctis.*

The Meaning of Suffrage

251. The just encounter God in death. He calls them to himself so as to share eternal life with them. No one, however, can be received into God's friendship and intimacy without having been purified of the consequences of personal sin. "The Church gives the name Purgatory to this final purification of the elect, which is entirely different from the punishment of the damned. The Church formulated her doctrine of faith on Purgatory especially at the Councils of Florence and Trent"[358].

Hence derives the pious custom of suffrage for the souls of the faithful departed, which is an urgent supplication of God to have mercy on the souls of the dead, to purify them by the fire of His charity, and to bring them to His kingdom of light and life. This suffrage is a cultic expression of faith in the communion of saints. Indeed, "the Church in its pilgrim members, from the very earliest days of the Christian religion, has honoured with great respect the memory of the dead; and 'because it is a holy and a wholesome thought to pray for the dead that they may be loosed from their sins' (2 *Mac* 12:46) she offers her suffrages for them"[359]. These consist, primarily, in the celebration of the holy sacrifice of the Eucharist[360], and in other pious exercises, such as prayers for the dead, alms deeds, works of mercy[361], and the application of indulgences to the souls of the faithful departed[362].

Christian Exequies

252. The Roman Liturgy, like other Latin and Oriental Liturgies, contains many and varied forms of suffrage for the dead.

The rite of Christian exequies consists traditionally of three parts. Because of the profoundly changed circumstances of life in the greater urban conurbations, these are often reduced to two or even only one part. The rite of Christian exequies are:[363]

---

[358] CCC 1031; cf. DS 1304; 1820; 1580.
[359] LG 50.
[360] SECOND COUNCIL OF LYONS, *Professio fidei Michaelis Paleologi* (6 Iulii 1274), in DS 856: St CYPRIAN, *Epistula* I, 2: CSEL 3/2, Vindobonae 1871, pp. 466-467; St AUGUSTINE, *Confessiones*, IX, 12, 32: CSEL 33/1, Vindobonae 1896, pp. 221-222.
[361] Cf. St AUGUSTINE, *De curis pro mortuis gerenda*,6: CSEL 41, Vindobonae 1900, pp. 629-631; St JOHN CHRISTOSOM, *Homilia in primam ad Corinthios*, 41, 5: PG 61, 494-495; CCC1032.
[362] Cf. EI, *Normae de Indulgentiis*, 3, p. 21; *Aliae concessiones*, 29, pp. 74-75.
[363] Cf. RITUALE ROMANUM, *Ordo exsequiarum*, cit., *Praenotanda*, 4.

• prayer vigil at the home of the deceased, or somewhere else as circumstances permit, during which family, friends and members of the Christian community gather to pray to God in suffrage, to hear the "the words of life eternal", and in their light, to see beyond this world by contemplating the risen Christ in faith; to comfort those who mourn the deceased; and to express Christian solidarity in accordance with the words of the Apostle "be sad with those in sorrow" (*Rm* 12:15)[364];

• the celebration of the Holy Eucharist, which is highly desirable when possible. In the celebration of the Holy Eucharist, the Christian community listens to "the word of God which proclaims the paschal mystery, assures us of the hope of meeting again in the Kingdom of God, enlivens our devotion to the dead and exhorts us to witness through a truly Christian life"[365]. The celebrant comments on the word of God in his homily, "avoiding any form of funerary eulogy"[366]. In the Holy Eucharist, "the Church expresses her efficacious communion with the departed: offering to the Father in the Holy Spirit the sacrifice of the death and Resurrection of Christ; she asks Him to purify His child of his sins and their consequences, and to admit him to the Paschal fullness of the table of the kingdom"[367]. A profound reading of the requiem Mass allows us to see how the Liturgy has made of the Holy Eucharist, that eschatological banquet, the true Christian *refrigerium* for the deceased;

• the *Rite of committal, the funeral cortege, and burial*; at the committal, the deceased is commended to God, "the final commendation by which the Christian community says farewell to one of its members before his body is buried"[368]. In the funeral cortege, mother Church, who has sacramentally borne all Christians

---

[364] This vigil, which is still called a "wake" in English speaking countries, is an act of faith in the resurrection, even though it may have lost all theological and historical significance, and an imitation of the women in the Gospel who came to anoint the body of Christ, and became the first witnesses of the resurrection.

[365] RITUALE ROMANUM, *Ordo exsequiarum*, cit., *Praenotanda*, 11.

[366] *Ibid.*, 41.

[367] CCC 1689.

[368] RITUALE ROMANUM, *Ordo exsequiarum*, cit., *Praenotanda*, 10.

in her womb during their earthly pilgrimage, now accompanies the body of the deceased to his place of rest, while he awaits the resurrection (cf. 1 *Cor* 15:42-44).

253. Every stage of the rite of obsequies should be conducted with the greatest dignity and religious sensibility. Hence, it is necessary for: the body of the deceased, which was the Temple of the Holy Spirit, to be treated with the utmost respect; funeral furnishings should be decorous and free of all ostentation; the liturgical signs, the cross, the paschal candle, the holy water and the incense, should all be used with the utmost propriety.

254. Christian piety has always regarded burial as the model for the faithful to follow since it clearly displays how death signifies the total destruction of the body. The practice eschews meanings that can be associated with mummification or embalming or even with cremation. Burial recalls the earth from which man comes (cf. *Gen* 2:6) and to which he returns (cf. *Gen* 3:19; *Sir* 17:1), and also recalls the burial of Christ, the grain which, fallen on the earth, brought forth fruit in plenty (cf. *John* 12:24).

Cremation is also a contemporary phenomenon in virtue of the changed circumstances of life. In this regard, ecclesiastical discipline states: "Christian obsequies may be conceded to those who have chosen to have their bodies cremated, provided that such choice was not motivated by anything contrary to Christian doctrine"[369]. In relation to such a decision, the faithful should be exhorted not to keep the ashes of the dead in their homes, but to bury them in the usual manner, until God shall raise up those who rest in the earth, and until the sea gives up its dead (cf. *Aps* 20:13).

Other Suffrage

255. The Church offers the sacrifice of the Holy Eucharist for the dead not only on the occasion of their funerals, but also on the third, seventh, and thirtieth day following their deaths, as well as on their

---

[369] *Ibid.*, 15; SUPREME CONGREGATION OF THE HOLY OFFICE, Instruction, *De cadaverum crematione*, 2-3, in AAS 56 (1964) 822-823; CIC, can. 1184, 5, § 1, 2.

anniversaries. The celebration of the Mass in suffrage for the souls of the faithful departed is the Christian way of recalling and prolonging, in the Lord, that communion with those who have crossed the threshold of death. On 2 November, the Church incessantly offers the holy sacrifice of the Mass for the souls of all the faithful departed and prays the Liturgy of the Hours for them.

The Church daily supplicates and implores the Lord, in the celebration of the Mass and at Vespers, that "the faithful who have gone before us marked with the sign of faith [...] may be given light, happiness and peace"[370].

It is important to instruct the faithful in the light of the celebration of the sacrifice of the Eucharist, in which the Church prays that all of the faithful departed, of whatever place or time, will be brought to the glory of the risen Lord, so as to avoid possessive or particular ideas that relate the Mass only to one's "own" dead[371]. The celebration of Mass in suffrage for the dead also presents an important opportunity for catechesis on the last things.

The Memorial of the Dead in Popular Piety

256. As with the Liturgy, popular piety pays particular attention to the memory of the dead and carefully raises up to God prayers in suffrage for them.

In matters relating to the "memorial of the dead", great pastoral prudence and tact must always be employed in addressing the relationship between Liturgy and popular piety, both in its doctrinal aspect and in harmonising the liturgical actions and pious exercises.

257. It is always necessary to ensure that popular piety is inspired by the principles of the Christian faith. Thus, they should be made aware of the paschal meaning of the death undergone by those who have received Baptism and who have been incorporated into the mystery of the death and resurrection of Christ (cf. *Rm* 6:3-10); the immortality of the soul (cf. *Lk* 23:43); the communion of Saints, through which "union with those who

---

[370] MISSALE ROMANUM, *Prex eucharistica I, Commemoratio pro defunctis.*
[371] Regarding Masses for the dead cf. *Institutio generalis Missalis Romani*, 355.

are still on their pilgrim journey with the faithful who repose in Christ is not in the least broken, but strengthened by a communion of spiritual goods, as constantly taught by the Church"[372]: "our prayer for them is capable not only of helping them, but also of making their intercession for us effective"[373]; the resurrection of the body; the glorious coming of Christ, who will "judge the living and the dead"[374]; the reward given to each according to his deeds; life eternal.

Deeply rooted cultural elements connoting particular anthropological concepts are to be found among the customs and usages connected with the "cult of the dead" among some peoples. These often spring from a desire to prolong family and social links with the departed. Great caution must be used in examining and evaluating these customs. Care should be taken to ensure that they are not contrary to the Gospel. Likewise, care should be taken to ensure that they cannot be interpreted as pagan residues.

258. In matters relating to doctrine, the following are to be avoided:

• the invocation of the dead in practices involving divination;

• the interpretation or attribution of imaginary effects to dreams relating to the dead, which often arises from fear;

• any suggestion of a belief in reincarnation;

• the danger of denying the immortality of the soul or of detaching death from the resurrection, so as to make the Christian religion seem like a religion of the dead;

• the application of spacio-temporal categories to the dead.

---

[372] LG 49.
[373] CCC 958.
[374] DS 150; MISSALE ROMANUM, *Ordo Missae, Symbolum Nicaeno-Constantinopolitanum.*

259. "Hiding death and its signs" is widespread in contemporary society and prone to the difficulties arising from doctrinal and pastoral error.

Doctors, nurses, and relatives frequently believe that they have a duty to hide the fact of imminent death from the sick who, because of increasing hospitalization, almost always die outside of the home.

It has been frequently said that the great cities of the living have no place for the dead: buildings containing tiny flats cannot house a space in which to hold a vigil for the dead; traffic congestion prevents funeral corteges because they block the traffic; cemeteries, which once surrounded the local church and were truly "holy ground" and indicated the link between Christ and the dead, are now located at some distance outside of the towns and cities, since urban planning no longer includes the provision of cemeteries.

Modern society refuses to accept the "visibility of death", and hence tries to conceal its presence. In some places, recourse is even made to conserving the bodies of the dead by chemical means in an effort to prolong the appearance of life.

The Christian, who must be conscious of and familiar with the idea of death, cannot interiorly accept the phenomenon of the "intolerance of the dead", which deprives the dead of all acceptance in the city of the living. Neither can he refuse to acknowledge the signs of death, especially when intolerance and rejection encourage a flight from reality, or a materialist cosmology, devoid of hope and alien to belief in the death and resurrection of Christ.

The Christian is obliged to oppose all forms of "commercialisation of the dead", which exploit the emotions of the faithful in pursuit of unbridled and shameful commercial profit.

260. In accordance with time, place and tradition, popular devotions to the dead take on a multitude of forms:

• the novena for the dead in preparation for the 2 November, and the octave prolonging it, should be celebrated in accordance with liturgical norms;

• visits to the cemetery; in some places this is done in a community manner on 2 November, at the end of the parochial mission, when the parish priest takes possession of the parish; visiting the cemetery can also be done privately, when the faithful go to the graves of their own families to maintain them or decorate them with flowers and lamps. Such visits should be seen as deriving from the bonds existing between the living and the dead and not from any form of obligation, non-fulfilment of which involves a superstitious fear;

• membership of a confraternity or other pious association whose objects include "burial of the dead" in the light of the Christian vision of death, praying for the dead, and providing support for the relatives of the dead;

• suffrage for the dead through alms deeds, works of mercy, fasting, applying indulgences, and especially prayers, such as the *De profundis*, and the formula *Requiem aeternam*, which often accompanies the recitation of the *Angelus*, the rosary, and at prayers before and after meals.

CHAPTER EIGHT

Shrines and Pilgrimages

261. The relationship between the Liturgy and popular piety is probably most evident at shrines. These are often dedicated to the Holy Trinity, to Christ our Saviour, to the Blessed Virgin Mary, to the Saints or Beati. "At shrines more abundant means of salvation are to be provided for the faithful; the word of God is to be carefully proclaimed; liturgical life is to be appropriately fostered especially through the celebration of the Eucharist and penance; and approved forms of popular piety are to be fostered"[375].

Pilgrimage is closely connected with shrines, and itself an expression of popular piety.

Even though weakened by the effects of secularism, interest in shrines and pilgrimage remains high among the faithful.

In view of the object of this Directory, it would seem appropriate to offer some guidelines for the pastoral activities of shrines, and for pilgrimages so that they may be conducted in accordance with a correct understanding of the relationship between Liturgy and popular piety.

The Shrine

Principles

262. In accordance with Christian revelation, the risen Christ is the supreme and definitive sanctuary (cf. *John* 2:18-21; *Ap* 21:22) around which the community of the disciples gathers. In turn, that community is the new dwelling place of the Lord (cf. 1 *Pt* 2:5; *Eph* 2:19-22).

Theologically, a shrine, which often derives from popular piety, is a sign of the active and saving presence of the Lord in history, and a place of respite in which the people of God on its journey to

---

[375] CIC, can 1234, §1.

the heavenly City (cf. *Heb* 13:14), can renew its strength for the pilgrim journey[376].

263. Shrines, like churches, have enormous symbolic value: they are icons "of the dwelling place of God among men" (*Ap* 21:3) and allude to "the mystery of the Temple" which was fulfilled in the Body of Christ (cf. *John* 1:14; 2:21), in the ecclesial community (cf. 1 *Pt* 2:5) of the faithful (cf. 1 *Cor* 3:16-17; 6:19; 2 *Cor* 6:16). To the faithful, shrines represent:

● a memorial to an original extraordinary event which has given rise to persistent devotion, or a witness to the piety and gratitude of a people that has received many benefits;

● privileged places of divine assistance and of the intercession of Blessed Virgin Mary, the Saints or the Beati, in virtue of the frequent signs of mercy that have been shown in them;

● signs of cosmic harmony and reflections of divine beauty because of their physical positioning which is often elevated, solitary and austere;

● a call to conversion because of what is preached in them, an invitation to redouble the life of charity and the works of mercy, and an exhortation to follow Christ;

● places dedicated to consolidating the faith, to growth in grace, refuge and consolation in affliction, by virtue of the sacramental life practised in them;

● particular interpretations and prolongations of the Word of God by virtue of the Gospel message proclaimed in them;

---

[376] Cf. PONTIFICAL COUNCIL FOR THE PASTORAL CARE OF MIGRANTS AND ITINERANTS, *The Shrine. memory, presence and prophecy of the living God.* (8.5.1999), Libreria Editrice Vaticana, Città del Vaticano 1999.

• an encouragement to cultivate an eschatological outlook, a sense of transcendence and to learn to direct their earthly footsteps towards the sanctuary of Heaven (cf. *Heb* 9:11; *Ap* 21:3).

"Christian shrines have always been, and continue to be, signs of God, and of His intervention in history. Each one of them is a memorial to the Incarnation and to the Redemption"[377].

Canonical Recognition

264. "The term shrine signifies a church or other sacred place to which the faithful make pilgrimages for a particular pious reason with the approval of the local ordinary"[378].

A prior condition for the canonical recognition of a diocesan, national or international shrine is the respective approval of the diocesan bishop, the Conference of Bishops, or the Holy See. Canonical approval is an official recognition of a sacred place and for the specific purpose of receiving the pilgrimages of the people of God which go there to worship the Father, profess the faith, and to be reconciled with God, the Church and one's neighbour, and to implore the intercession of the Mother of God or one of the Saints.

It should not be overlooked, however, that many other places, often humble little churches in the cities or in the countryside, locally fulfill the same functions as shrines, even without canonical recognition. These also form part of the "topography" of the faith and of the popular piety of the people of God[379], of a particular community living in a specific geographical area, on its journey towards the heavenly Jerusalem in faith (*Ap* 21).

The Shrine as Place of Cultic Celebration

265. Shrines have an important cultic function. The faithful visit shrines to participate in the liturgical celebrations and the various pious exercises practised there. This fact, however, should not

---

[377] JOHN PAUL II, *Allocution to the rectors of French Shrines* in *Insegnamenti di Giovanni Paolo II*, IV/I (1981), Libreria Editrice Vaticana, Città del Vaticano 1981, p. 138.
[378] CIC, can 1230. For the concession of indulgences see EI, *Aliae concessiones*, 33, §1, 4E, p. 77.
[379] Cf. JOHN PAUL II, Encyclical Letter *Redemptoris Mater*, 28.

cause the faithful to overlook the Gospel teaching according to which no specific place is decisive for authentic worship of the Lord (cf. *John* 4:20-24).

Exemplary liturgical celebration

266. Those in charge of shrines should ensure that the quality of the liturgy celebrated at the shrines is exemplary: "Among the functions ascribed to sanctuaries, and confirmed by the *Code of Canon Law*, is that of fostering the Liturgy. This is not to be understood as increasing the number of liturgical celebrations, but in terms of improving the quality of liturgical celebration. The rectors of sanctuaries should be aware of their responsibility to ensure that this goal is reached. They should realise that the faithful who come to a shrine from diverse places should be able to return comforted in spirit, and edified by the liturgical celebrations: by their capacity to communicate the message of salvation, by the noble simplicity of their ritual expression, and by the faithful observance of the liturgical norms. Rectors of shrines are well aware that the effects of exemplary liturgical celebration are not limited to the liturgical actions celebrated in shrines: both priests and pilgrims take back to their own places the strong cultic impressions that they have experienced in shrines".[380]

Celebration of the Sacrament of Penance

267. For many of the faithful, a visit to a shrine is a propitious occasion on which to avail of the Sacrament of Penance. It is, however, necessary to encourage the various constitutive elements of the Sacrament of Penance:

• the place of celebration: in addition to the traditional confessionals located in the church, it is desirable that a confessional chapel be provided for the celebration of the Sacrament of Penance and in which space is available for community preparation, and for penitential

---

[380] CONGREGATION FOR DIVINE WORSHIP, Circular Letter *Orientations and Proposals for the Celebration of the Marian Year*, 75.

celebrations. These should always respect the canonical norms relating to the Sacrament of Penance as well as the privacy which is needed for confession. It should also provide some possibility for dialogue with the confessor.

• preparation for the Sacrament: sometimes, the faithful require assistance in preparing for confession, especially in directing the mind and heart to God through a sincere conversion, "since the essence of Penance consists of this"[381]. The *Ordo Paenitentiae*[382] provides for celebrations designed to assist preparation for confession through a fruitful celebration of the Word of God; or at least some form of suitable preparatory material being placed at the disposal of the faithful, so as to prepare them not only for the confession of sins, but also for a sincere amendment of life.

• choice of the *ritual action*, to lead the faithful to discover the ecclesial nature of Penance; in this respect *the Rite for the reconciliation of several penitents with individual confession and absolution* (the second rite of Penance), properly prepared and conducted, should not be exceptional, but a normal celebration of the Sacrament of Penance especially at particular times of the Liturgical Year. Indeed, "communal celebration manifests more clearly the ecclesial nature of penance"[383]. Reconciliation without individual confession and absolution is a completely exceptional and extraordinary form of the Sacrament of Penance, and may not be considered interchangeable with the ordinary form of the Sacrament. The use of general absolution cannot be justified solely by the presence of great numbers of the faithful, as happens on feast days and pilgrimages[384].

Celebration of the Eucharist

268. "The celebration of the Eucharist is the climax and pivot of all pastoral activity in shrines"[385]. Great care should be devoted to the

---

[381] RITUALE ROMANUM, *Ordo Paenitentiae*, cit., 6 a.
[382] Cf. *Ibid, Appendix II, Specimina celebrationum panitentialium*, 1-73.
[383] *Ibid., Praenotanda*, 22.
[384] Cf. *CIC, can. 961, §2*.
[385] *Collectio missarum de Beata Maria Virgine, Praenotanda*, 30.

celebration of the Eucharist so that its exemplary celebration may lead the faithful to a deep encounter with Christ.

It can happen that different groups wish to celebrate the Eucharist at the same time. This practice is not consistent with the ecclesial dimension of the Eucharistic mystery, in that the celebration of the Eucharist, rather than being and expression of fraternity becomes and expression of individualism which fails to reflect the communion and universality of the Church.

A simple reflection on the nature of the Eucharistic celebration, "sacrament of holiness, sign of unity, and bond of charity"[386], should be sufficient to persuade priests who lead pilgrim groups to celebrate the Eucharist with other groups of the same language. On occasions when pilgrims come together from different countries, it is important that the Creed and the Our Father be sung in Latin using the simpler melodies[387]. Such celebrations offer a truer image of the Church and of the Eucharist, and afford the faithful an opportunity for mutual encounter and reciprocal enrichment.

Anointing of the Sick

269. The *Ordo unctionis infirmorum cumque pastoralis curae* provides for the communal celebration of the Anointing of the Sick, especially on the occasion of a pilgrimage to a shrine[388]. Such is perfectly in accord with the nature of the Sacrament: obviously, where the imploration of the Lord's mercy is more intense, there too will the maternal solicitude of the Church be more sought by her children who, through sickness or old age, begin to be in danger of death[389].

The Rite is to be conducted in accordance with the stipulations of the Ordo. "When several priests are available, each priest lays on hands and administers the anointing with the formula to each sick person in the group; the prayers, however, are to be recited by the principal celebrant"[390].

[386] SC 47.
[387] Cf. *Institutio generalis Missalis Romani*, 41.
[388] Cf. n. 83.
[389] Cf. CIC, can. 1004.
[390] RITUALE ROMANUM, *Ordo unctionis infirmorum eorumque pastoralis curae*, cit., 90.

Celebration of the Other Sacraments

270. In addition to the celebration of the Sacraments of Penance, Holy Eucharist, and the Anointing of the Sick, the other sacraments are occasionally celebrated. This requires particular care on the part of the rectors of shrines to ensure that the dispositions of the local bishop are observed and that additionally:

• they seek to build a genuine understanding and develop a fruitful collaboration between shrine and parish community;

• they consider the nature of every sacrament; for example, since the Sacraments of Christian initiation require preparation and effect the insertion of the Baptized into a particular ecclesial community, they should normally be received in the parish;

• they should ensure that the celebration of every sacrament has been preceded by adequate preparation: the rectors of shrines may not proceed to the marriage of any couple unless they shall have obtained the permission of the Ordinary or the parish priest[391];

• they should evaluate carefully the multiple and unpredictable circumstances that can arise, and for which it is not always possible to establish norms.

Celebrating the Liturgy of the Hours

271. A visit to a shrine, which is always a special occasion of private and community prayer, affords a valuable opportunity to assist the faithful in appreciating the beauty of the Liturgy of the Hours, and to allow them to participate in the daily praise which the Church, on her earthly pilgrimage, raises up to the Father, through Christ in the Holy Spirit[392].

Rectors of shrines, therefore, are to make provision for the worthy and opportune celebration of the Liturgy of the Hours, especially

---

[391] Cf. CIC, can. 1115.
[392] Cf. *Institutio Generalis de Liturgia Horarum*, 27.

Morning and Evening prayer, in the liturgical programmes proposed for pilgrims. In this respect, a votive office connected with the shrine could be used either in whole or part[393].

During the course of the pilgrimage to a shrine, priests will ensure that some hour of the Divine Office is recited by the faithful.

Sacramentals

272. From earliest times, the Church is familiar with the practice of blessing people, places, food, and other objects. In our times, the custom of blessings presents some delicate concerns because of ancient practices or customs deeply rooted amongst the faithful. The question is obviously more pertinent in shrines where the faithful come to implore the graces and assistance of the Lord through the intercession of Our Lady of Mercy, or of the Saints, and request the most varied of blessings. Correct pastoral practise in dispensing blessings demands that the rectors of shrines:

• proceed gradually and prudently in applying the principles contained in the *Rituale Romanum*[394], which are based on the fundamental principle that a blessing is an authentic expression of faith in God, the giver of all good things;

• give due importance - where possible - to the two elements which constitute the "typical structure" of a blessing: proclamation of the Word of God which makes sense of the sacred sign, and the prayer with which the Church praises God and implores his assistance[395], as recalled when the ordained minister makes the sign of the cross;

• give precedence to community celebrations over individual or private celebrations and to educate the faithful to active and conscious participation[396].

---

[393] Cf. *ibid.*, 245.

[394] Cf. RITUALE ROMANUM, *De Benedictionibus*, cit., *Praenotanda*, 1-34.

[395] Cf. *ibid.*, 22-24.

[396] Cf. *ibid.*, 24 a.

273. It is, therefore, desirable that the rectors of shrines provide for the celebration of blessings at specific times during the day[397], especially during those periods when there is a notable increase in the number of pilgrims. From these celebrations, which should be marked by dignity and authenticity, the faithful should be able to grasp the true meaning of a blessing, an the importance of commitment to observing the commandments of God, which is "implied by asking for a blessing"[398].

Shrines as Places of Evangelization

274. Innumerable centres of social communications broadcast news and messages of all kinds every day of the week. A shrine, however, is a place for the proclamation of a message of life: the "Gospel of God" (*Mk* 1:14; *Rm* 1:1), or the "Gospel of Jesus Christ" (*Mk* 1:1), that is the good news coming from God about Jesus Christ: he is the Saviour of all mankind, by whose death and resurrection heaven and earth have been reconciled for ever.

The fundamental points of that message must be proposed, either directly or indirectly, to the faithful who make pilgrimage to shrines: the programme outlined in the Sermon on the Mount; the joyful proclamation of the goodness and fatherhood of God and of His loving providence; the commandment of love; the salvific significance of the Cross; the transcendent end of human life.

Many shrines are effective places for the proclamation of the Gospel: in the most varied of ways the message of Christ is transmitted to the faithful as a call to conversion and an invitation to follow Christ, as an exhortation to perseverance, as a reminder of the demands of justice, as a word of consolation and peace.

The fact should not be overlooked that many shrines support the missions ad *gentes* in various ways and fulfil an important role of evangelization in the Church.

---

[397] Cf. *ibid.*, 30.
[398] Cf. *ibid.*, 15.

Shrines as Charitable Centres

275. The exemplary role of shrines is also expressed through charity. Every shrine in so far as it celebrates the merciful presence of the Lord, the example and the intercession of the Blessed Virgin Mary and the Saints, "is in itself a hearth radiating the light and warmth of charity"[399]. In common parlance and in the language of the poor "charity is love expressed in the name of God"[400]. It finds concrete expression in hospitality and mercy, solidarity and sharing, assistance and giving.

Many shrines are centres mediating the love of God and fraternal charity on the one hand, and the needs of mankind on the other. This is made possible by the generosity of the faithful and the zeal of those responsible for the shrines. The charity of Christ flourishes in these sanctuaries which seem to be an extension of the maternal solicitude of Our Lady and of the compassionate presence of the Saints expressed:

• in the creation and development of permanent centres of social assistance such as hospitals, educational institutions for needy children, and in the provision of homes for the aged;

• "in the hospitality extended to pilgrims, especially the poor, to whom the opportunity for rest and shelter should be offered, in so far as possible;

• in the solicitude shown to the old, the sick, the handicapped, to whom particular attention is always given, especially in reserving for them the best places in the shrine: without isolating them from the other pilgrims, celebrations should be made available at convenient times, taking into account their ability to participate at them; effective collaboration should also exist between the shrines and those who generously provide for transport;

---

[399] CENTRAL COMMITTEE FOR THE MARIAN YEAR, *Marian Sanctuaries*, 4 (Circular Letter 7. 10. 1987).
[400] *Ibid.*

• in availability and service to all who come to shrines: educated and uneducated members of the faithful, poor and rich, locals and strangers"[401].

The Shrine as Cultural Centre

276. Shrines are often of cultural or heritage significance in themselves. They synthesize numerous expressions of popular culture: historical and artistic monuments, particular linguistic and literary forms, or even musical compositions.

In this perspective, shrines can often play an important role in the definition of the cultural identity of a nation. Since a shrine can produce a harmonious synthesis between grace and nature, piety and art, it can also be presented as an example of the *via pulchritudinis* for the contemplation of the beauty of God, of the mystery of the *Tota pulchra*, and of the wonderful accomplishment of the Saints.

The tendency to promote shrines as "cultural centres" must also be acknowledged. Such efforts include the organisation of courses and lectures, from which important publications can derive, as well as the production of sacred "representations", concerts and other artistic and literary activities.

The cultural activities of a shrine are undertaken as collateral initiatives in support of human development. They are secondary to the shrine's principal functions as a place of divine worship, of evangelization and charity. The rectors of shrines will therefore ensure that the cultic functions of such places will not be superceded by any cultural activities taking place in them.

Sanctuaries and Ecumenical Commitment

277. The shrine, as a place of proclamation of the Word, of call to conversion, of intercession, of intense liturgical life, and of charitable works, is, to a certain extent, a "spiritual benefit" shared with our brothers and sisters not in full communion with

---

[401] CONGREGATION FOR DIVINE WORSHIP, Circular Letter, *Orientations and proposals for the Celebration of the Marian Year*, 76.

the Catholic Church, in accord with the norms of the *Ecumenical Directory*[402].

In this sense, the shrine is called to be a place of ecumenical commitment, fully aware of the grave and urgent need for the unity of those who believe in Christ, the one Lord and Saviour.

Rectors of shrines will therefore make pilgrims aware of that "spiritual ecumenism" of which *Unitatis redintegratio*[403] and the *Directory on Ecumenism*[404] speak, and which should be constantly remembered by the faithful in their prayers, in the celebration of the Eucharist and in their daily lives[405]. Prayers for Christian unity should therefore be intensified in shrines especially during the week of prayer for Christian unity, as well as on the solemnities of the Ascension and Pentecost, in which we remember the community of Jerusalem united in prayer while awaiting the coming of the Holy Spirit to confirm their unity and their universal mission[406].

Were the opportunity to arise, the rectors of shrines should encourage prayer meetings for Christians from various confessions from time to time. These meetings should be carefully and collaboratively prepared. The Word of God should be preeminent in them and they should include prayers drawn from the various Christian denominations.

In certain circumstance, and by way of exception, attention may be given to persons of different religions: some shrines, indeed, are visited by non-Christians who go there because of the values inherent in Christianity. All acts of worship taking place in a shrine must always be clearly consistent with the Catholic faith, without ever attempting to obfuscate anything of the content of the Church's faith.

278. Ecumenical endeavour in shrines dedicated to Our Lady pose special considerations. At a supernatural level, Our Lady, who gave birth to our Saviour and was the first and perfect disciple, played an

---

[402] Cf. PONTIFICAL COUNCIL FOR THE PROMOTION OF CHRISTIAN UNITY, *Directoire pour l'application des Principes et des Normes sur* L'Oecuménisme (25.3.1993): AAS 85 (1993) 1039-1119.
[403] N.8.
[404] N. 25, in AAS 85 (1993) 1049.
[405] Cf. *ibid.*, n. 27, p. 1049.
[406] cf. *ibid.*, n. 110, p. 1084.

important role in promoting unity and concord among the disciples of the Lord. Hence the Church refers to her as the *Mater unitatis*[407]. At the historical level, different interpretations of her role in the history of salvation have provoked divisions among Christians. On the other hand, it must be recognised that the Marian role is beginning to bear fruit in ecumenical dialogue.

Pilgrimage

279. Pilgrimage is a universal religious experience and a typical expression of popular piety[408]. It is invariably connected with a shrine, for which it is an indispensable component[409]. Pilgrims need shrines, and shrines need pilgrims.

Biblical Pilgrimage

280. In the Bible, pilgrimage, with its religious symbolism, goes back as far as that of the Patriarchs Abraham, Isaac and Jacob to Sichem (cf. *Gn* 12:6-7; 33:18-20), Bethel (cf. *Gn* 28:10-22; 35:1-15) and Mamre (*Gn* 13:18; 18:1-15) where God showed himself to them and made a commitment to give them the "promised land".

For the tribes of Israel delivered from Egypt, Sinai, the mountain on which God revealed himself to Moses (cf. *Ex* 19-20) became a sacred place and the crossing of the desert became a journey to the promised land: the journey had God's blessing, the Ark (*Num* 9:15-23) and the Tabernacle (cf. 2 *Sam* 7:6) symbolised the presence of God among his people, leading them and protecting them by the Cloud (cf. *Num* 9:15-23).

---

[407] Cf. *Collectio missarum de Beata Maria Virgine*, Form. 38: "Sancta Maria Mater Unitatis"; St AUGUSTINE, *Sermo* 192, 2: PL 38, 1013; PAUL VI, Homily on the Feast of the Presentation of Our Lord in the Temple, (2.2.1965), in *Insegnamenti di Paolo VI*, III (1965), Tipografia Polyglotta Vaticana, Città del Vaticano 1966, p. 68; JOHN PAUL II, Homily at the Shrine of Jasna Gora (4.6.1979) in *Insegnamenti di Giovanni Paolo II*, II/1 (19799, Libreria Editrice Vaticana, Città del Vaticano 1979, p. 1418; Angelus discourse (12.6.1988) in *Insegnamenti di Giovanni Paolo II*, XI/2 (1988), Libreria Editrice Vaticana, Città del Vaticano 1989, p. 1997.
[408] Cf. PONTIFICAL COUNCIL FOR MIGRANTS AND *ITINERANTS*, *Pilgrimage in the Great Jubilee of 2000* (25.4.1998), Libreria Editrice Vaticana, Città del Vaticano, 1998.
[409] According to the Code of canon Law, the frequency of pilgrimages is an integral element of the concept of shrine: "The term shrine signifies a church or other place to which the faithful make pilgrimages for a particular pious reason with the approval of the local ordinary" (can. 1230).

When Jerusalem became the place of the Temple and the Ark, it became a city-shrine for the Jews and the object of their "holy journey" (*Ps* 84:6), in which the pilgrim encountered "cries of joy and praise and an exultant throng" (*Ps* 42:5), and appeared in his presence in "God's house" (cf. *Ps* 84:6-8)[410].

The men of Israel were obliged to present themselves before the Lord three times each year (cf. *Ex* 23:17), in the Temple in Jerusalem: this gave rise to the pilgrimage to the Temple on the feast of the Pasch, of the feast of weeks (Pentecost) and of tents; every religious family, such as that of Jesus (cf. *Lk* 2:41), went to Jerusalem for these feast of the Passover. Jesus went on pilgrimage to Jerusalem during his public ministry (cf. *John* 11:55-56); St Luke presents the saving mission of Jesus as a mystic pilgrimage (cf. *Lk* 9:51-19:45) whose object is Jerusalem, the messianic city, the place of his sacrifice and of his exodus to the Father: "I came from the Father and have come into the world and now I leave the world to go to the Father"(*John* 16:28). The Church began her missionary journey during a gathering of pilgrims in Jerusalem when "there were devout men in Jerusalem from every nation under heaven" (*Acts* 2:5) to celebrate Pentecost.

Christian Pilgrimage

281. When Jesus accomplished in himself the mystery of the Temple (cf. *John* 2:22-23) and had passed from this world to the Father (cf. *John* 13:1), thereby going through the definitive exodus in his own person, no pilgrimage was binding any longer on his disciples: their entire lives now become a pilgrimage towards the sanctuary of heaven and the Church is seen as an "earthly pilgrimage"[411].

The Church, however, because of the harmony between her teaching and the spiritual values inherent in pilgrimage, has not only regarded pilgrimage as a legitimate form of piety but has encouraged it throughout her history.

---

[410] The significance of the pilgrimage is borne out in the "canticles of ascent", psalms 120-134, used by those going up to Jerusalem. In their Christian interpretation, these express the Church's joy as she journeys on her earthly pilgrimage to the heavenly Jerusalem.

[411] MISSALE ROMANUM, *Prex eucharistica III, Intercessiones.*

282. With a few exceptions, pilgrimage did not form part of the cultic life of the Church for the first three centuries of her history: the Church feared contamination from the religious practices of Judaism and paganism, where pilgrimage was much practised.

During this period, however, the basis was laid for a revival of the practice of pilgrimage with a Christian character: the cult of the martyrs, to whose tombs many of the faithful went to venerate the mortal remains of these outstanding witnesses to Christ, logically and gradually became a successor to the "pious visit" and to the "votive pilgrimage".

283. In the Constantinian era, following the rediscovery of the places associated with the Passion of Our Lord and the of the relics of the Passion, Christian pilgrimage made significant progress: pilgrimage to Palestine was especially important in this regard, since its holy places, starting with Jerusalem made it a "Holy Land". Contemporary accounts make this clear, as can be seen in the fourth century *Itenerarium Burdigalense* and the *Itenerarium Egeriae*.

Basilicas were built on the site of the "holy places": the *Anastasis* on the Holy Sepulchre, the *Martyrium* on the Mount Calvary, and quickly became places of pilgrimage. The sites associated with the infancy and public life of Christ also became places of pilgrimage. Pilgrimages began to be made to some of the site associated with the Old testament, such as Mount Sinai.

284. The middle ages were the golden age of pilgrimage. Apart from their strictly religious function, they played an extraordinary part in the development of Western Christianity, the amalgamation of various nations, and to the interchange of ideas and values from every European civilisation.

There were numerous places of pilgrimage. Jerusalem, despite its occupation by the muslims, still remained a great spiritual attraction for the faithful, and gave rise to the crusades whose purpose was to make Jerusalem accessible to the faithful who wished to visit the Holy Sepulchre. Numerous pilgrims flocked to venerate the instruments of the Passion: the tunic, the holy towel of

Veronica, the holy stairs, and the holy shroud. Pilgrims came to Rome to venerate the tombs of the Apostles Peter and Paul *(ad Limina Apostolorum)*, the catacombs and basilicas, in recognition of the service rendered to the universal Church by the successor of Peter. The shrine of Santiago de Compostela from the ninth to the sixteenth centuries was frequented by countless pilgrims. They came on foot from various countries and reflect an idea of pilgrimage that is at once religious, social, and charitable. The tomb of St Martin of Tours was another important centre of pilgrimage, as was Canterbury, the place of the martyrdom of St Thomas à Becket. These places of pilgrimage had enormous influence throughout Europe. Monte Gargano in Apulia, San Michele della Chiusa in the Piemonte, and Mont St Michel in Normandy, all dedicated to St Michael the Archangel, were important pilgrim centres, as were Walsingham, Rocamadour and Loreto.

285. Pilgrimage declined in the modern period because of changed cultural circumstances, the events surrounding the protestant movement and also because of the influence of the enlightenment: the journey to a distant country become "a spiritual journey", or an "interior journey", or a "symbolic procession" reduced a short walk as in the case of the *via Crucis.*

The second half of the nineteenth century saw a revival or pilgrimage, but in a much changed form: the goal of such pilgrimage becomes a particular shrine which embodies the faith or cultural identity of specific nations: shrines can mentioned in this context such as Altoeting, Antipolo, Aparecida, Assisi, Caacupé, Coromoto, Czestochowa, Ernakilam-Angamaly, Fatima, Guadalupe, Kevelaer, Knock, La Vang, Loreto, Lourdes, Mariazell, Marienberg, Montevergine, Montserrat, Nagasaki, Namugongo, Padova, Pompei, San Giovanni Rotondo, Washington, Yamoussoukro etc...

Spirituality of Pilgrimage

286. Despite change, pilgrimage has maintained the essential traits of its spirituality throughout the ages, down to our own time.

Eschatological Dimension

The original and essential quality of pilgrimage: a pilgrimage, or "journey to a shrine", is both a moment in and parable of, our journey towards the Kingdom; it affords an opportunity for the Christian to take greater stock of his eschatological destiny as *homo viator*: journeying between the obscurity of the faith and the thirst for the vision of clarity, tribulation and the desire for everlasting life, the weariness of the journey and the rest awaiting, between exile and homeland, between frenetic activity and contemplation[412].

The exodus event, Israel's journey towards the promised land, is also reflected in the spirituality of pilgrimage: the pilgrim is well aware that "there is no eternal city for us in this life" (*Hb* 14:14), and that beyond the immediate objective of a particular shrine and across the desert of life, we find our true Promised Land, in heaven.

Penitential dimension

Pilgrimage is also a journey of conversion: in journeying towards a shrine the pilgrim moves from a realisation of his own sinfulness and of his attachment to ephemeral and unnecessary things to interior freedom and an understanding of the deeper meaning of life. As has already been said, a visit to a shrine can be a propitious occasion for the faithful and is often undertaken in order to avail of the Sacrament of Penance[413]. In the past - as in our own times - pilgrimage itself has been seen as a penitential act.

When the pilgrim returns from a genuine pilgrimage, he does so with the intention of "amending his life", and ordering it more closely to God, and to live in a more transcendent way.

Festive dimension. The penitential aspect of pilgrimage is complemented by a festive aspect: the festive dimension also lies at the heart of pilgrimage, and arises from many anthropological reasons.

The joy of a Christian pilgrimage is a continuation of the joy experienced on Israel's pious pilgrimage to Jerusalem: "I rejoiced when I heard them say: 'let us go up to God's house'" (*Ps* 122:1);

[412] Cf. St AUGUSTINE, *Tractatus CXXIV In Iohannis Evangelium*, 5: CCL 36, Turnholti 1954, p. 685.
[413] Cf., supra n. 267.

pilgrimage can be a break from the monotony of daily routine; it can be an alleviation of the burdens of every day life, especially for the poor whose lot is heavy; it is an occasion to give expression to Christian fraternity, in moments of friendship meeting each other, and spontaneity which can sometimes be repressed.

Worship dimension

Pilgrimage is essentially an act of worship: a pilgrim goes to a shrine to encounter God, to be in His presence, and to offer Him adoration in worship, and to open his heart to Him.

During his visit to the shrine, the pilgrim completes many acts of worship which are properly Liturgical or drawn from popular piety. He performs different kind of prayers: prayers of *praise and adoration* to the Lord for his goodness and holiness; prayers of *thanksgiving* for the gifts he has given; prayers in *discharge of a vow*; prayers *imploring the graces* necessary in life; prayers *asking* for *forgiveness* of sins committed.

Frequently, the pilgrim's prayers are directed to Our Lady, or to the Angels and Saints who are regarded as powerful intercessors with God. The icons venerated at pilgrim shrines are signs of the presence of the Mother of God and the Saints who surround the Lord in his glory, "living for ever to intercede for us" (*Hb* 7:25), and always present in the community gathered in his name (cf. *Mt* 18:20; 28:20). Sacred images, whether of Christ, his Mother, the Angels and Saints, are signs of the divine presence and of God's provident love; they bear witness to the prayers of generations raised up to God in supplication, to the sighs of the afflicted, and to the thankful joy of those who have received grace and mercy.

Apostolic dimension

The pilgrim's journey, in a certain sense, recalls the journey of Christ and his disciples as they travelled throughout Palestine to announce the Gospel of salvation. In this perspective, pilgrimage is a proclamation of faith in which pilgrims become "errant heralds of Christ"[414].

---

[414] SECOND VATICAN COUNCIL, Decree *Apostolicam actuositatem*, 14.

Dimension of communion. The pilgrim who journeys to a shrine is in a communion of faith and charity not only with those who accompany him on the "sacred journey" (cf. *Ps* 84:6), but with the Lord himself who accompanies him as he once accompanied the disciples on the road to Emmaus (cf. *Lk* 24:13-35). He travels with his own community and through that community, he journeys with the Church in heaven and on earth. He travels with all of the faithful who have prayed at that shrine down through the centuries. He appreciates the natural beauty which surrounds the shrine and which he is moved to respect. The pilgrim journeys with mankind whose sufferings and hopes are so clearly evident at the shrine, especially as represented through art.

Conducting a Pilgrimage

287. As the shrine is a place of prayer, a pilgrimage is a journey of prayer. Each stage of the pilgrim journey should be marked by prayer and the Word of God should be its light and its guide, its food and its sustenance.

The success of a pilgrimage, seen as an act of worship, and of the spiritual fruits deriving from it, require careful planning of the various celebrations that will take place during the pilgrimage, and adequate highlighting of their various phases.

The beginning of the pilgrimage should be an occasion of prayer, preferably in the parish church or in some other suitable church, with the celebration of the Holy Eucharist or a part of the Liturgy of the Hours[415], or with a special blessing for pilgrims[416].

The *final* stage of the pilgrimage should be characterised by intense prayer. It should preferably, be travelled on foot in processional form, and interspersed with prayer, hymns and pauses at the shrines marking the route to the sanctuary.

The *reception* of the pilgrims could be a suitable moment for a "threshold liturgy", placing the pilgrims and the keepers of the shrine in a perfect context of faith; where possible, the latter should

---

[415] Cf. *RITUALE ROMANUM, De Benedictionibus, Ordo ad benedicendos peregrinos*, cit., 407.
[416] Cf. *ibid.*, 409-419.

join with the pilgrims in the final phase of the pilgrim journey.

The *time* spent in the sanctuary constitutes the most important part of the pilgrimage and should be marked by a commitment to conversion, ratified by reception of the Sacrament of Penance; by private prayer of thanksgiving, supplication, or of intercession, in accordance with the nature of the shrine or the objectives of the pilgrimage; by celebration of the Holy Eucharist, which is the climax of the pilgrimage[417].

The *conclusion* of the pilgrimage should be marked by a moment of prayer, either in the shrine itself or at the church from which the pilgrimage departed[418]. The pilgrims should give thanks to God for the gift of the pilgrimage and ask the Lord for his assistance in living out the Christian vocation more generously when they return to their homes.

From antiquity, pilgrims have always brought home souvenirs of their pilgrimage, in recollection of the shrine that they had visited. Care should be taken to ensure that object, images, and books available in shrines transmit authentically the spirit of the shrine. Care should also be taken to ensure that shops or stalls are not set up within the sacred space of the sanctuary, and that even the appearance of commerce be excluded.

Conclusion

288. Both parts of this Directory contain many directives, proposals, and guidelines to encourage and clarify popular piety and religiosity, and to harmonise it with the Liturgy.

In referring to specific traditions and diverse circumstances, the Directory wishes to set forth some basic presuppositions, to reiterate various directives, and to make some suggestions so as to promote fruitful pastoral activity.

With the assistance of their collaborators, especially of the rectors of shrines, it is for the Bishops to establish norms and practical guidelines in relation to this matter, taking into account local traditions and particular manifestations of popular piety and religiosity.

---

[417] Cf. supra nn. 265-273.
[418] Cf. RITUALE ROMANUM, *De benedictionibus, Ordo benedictionis peregrinorum ante vel post reditum*, cit., 420-430

Index of Biblical References

The biblical reference is followed by the number of the relevant paragraph of the Directory where it is cited: where the reference alludes to a biblical text rather than a direct citation, the paragraph number is given in italics.

Old Testament

Genesis

1:12	181
2:6	*254*
2:9	*109*
2:17	*249*
3:3	*249*
3:19	*249, 254*
3:24	*214*
8:1-15	*280*
12:6-7	*280*
13:18	*280*
21:17	*214*
22:11	*214*
28:10-22	*280*
33:18-20	*280*
35:1-15	*280*

Exodus

12:1	*175*
13:2.12-13	*218*
14:8-31	*245*
19:6	*76*
19-20	*280*
19-24	*76*
23:17	*280*

Leviticus

11:44-45	*76*
12:1-8	*120*
19:2	*76*

Numbers

9:15-23	*280*
10:33-36	*280*

Deuteronomy

8:3	*126*

2 Samuel

6:12-19	*245*
7:5-16	*218*
7:6	*280*

I Kings

19:4-8	*214*

I Chronicles

17:11-14	*218*

Tobit

12:15	*214*

II Maccabees

12:46	*251*

Psalms

42:5	280
84:6-8	*280, 286*
89[88]:2	*154*
91:11	*214*
103:20	*213*
122:1	*286*
137:1	*215*

Wisdom

1:13	*249*

Sirach

17:1	*159, 254*

Isaiah

6:3	*215*
6:1-4	*214*
7:14	*118*
9:5	*108*
9:6	*18*
11:1	*181*
52:13 - 53:12	*137*
53:3	*136*
53:4-5	*175*

Daniel

3:49-50	*214*
6:23	*214*

Zechariah

12:10	*167*

Malachi

3:20	*98*

205

Index of Biblical References

Index of Persons and Places

Each entry is followed by a reference to a paragraph number in the Directory; when the reference is to a note, the number if followed by *.

Analytical Index

The entry is followed by the number of the relevant paragraph of the Directory; where the reference is to a footnote the number is followed by an asterisk (*).

A

Act of Reparation
formula to implore mercy and to make reparation the the Sacred Heart of Jesus 171.

Actions
as a language of popular piety 15.

Adaptation
between liturgical forms and popular piety in the IV century 24; the process of a. and inculturation of a pious practice 92.

Adoration of the Blood of Christ
Hour of a. and its purpose 178.

Advent
harmonisation with the a. liturgy. 96-105; a. wreath 98; a. processions. 99; the winter season 100; the memory of the Virgin Mary 101-102 and191; Christmas novena 103; Christmas crib 104; spirit of a. and popular piety 105.

Advent season
See Advent.

Advent wreath
composition and purpose 98.

Akathistos
hymn to the Mother of God in the Byzantine rite 207.

Almsgiving
as intercession for the deceased 251.

Altar
Placing of relics under the a. during dedication 237; on not placing relics or images of the saints on the a. 237 and 244.

Angels
teaching of the Church, witness of Scripture and Tradition 213-214; veneration of the a. in particular days, circumstances and conditions 215; devotion of the faithful to the a., nature of the guardian a. 216; possible deviations 217.

Angelus
linked to the feast of the Annunciation 187; significance and form of the a. 195; accompanying the *Angelus Dei* 216 and the *Requiem aeternam* 260.

Angelus Dei
invoking the guardian angel, often accompanying the *Angelus Domini* 216.

Anointing of the Sick
celebrated in the shrines 269.

Anthropology
anthropological dimension of symbolism and expressions of popular piety 12; anthropological values and marian feasts 187 and in the feasts of the saints 232-

211

233; anthropological content of procession 247.

Antiquity, Christian
link between liturgy and popular piety in a. 23-27.

Apocrypha
the spread of apocryphal literature in the Middle Ages and its influence on iconography 30; a. on the life of Mary 23*.

Apostolic See
teachings concerning popular piety 2. See Dicastery, Magisterium.

Apostolic Tradition
witness of elements of popular matrix 23.

Apparitions
in the context of private revelations 90; a. of Fatima 174 and 189.

Art
veneration of sacred images and the artistic patrimony 18; baroque culture 41; inculturation and artistic expression 92; artistic value of sacred images 243; a. in the sacred shrines 276.

Ash Wednesday
its meaning 125.

Associations
birth of a. in the Middle Ages 31; a. of the faithful as subjects of popular piety 69; a. and the practice of pious exercises 72, of the marian Saturday 188, of the acts of consecration to Mary 204; "Association of the Holy Family" 112; a. and pious devotions for

the deceased 260; a. and the care of pilgrims at shrines 275.
See Confraternities.

Assumption of the Blessed Virgin Mary *(solemnity)*
the solemnity of the a. 180 and expressions of popular piety 181.

Ave Maria
in the context of the *Angelus Domini* 195 and of the rosary 197.

B

Baptism
feast of the Baptism of the Lord 119; b. and consecration to Mary 204; b. and the meaning of dying in Christ 250.
See Initiation, Christian.

Baptismal vespers
on Easter Sunday 245.

Bishop/s
competence and responsibilities of the b. concerning popular piety 1, 3, 5, 18, 21; teachings of Conference/s of B. on popular piety 2; the B. as recipients of this Directory 5; approval from the B. of a diocesan shrine 264 and its relationship to the B. 270; the competence of the B. to give norms and guidelines concerning popular piety according to the local traditions 288. See Ordinary.

Blesseds
when they may be named in the litany of saints 235. See Saints.

Blessing
the development of rites of b. in the Middle Ages, where one finds, along

with the elements of Christian faith, some aspects of other creeds 32-33; pastoral use of rites of b. at sacred shrines 272-273; b. of children 112; of homes 118, 152; of candles 120; of a mother 121; of eggs 150; of the family table 68, 109, 150, 260; of families 152; with the Most Blessed Sacrament 163; of herbs 181; of rosary beads 198; of medals 206; of fire 225; with relics of the saints 237; of sacred images 244; of pilgrims 287.

Blood of Christ
Veneration and devotion 175-179; scriptural foundations 175-176; in liturgical worship 177; in popular piety 178; prayerful meditation on the "seven wounds" 178, iconography 179. See Body and Blood of Christ; "Via Sanguinis".

Body and Blood of the Lord
the solemnity 160-163 and 177; institution of the feast of the B. 160; eucharistic procession 162-163 and 245. See Blood of Christ.

Burial
internment and cremation 252-254. See Funeral rites.

Byzantine rite
memorial of Mary in Advent 101, in the month of August 190*; the hymn Akathistos 207.

C

Calendar
link between pious marian devotions and general celebrations of the c. or of the particular c. of the diocese or religious family 187; celebrations of the saints in the particular c. and in the general Roman c. 227-229; directions and norms of the Roman c. concerning the celebrations of the saints 229.

Catechesis
the lack of c. in the Middle Ages as a threat to the correct expression of the Christian faith 33; the work of c. in the missions also through pious practices 36; the promotion of c. and Giustiniani and Querini 37; the formative purpose of parish catechesis 39; c. of adults on Sunday at the time of the Catholic reform 42; c. supports a healthy relationship between liturgy and popular piety 49; c. concerning the Christian meaning of Sunday 95; pious devotions as a means of c. 189; c. and devotion to the saints 212-213; c. concerning sacred images 239; need for c. on the meaning of intercession for the deceased 255.

Catechism of the Catholic Church
private revelations 90; the mystery of the Trinity 157*; marian devotion 183* and commentary on the Ave Maria 197*; danger of naive credulity 206*; Purgatory 210* and 251; the angels 213* and 215*; sacred images 238*, 239, 240*; faith in the resurrection of the dead 248*; death 249*; intercession for the deceased 251*, 252* and 257*.

Catholic reform
historical period 41-43.

Celebrations of the Word
importance of listening to God's word in Marian devotions 193-194.

Cemetery
procession to the c. on the 2nd November and in the funeral rites 245; visiting the c. 260.

Charism
relationship between ministry and c. concerning the expression of popular piety 84.

Charity
forms of compassion and c. 6; c. as a value in popular piety 61; the practice of c. in confraternities and associations 69; forms of c. linked with infancy and human life 113; the c. of the Sacred Heart of Jesus 166; shrines as places of c. 263 and 275.

Children
feast of the Holy Innocents and the protection of infants and c. 113.

Christ
See Jesus Christ

Christmas
origin 25 and 27; liturgical time and expressions of popular piety 106-119; Christmas tree 109; Christmas dinner 109; spirituality of Christmas 108; midnight Mass 111; Christmas Eve 109-111; crib 104 and 109.

Christmas Tree
symbolism of the c. 109.

Church
the C.'s care for popular piety1; liturgy and popular piety in the light of the Magisterium of the C. 2, 60-75; the faith of the C. is expressed in forms of prayer 16; the C. as people of God 44;

popular piety belongs to the life of worship of the C. 50; the C. as a worshipping community 81-86; the "ecclesiological principle" of Christian worship 84; recognising the authority of the C. in the context of private revelations 90; precept of the C. to confess one's serious sins at least once per year and of receiving Holy Communion at least once per year 125; Mary as icon of the C. 147, 180; image of the C. as spouse 179; Magisterium of the C. and Marian devotions 185-186; popular piety as a means of promoting an ecclesial vision of Mary189; the *Akathistos* prayer contains the faith of the early Church in Mary 207; doctrine of the C. on the saints 208-212, on angels 213-214, on sacred images 240; faith of the C. in eternal life 248.

Commemoration of the faithful departed
on the 2nd November and related intercessions for the deceased 245, 255 and 260.

Common Priesthood
c. and popular piety 85-86.

Conference/s of bishops
teachings of C. on popular piety 2; C. pious devotions regarding a nation or a large region 92; competence of the C. concerning rogation days 245 and the recognition of "national" shrines 264. See Documents of the Conferences of bishops.

Confirmation
gift of the Holy Spirit 156; baptism and c. as the basis of consecration to God 204.

Confraternities
birth, development and purpose of c. in the Middle Ages 31 and in the post-tridentine era 41; c. as subjects of popular piety and their forms of piety, devotions and charity 69; the practice of pious devotions in c. 72; representations of the passion fostered by c. 144; c. and devotion to the faithful departed 260.

Consecrated life
and the feast of the Presentation of the Lord 122.

Consecration of families
c. to the Holy Family 112, to the Sacred Heart of Jesus 171.

Consecration to Mary
c. to the Immaculate Heart of Mary 174; significance of the act of c. 204.

Consecration to the Sacred Heart of Jesus
personal c. 68, of the family 171.

Contemporary era
Liturgy and popular piety in the c. 44-46.

Coptic rite
memorial of Mary in Advent 101, 190.

Council
of Chalcedon 207; of Carthage III 26*; of Constantinople I 207*; of Ephesus 207; of Florence 210*, 251; Lateran V 38; of Lyons II 251*; of Nicea I 207; of Nicea II 238 (*Definitio de sacris imaginibus* 18*, 28, 238*, 239*, 240*); of Trent 38, 39, 251 (*Decretum de invocatione, veneratione et reliquiis Sanctorum et sacris imaginibus* 8*, 18*, 38*, 236*, 239*, 240*, 241*; *Decretum de peccato originali* 349*; *Decretum de purgatorio* 38*; *Decretum de sacramentis* 38*; *Decretum de ss. Eucharistia* 38*; *Decretum de reformatione generali* 38; *Decretum super petitione concessionis calicis* 38*; *Doctrina de communione sub utraque specie et parvulorum* 38*; *Doctrina de sacramento extremæ unctionis* 38*; *Doctrina de sacramento matrimoniii* 38*; *Doctrina de sacramento ordinis* 38*; *Doctrina de sacramento pænitentiæ* 38*; Doctrina de ss. Missæ sacrificio 38*); Vatican II 1, 2, 12, 46, 60, 70, 227, 228, 236 (Documents: *Ad gentes* 156*; *Apostolicam actuositatem* 183*, 286*; *Christus Dominus* 5*; *Dei Verbum* 76*, 87*, 88*; *Gaudium et spes* 100*, 156*, 248*; *Lumen gentium* 5*, 70*, 83*, 183*, 204*, 205*, 207*, 210*, 212*, 251*, 257*; *Optatam totius* 183*; *Presbyterorum Ordinis* 183*; *Sacrosanctum Concilium* 7*, 11*, 18*, 46, 50-59, 67*, 70*, 71*, 72*, 73*, 81*, 83*, 94*, 95*, 171*, 175*, 180*, 201*, 209*, 228*, 229*, 237*, 268*; *Unitatis redintegratio* 182*, 277).

Cremation
practice and canonical legislation 254.

Cross
the veneration of the C. 127-128; sign of triumph, of blessings 128; adoration of the C. 159.

Crucifix
veneration of the C. 127-129

Culture
Gospel and c. meet in popular piety 63,

91-92; discerning the values of the c. 95; 243, sacred images carry the mark of their surrounding c. 257; the shrine as a place of c. 276. See Inculturation

Customs
c. and pious devotions 72.

D

Dance
as religious expression in some popular traditions 17.

De profundis
psalm for the deceased 260.

Deacons
the care of the d. in promoting liturgical life and popular piety 1; among those to whom this directory is addressed 5.

Death
the meaning of Christian d., in the light of the faith 248-250; the concealment of d. 259. See Cremation, Deceased, Funeral rites.

Deceased
primitive traces in popular practice concerning the memory of the d. 23; prayers and intercession for the d. in the Middle Ages 32; the memory of the d. and intercession for them in the Liturgy and in popular piety 248-260; procession to the c. on the 2nd November and in the funeral rites 245, visiting the cemetery 260; Christian meaning of death 249; celebration of the Eucharist 251-252 and 255; the souls in Purgatory 251; intercession 251-255; the funeral rites 252-254;

burial 252-254; cremation 254; remembrance of the d. in the Liturgy of the hours 255; popular piety towards the d. 256-260 the dangers to be avoided 258-259; customs and traditions concerning the worshipping of the d. 257; immortality of the soul 257-258; novena for the d. 260. See Funeral rites, Indulgences, Intercession

Demons
erroneous beliefs 217.

Devotio moderna
its influence 34-35.

Devotions
meaning of the term (exterior acts animated by an interior disposition) 8.

Dicasteries of the Holy See
Congregation of Rites: Decree *Quemadmodum Deus* 220*; Decree *Maxima redemptionis nostrae mysteria* 143*; Instruction *Eucharisticum mysterium* 2*, 141*, 164*; Congregation for the Doctrine of the Faith, Letter *Orationis forma* 57*; (Congregation of the Holy Office), Instruction *De cadaverum crematione* 254*; Congregation for Bishops, *Directory for the Pastoral Ministry of Bishops* 5*, 75*; Congregation for the Clergy: *Directory for the Ministry and Life of Priests* 197*; General Directory on Catechesis 2*, 59*; Congregation for Divine Worship, Instruction *De Calendariis particularibus* 231*; Congregation for Divine Worship, Letter on the preparation and celebration of the Easter Feasts 138*, 139*, 140*, 141*, 145*, 146*, 156*; Lettera circolare *Guidelines and*

proposals for celebrating a marian year 66*, 73*, 183*, 184*, 186*, 188*, 190*, 191*, 194*, 195*, 197*, 199*, 200*, 202*, 203*, 204*, 205*, 266*, 275*; Congregation for Divine Worship and the Discipline of the Sacraments, Instruction *Varietates legitimae* 6*, 12*, 21*, 66*, 92*; *Notification on devotion to the Beatified* 236*; Penitenzieria Apostolica, *Enchiridion Indulgentiarum* 72*; Pontifical Council for Culture, *Per una pastorale della Cultura* 91*; Pontifical Council for the Pastoral Care of Migrants and Travellers, *Il Santuario. Memoria, presenza and profezia del Dio vivente 262*; Il Pellegrinaggio nel Grande Giubileo del 2000* 279*; Pontifical Council for Christian Unity, *Directoire pour l'application des Principes et des Normes* sur *l'Oecuménisme* 155*, 182*, 277*.

Directory
nature 4; purpose 4; structure 4; those to whom this d. is addressed 5; terminology 6-10.

Divination
on not invoking the dead for purposes of d. 258.

Divine mercy
the devotion to the D. on the second Sunday of Easter 154.

Documents of the Conferences of Bishops
General Episcopal Conference of Latin-America, *Documento di Puebla* 2*, 58*, 61*, 62*, 63*, 64*, 66*, 74*; *Documento de Santo Domingo* 2*; Episcopal Conference of Spain,

Episcopal Commision for Liturgy, *Evangelización y renovación de la piedad popular* 2*; National Secretariat for Liturgy, *Liturgia y piedad popular*, Directorio Litúrgico-Pastoral 2*; Italian Episcopal Conference, Commission for Liturgy, Pastoral letter *Il rinnovamento liturgico in Italia* 74*.

Dormition of Mary
Eastern solemnity on the 15th August 23* and 190*.

Dress
to wear a particular d. 15, distinctive sign of some confraternities 69; the scapular as a reduced form of religious d. 205.

Dying
commendation to Saint Joseph 220-221 and to the intercession of the saints 235.

E

East
Liturgy, iconography, hymnody in the E. in the Middle Ages 28; the Blessed Virgin Mary in Advent in the calendar of the Christian E. 101; the feast *Hypapante* in the byzantine E. 120; spread of the *Trisagio* 159; marian months in the E. 190; *Akathistos* hymn 207; veneration of the saints 208; iconography 243.See Byzantine rite , Coptic rite.

Easter
E. Sunday and popular piety 148-151. See Eastertide, Easter Triduum.

F

Family

the f. as subject of popular piety 68; feast of the Holy Family and the carrying out of the Christian family's rites and moments of prayer (dedication to the Holy Family, blessing of children, renewal of marriage vows, engaged couple's exchange of promises) 112; blessing of the family table 68, 109, 150, 260; annual blessing of familes in their homes 152, the consecration of the family to the Sacred Heart of Jesus 68, 171; readings and reflections on the f. in God's word 68; f. and pious practices 72.

Fasting

linked to sacred times 25; f. during Lent 126.

Father (God)

the mystery of God's paternity 79-80.

Fatima

apparitions at F. and devotion to the Immaculate Heart of Mary 174; gatherings for marian prayer recalling F. on the 13th of every month 189; shrine of F. 285.

Feast

times of f. 20; the source of f. days 33; marian f. and pious exercises 187; preparation for f. 189; convergent elements in the f. of a saint 227, its preparation and celebration 230-234; f. and their religious and anthropological content 232-233.

First Fridays

practice of the nine f. 42, 171.

Formation

f. of priests and faithful 11; the importance of f. for popular piety 59. See Catechesis.

Forty Hours

Eucharistic devotion 165

Friday

memorial of the Passion 130. See First Fridays.

Funeral rites

prayers that the angels might accompany the soul of the deceased into paradise 215; procession to the cemetery 245; rites 252-254. See Deceased.

G

Good Friday

liturgical meaning and demonstrations of popular pity 142-145; the procession of the "dead Christ" 142-143; the representation of the Passion 144; the devotion to Our Lady of Sorrows 145; the " reproaches " 159.

Gregory the Great

reference to a fruitful relationship between Liturgy and popular piety 27.

Guadalupe (Our Lady of)

the feast 102; the shrine 207*, 285.

24–27; i. in the 124th to the 16th centuries 36 and 43; i. and popular piety 91-92. See Culture.

Indulgences
pious exercises and i. 72; i. for the souls of the deceased 251.

Initiation, Christian
i. and the common priesthood 85; i. and Lent 124; celebration of i. and mystagogy during eastertide 191.

Innocent (Saint)
increasing value of feasts 113.

Institutes, religious
and this Directory 5; pious practices of religious families 72; the Saturday memorial of Mary and religious communities 188; formulas of Marian litanies used in Orders and i. 203.

Intercession
purpose and forms of i. for the dead 248-260; meaning of i. and their various forms 251 and 255.See Deceased, Funeral rites.

J

Jansenism
influence of j. in returning purity to Liturgy 42; g. and devotion to the Sacred Heart of Jesus 170.

Jesus Christ
the mystery of J. at the centre of the life of worship 77-80; the mysteries of the infancy of J. and devotions 34, 79, 108; memorial of the name of J. 107; the mysteries of the Passion of J. and devotions 34, 41, 62, 79, 129, 144;

reading and meditation on the Passion of J. during Lent and on Good Friday130, 142; veneration and devotion to the crucifix and the cross during Lent and its adoration on Good Friday 127-129, 142-143, 159; procession of the "dead Christ" on Good Friday 142-143; procession with the image of the Risen One on Easter Sunday 149; Sacred Heart of J. (solemnity and devotions) 42, 166-173, 206; devotions and worship to the Blood of J. 175-179; Christological titles 176; the death of the faithful in the light of the mystery of Christ 250; See Baptism (of the Lord), Sacred Heart of Jesus, Sunday, Epiphany of the Lord, Eucharist, Christmas, Easter, Passion of the Lord, Presentation of the Lord, Blood of Christ, Good Friday, "Via Crucis", "Via Lucis".

John Paul II
directives concerning popular piety 2; family 68; examples of the "Via Crucis" over which he presided 139*; consecration to the Immaculate Heart of Mary 174* and the act of consecration to Mary 204*; *Akathistos* hymn 207; Documents: Allocution to the Rectors of French Shrines 263*; Allocution to the bishops of Abruzzo and Molise 65*, 66*; Allocution to the bishops of Basilicata and Puglia 61*; Discourse to the Fourth Latin-american Episcopal Conference at Santo Domingo 64*; Discourse at the *Angelus* in Mexico City 102; Discourse at the Angelus 278*; Discourse at Popayan 65*; Apostolic constitution *Divinitus perfectionis magister* 210*; Apostolic constitution Pastor Bonus 3*, 21; Apostolic exhortation

228*, 230*; *Collectio missarum de Beata Maria Virgine* 149*, 184*, 188*, 193*, 268*, 278*; *Institutio generalis de Liturgia Horarum* 67*, 68*, 110*, 245*, 271*; *Institutio generalis Missalis Romani* 237*, 244*, 255*, 268*; *Liturgia Horarum* 113*, 149*, 177*, 188*, 215*, 231*; *Missale Romanum* 39*, 40*, 79*, 80*, 108*, 115*, 116*, 124*, 177*, 182*, 188*, 210*, 211*, 215*, 220*, 234*, 248*, 249*, 250*, 255*, 257*, 281*; *De Benedictionibus* 112*, 121*, 150*, 152*, 198*, 205*, 206*, 243*, 244*, 272*, 273*, 287*; *De sacra communione et de cultu mysterii eucharistici extra Missam* 161*, 162*, 163*, 164*, 165*, 245*; *Martyrologium Romanum* 227; *Ordo coronandi imaginem Beatae Mariae Virginis* 203*; *Ordo dedicationis ecclesiae et altaris* 237*, 244*; *Ordo exsequiarum* 215*, 252*, 254*; *Ordo Paenitentiae* 215*, 267; *Ordo unctionis infirmorum eorumque pastoralis curae* 130, 215*, 221*, 269; *Rituale Romanum* 181*, 225*.

Liturgical movement
development of the l. in the twentieth century 46.

Liturgical traditions
formation and development of the various liturgical traditions 26.

Liturgical year
Primacy of the l. over devotions 11, 94; celebration of the l. and popular piety 94-182; harmonising the 'marian months' with the l. 191; veneration of the saints and blesseds during the l.. 209. See also Advent, Sunday, Christmas, Lent, Palm Sunday, Pentecost, Holy week, Paschal triduum, Eastertide, Ordinary time.

Liturgy
connection between L. and popular piety 2, 47-58; primacy of the L. 11; causes of imbalance between L. and popular piety 48-49; teaching of the Magisterium concerning the harmonisation between L. and popular piety 60-75; L. and pious exercises 73-74; the Church as worshipping community 81.

Liturgy of the hours
ecclesial praise of God 81; office of readings on Christmas night, before Holy Mass 110; connection between the L. and Eucharistic adoration 165; L. for the deceased 255; L. in the shrines 271, at the beginning of a pilgrimage and during the journey 271 and 287.

M

Magic
incompatibility between popular piety and m. rites, superstitions and spiritism 12.

Magisterium
teaching of the M. on Liturgy and popular piety 60-75; the value of popular piety 61-64; warning on the dangers 65-66; approval of pious exercises 72; M. and pious exercises 70-74, 192-207, and marian pious exercises 185-186; the renewal of popular piety 75. See Pius XII, Paul VI, John Paul II, Dicasteries of the Holy See, Documents of the Conferences of bishops, *"Marialis cultus"*, *"Sacrosanctum Concilium"*.

Marialis cultus
Apostolic exhortation of Paul VI on Marian devotion 2*, 61*, 73*, 74*, 75*, 101*, 123*, 165*, 180*, 182*, 184*, 185*, 186*, 195*, 197*, 201*, 207*.

Marian months
origin and purpose 190-191.

Marriage
renewal of m. vows 112.

Martyrology
the proclamation of the birth of the Lord in the formula of the Roman M. 111; book that lists the names of many saints and blesseds, for liturgical use 227.

Martyrs
popular use of the cult of m. 23; memorials of the m. 25; pilgrimages to the tombs of the m. 32 and 282; the cult of m. 208 and 227.

Mary, Blessed Virgin
the veneration of M. 183-207; act of consecration to M. 204; Mother of Sorrows 136 and 145; *Akathistos* 207; *Angelus Domini* 31 and 195; Assumption 180-181; Advent and M. 101-102; Carmel 205; Immaculate Heart of M. 174 and 206; ecumenical dimension of marian piety 207 and 278; Eucharist and M. 165; Fatima 174, 189, 285; Guadalupe 102 and 285; iconography 23; Christian initiation and M. 191; Immaculate Conception (solemnity, novena) 102 and 181; marian litanies 203; Mother of God (solemnity) 115-117; votive medals 206; marian months 190-191; novenas 189; *Ora della desolata and Planctus Mariae*, pious exercises on Good Friday 145; *Ora della Madre*, pious exercises of Holy Saturday 147; Word of God and M. 193-194; Easter and M. 149, 151, 191; marian piety: primitive expressions 23, in the Middle Ages 32, in the post-tridentine age 41; marian pious exercises185-186, 192-207, and their times 187-191; Presentation (feast of the 2nd February and devotions) 120-121; *Regina caeli* 196; Rosary 197-202; Saturday memorial 188; marian shrines 284-285; scapular 205; *Via Matris*, lenten pious exercise 136-137.

May
practice and guidelines concerning the month of m. 190-191.

Medals
carrying votive m. 15; distinctive sign of some confraternities 69; Marian medals, the "miraculous medal" 206.

Middle Ages
relationship between Liturgy and popular piety 28-33.

Mission
the m. "ad gentes" in Africa, America and the Far East 36; m. and local culture 43; missionary character of the Epiphany 118; "day of suffering for the missions" 156; pious exercises and the missionary imperative 186; the shrine as a place of evangelisation and of cooperating with the m. "ad gentes" 274.

Modern era
Liturgy and popular piety in the m. 34-43.

Planctus Mariae
marian pious exercise on Good
Friday 145.

Popular piety
Angels 213-217; liturgical year 94-
182; 16; approval of texts 16; blessings
272-273; singing 17; Church 81-84;
Constitution *Sacrosanctum Concilium*
50-58; culture 63; Sacred Heart of
Jesus 166-173; deceased 248-260;
ecumenism 12, 155, 182, 277-278;
Eucharist 160-165; evangelisation 2,
21, 66, 80; family 68; formation 59;
images and iconography 18, 238-244;
inculturation 58, 66, 91-92; language
of p. 14-20; Liturgy in relationship to
p. 2, 13, 47-58, 94; places19, 33;
Magisterium 60-75; Blessed Virgin
Mary 183-207; music 17; Word of God
87-89; pilgrimage 279-287; dangers
and risks 65-66; personal piety 23;
pious exercises 70-74; theological
principles 11-13, 76-92; processions
245-247; teachings of the Holy See and
the Episcopal Conferences 2; relics
236-237; responsibility 21; private
revelations 90; renewal 12, 75, 76-92;
common priesthood p. 85-86; Saints
208-247; shrines 262-279; subject of p.
67-69; history: Christian antiquity 23-
27, contemporary age 44-46, modern
age 34-43, medieval period 28-33;
special themes of p. 62; times 20, 32;
terminology 6, 9; texts 16; Trinity 76-
80, 157-159; values 61-64.

Popular religiosity
terminology 5, 10

Post-tridentine era
Liturgy and popular piety in the p. 39-41.

Prayer
ancient forms of personal p. 23; p.
manuals 41; personal p. and private,
methods of p. 82-83; animated by the
Spirit, p. as opening to God and
neighbour 156; p. before the Most
Blessed Sacrament 165; p. is helped by
sacred images 240; the p. of a pilgrim
at a shrine 286.

Presentation of the Lord
liturgical feast and its relationship to
popular piety 120-123.

Priests
popular piety and the ministry of the p.
1, among those to whom this Directory
is addressed 5.

Private revelations
their role 90.

Procession/s
meaning and form 245-247; p.: of
Advent 99; for the Presentation of the
Lord 120; in Holy Week 138; of the
palms - olive branches 139; on Holy
Thursday 141; on Good Friday 142-
143, 245; Easter 149; Eucharistic 162-
163 and 245; with relics 237, 245; with
sacred images 239; with the holy oils
245; on rogation days 245; Lenten
stations 245; baptismal vespers 245;
Viaticum 245; to the cemetery 245;
votive 246.

Protestantism
the rise of p. 38, its development 41
and its objections 208.

Public Squares
places of popular piety 19.

Sacred representations
in the Middle Ages 32; of the
Passion 144.

Sacred Scripture
insufficient knowledge of S. in the
Middle Ages 30; the separation from S.
during the period of catholic reform
41; reference to S. in the expression of
religious sentiment 87 and in pious
exercises 186; reference to S. in
eucharistic adoration 165; the S.
foundations for the devotion to the
Sacred Heart of Jesus 167 and to the
Blood of Christ 175; the relationship
between S. and hagiography 234.See
Word of God.

Sacrosanctum Concilium
the teaching of the Constitution on
Sacred Liturgy of the Vatican Council
II: 7*, 11*, 18*, 46, 50-59, 67*, 70*,
71*, 72*, 73*, 81*, 83*, 94*, 95*,
171*, 175*, 180*, 201*, 209*, 228*,
229*, 237*, 268*.

Saints
Development of the memorial of S. 27;
S. and confraternities 41; the
veneration of S., meaning and doctrine
208-212; the devotion to S. in the
Liturgy and in popular piety 226-247;
the celebration of S. 227-229; the feast
day (preparation, religious and
anthropological content) 230-233; S.
and the celebration of the Eucharist
234; Litanies 235; images 236; relics
236-237; processions 245-247; S.
pilgrimage centres 284. See Angels,
John the Baptist; Holy Innocents;
Joseph, Patron/s.

Santuary/ies
relevance for popular piety 19; s. in the
19th century 45; s. in honour of the
Holy Angels 216; meaning and
importance of s. 261-279; s. and
charity 275; s. and celebrations of
worship 265-273 (as exemplars of
Liturgy 266; Eucharist 261, 268;
christian initation 270; Liturgy of the
Hours 271; Marriage 270; Penance
261, 267; Sacramentals 272;
Sacraments 270; Anointing of the sick
269; s. and culture 276; s. and
ecumenism 277-278; expression of the
identity of faith and culture of a
country 285; s. and evangelisation 274;
canonical recognition of a s. 264;
souvenirs of a s. 287; theological and
symbolic content of s. 262-263;
welcoming of pilgrims to the s. and
their departure 287.

**Saturday Memorial of the Blessed
Virgin Mary**
the "first five Saturdays of the month"
and the devotion to the Immaculate
Heart of Mary 174; the memorial of the
Blessed Virgin Mary in the Saturday
Liturgy and in popular piety 188.

Scapular
Meaning and devotion 205.

Sects
hostility of sects towards popular piety
1; healthy popular devotion as an
antidote against the s. 64.

Sense of the Sacred
in reference to time and place 25.

Septenary
in preparation to a marian feast 189.

U

Unity
week of prayer for u. 155, 182; prayer for u. and the hymn *Akathistos* 207; the role of the shrines 277-278. See Ecumenism.

Urban IV
extension of the feast of Body and Blood of the Lord to the Latin Church 160.

V

Veni Creator Spiritus
hymn sung on 1st January 116; invocation of the Holy Spirit 156.

Veni Sancte Spiritus
invocation of the Holy Spirit 156.

Vernacular
v. and popular piety in the Middle Ages 32; demand for the v. in the Liturgy at the beginning of the sixteenth century 37; permission to use the Bible in the v. 42.

Via Crucis
scriptural 89; the pious exercise of the V. (its origin, meaning, and form) 131-135; on Good Friday 142; related to the "via lucis " 153.

Via Lucis
pious exercise in Eastertide 153.

Via Matris
meaning of the pious exercise, in harmony with themes of Lent 136-137.

Via Sanguinis
pious exercise in honour of the Blood of Christ 178.

Viaticum
v. and the reservation of the Body of the Lord 141, 164; procession to bring v. to the sick 245.

Visits to the Most Blessed Sacrament
Eucharistic devotion 165.

W

Winter time
meaning and value 100.

Word of God
reading and meditating the W. in families 68; W. and popular piety 87-89; the reading of the Passion of the Lord in Lent 130; celebrations of the W. marian piety 193-194; the W. in rites of blessing 272. See Sacred Scripture.

Work
invocation invocation of the Holy Spirit at the beginning of a w. or activity 156; Saint Joseph as a model for workers and craftsmen 220.

Worship
in the context of Christian revelation 76-80.